AUTONOMY AND CONTROL AT THE WORKPLACE

SOCIAL ANALYSIS
A Series in the Social Sciences
Edited by Richard Scase, University of Kent

BEYOND CLASS IMAGES:
Explorations in the Structure of Social Consciousness
Howard H. Davis

FUNDAMENTAL CONCEPTS AND THE SOCIOLOGICAL ENTERPRISE
C.C. Harris

URBAN PLANNING IN A CAPITALIST SOCIETY
Gwyneth Kirk

THE STATE IN WESTERN EUROPE
Edited by Richard Scase

Autonomy and Control at the Workplace

CONTEXTS FOR JOB REDESIGN

EDITED BY JOHN E. KELLY AND CHRIS W. CLEGG

CROOM HELM LONDON

©1982 John E. Kelly and Chris W. Clegg
Croom Helm Ltd, 2-10 St John's Road, London SW11

British Library Cataloguing in Publication Data

Autonomy and control at the workplace.
  1. Work design—Addresses, essays, lectures
  I. Kelly, John E. II. Clegg, Chris W.
  658.3'1423   T60.8

ISBN 0-7099-0410-X

Printed in Great Britain by
Biddles Ltd, Guildford, Surrey

CONTENTS

Notes on Contributors
List of Tables and Figures
Acknowledgments
Introduction

Frank Blackler is Head of the Department of Behaviour in Organisations at the University of Lancaster

Chris Clegg is a Research Fellow in the MRC/SSRC Social and Applied Psychology Unit at the University of Sheffield

Frans van Eijnatten is an Organisational Psychologist working in the Quality of Working Life Research Group at the University of Nijmegen in Holland

Mike Fitter is a Research Fellow in the MRC/SSRC Social and Applied Psychology Unit at the University of Sheffield

Denis Gregory is a Researcher at the Research Unit for the Wales Trades Union Congress

Friso den Hertog is a senior member of the Social Research Department at N.V. Philips Gloelampenfabrieken in Holland

John Kelly is a Lecturer in Industrial Relations at the London School of Economics and Political Science

Ceridwen Roberts was a Lecturer in Industrial Sociology at Trent Polytechnic, now working at the Department of Employment

Toby Wall is a Research Fellow in the MRC/SSRC Social and Applied Psychology Unit at the University of Sheffield

Stephen Wood is a Lecturer in Industrial Relations at the London School of Economics and Political Science

TABLES AND FIGURES

ACKNOWLEDGMENTS

Jenny Cox, Lou Hughes, Lynne Jarvis, June Staniland and Karen Thompson typed the various drafts and redrafts of these chapters. Lou also assisted with indexing, Lynne prepared the artwork and John Cordery checked out all the references. At the end of it all Judith Hallam typed the final copy. We would like to thank each of them for their help and tolerance.

INTRODUCTION

In its 1978 review of work organisation, the Social Science Research Council in Great Britain concluded that research in the area:-

> has been limited . . . . in its frame of reference so that important contextual factors have been neglected; there is a disciplinary imbalance in research efforts and inadequate development of multi-disciplinary investigations; research (and action) on work organisation have been formulated within a unitary and too narrowly commercial frame of reference, and in particular trade union interest and involvement have been far too limited (SSRC, 1978, p. 35).

Certainly, studies of what has variously been labelled as job enrichment, work restructuring or job redesign, have been dominated historically by psychological concerns and levels of analysis. For example, many of the classic contributions to the field have been produced by researchers trained in psychological concepts and methods. Indeed, in one sense, the psychological approach to job redesign has been so successful that other groups (for example consultants and academics from management departments) have also adopted a distinctly psychological orientation. Within this tradition interest has developed from 'fitting the man to the job', to 'fitting the job to the man', and consequently it is hardly surprising that much emphasis has been placed on trying to understand the interaction between the task and the person, with job performance, job satisfaction (or morale) and motivation by far the most frequently-cited outcomes. These analyses at the level of the individual, have often been relatively context-free, partly perhaps because contextual variables have been outside the areas of expertise of investigators, who in addition have often either assumed or appear to have assumed that the interests of the organisation and the employees are shared. Furthermore, the most prevalent research designs have incorporated quantitative approaches, a tendency which has led to an emphasis in the literature on correlational and multivariate statistical evidence.

The net result of this historically derived nexus of concepts, methods and perspectives is that the origins, dynamics and consequences of job redesign initiatives remain under-investigated. Rarely have we seen more than glimpses of the organisations within which such developments are engineered, for example of their information, control and authority systems, departmental and organisational structures, or collective bargaining arrangements.

We must of course acknowledge and consider two possible exceptions to this rather idealised portrayal. First, some case studies do in fact discuss wider features of organisations, such as the nature and layout of technology and machinery, payment and other reward systems, or systems of consultation and representation. Such discussions clearly mark a recognition of the significance of context and constitute an advance over the relatively narrow emphases of more conventional approaches. Usually however, such discussions are rather anecdotal and features of organisations are selected for inclusion primarily on the basis of whether they might hinder the successful implementation of a job redesign scheme. In short, the majority of these discussions consist, in essence, of "how-to-do-it" guides sometimes presented in the form of a checklist of factors for consideration, and few attempts have been made to integrate these factors into a coherent theoretical framework.

The other arguable exception to our characterisation of the field is the 'Quality of Working Life (QWL) Movement'. This can be traced back to 1970 or thereabouts, and consists of a reaction, similar to our own, against the emphases on job content, the measurement of job characteristics, and the use of outcome variables such as job performance and job satisfaction. Writers in the QWL tradition have adopted a far more holistic approach and have sought to place the phenomenon of job redesign in a societal context through consideration, for example, of national and international systems of government, education, industrial relations and law. Unfortunately for those of us trying to understand the meaning and impact of job redesign at the organisational level, much of the work in this tradition has been pitched at a rather macroscopic and abstract level of analysis, and thereby, in this context, lacks specificity.

This book has its origins in our desire to try and rectify some of the omissions characterised above, in particular by relating changes in local autonomy and control through job redesign to specific organisational processes and structures. The concept of autonomy is central to all theories of job redesign and is thought to be causally

related to job satisfaction, motivation, and, in some formu-
lations, to alienation. But having argued the need to examine
job redesign in its organisational context, it immediately
follows we also consider the concept of control, whether this
be at job, departmental or organisational level. Thus the
interaction between the autonomy arising from job redesign and
the pattern of control that is characteristic of organisations,
constitutes a central focus of this book. Our aim then is to
re-examine the phenomenon of job redesign in a series of
different, but related contexts, by including accounts from
people trained in a range of social science disciplines
utilising different frames of reference.

Six of the chapters were first presented in a symposium
at the annual conference of the British Psychological Society
in 1979. Those papers have been rewritten and two further
chapters added, one of which presents a social and psychological overview of job redesign, whilst the other examines its
future prospects. Almost all the authors employ case study
material in the development of their arguments, a method
which allows examination in some detail of organisational
processes surrounding the development, implementation and
subsequent evaluation of job redesign. Whilst it is difficult
to know how far we can generalise such findings, the shared
orientation is that we should first try and understand what
actually happens in specific organisations, thereby working
from the particular to the general.

Some comments on the contributors are also appropriate.
From the outset we sought authors who share a real interest
in, and practical experience of, job redesign, along with the
particularistic orientation described above. They each
believe job redesign either is, or could be, a significant
phenomenon. Thereafter we were anxious to call on people
whose views differ, perhaps as a result of their professional
roles, and/or their ideological commitments, and/or their
disciplinary backgrounds. It is worth noting that contributions from psychologists have been welcomed: our earlier
comments on the psychological emphasis in this area relate to
the imbalance of disciplinary effort (something which
individual psychologists can't do much about), and to their
focussed perceptions of the issues (which they can). The
psychologists in this volume have sought, in these pages and
in their other work, to incorporate analyses of organisational
context.

In the first chapter, Toby Wall offers a social and
psychological perspective on job redesign. He describes the
term and offers an account of the current interest in the
phenomenon, placing particular emphasis on its political
promotion as an aspect of social policy. He reviews the
evidence on the human and organisational consequences of job
designs, and then examines three particular problems of
diffusion by which he accounts for the gap between policy and
practice. He stresses divergent interpretations of the

relevance and meaning of job redesign, the fact that it can cut across many organisational activities, and our lack of knowledge in this area, three issues to which we return again and again in this book. His conclusion is that we should keep an open mind on the prospects for job redesign drawing the distinction between how the technique is currently used and how it might be used, pointing to the need for continued pragmatic empirical evaluations of the phenomenon.

The next three chapters can be grouped in that each adopts a critical approach to job redesign, albeit from different perspectives. Thus John Kelly, in chapter 2, offers a radical critique of the classical approaches to job redesign, his criticisms covering the assumptions underlying such theories, their core propositions, and their empirical support. He draws on the work of Marx, Taylor and Baldamus to offer an economic and structural account of job redesign, which he supports through analyses of case study material. He concludes that the difficulties with the classical theories stem from inadequate conceptualisations of the employment relationship and proffers an explanation of the impact of job redesign in terms of changes in pay, labour intensification and elimination, and flowline organisation.

In chapter 3, Denis Gregory presents a trade union perspective on job redesign. He points to excessive use of jargon, scepticism over alleged benefits, the predominance of managerial initiatives and the problems of relating it to collective bargaining as explanations of traditional 'defensive' union responses to job redesign. He argues that the central issue is one of control, that control at job level also embraces issues such as health and safety and hours of work, and that these should be jointly explored through collective bargaining processes. He is highly sceptical of managerial responses to positive trade union efforts towards participating in 'control' and considers the future prospects for job redesign by discussing the impact of micro-technology. He concludes that trade unions are now ready to bargain collectively about a new set of production relationships within a post-industrial society, where work and leisure are radically reconstructed on a high technology base.

Ceridwen Roberts and Steve Wood, in chapter 4, use a detailed description of a case study analysed from a sociological perspective, in order to explore empirically the middle ground between the view that job redesign is trivial and the more optimistic 'domino theory' of Bosquet, whereby job redesign initiatives are seen to create a demand for participation in other spheres. Their analysis focusses on power and control within a strongly unionised multiplant organisation which experimented with job redesign, and demonstrates that it should be analysed as part of the process of bargaining in which the various parties endeavour to pursue their interests. The outcome of this process cannot be assumed in advance because trade unions actively respond to, modify and sometimes

reverse management initiatives, dependent on the balance of
power.

The next three chapters also go together insofar as they
present detailed studies of the process of redesign and the
organisational impact of it. Thus in chapter 5, Friso den
Hertog and Frans van Eijnatten develop the theme of diffusion,
drawing on extensive practical experience within the Philips
Organisation to demonstrate why job redesign hasn't "taken
off". Two reasons are given: failures to take account of the
process of reorganising jobs and of the broader organisational
context within which the activity takes place. Their chapter
focusses on the process of change, using local case studies to
demonstrate there is "no one best way", instead offering five
practical paradigms, each of which places such exercises
within the organisational context, to guide the redesign
strategy.

Chris Clegg, in chapter 6, and Mike Fitter in chapter 7,
go on to consider the impact of job redesign within an
organisation. They analyse the same case study, both
explicitly adopting a systems view of the situation. Chris
Clegg describes the consequences of how jobs are designed
before and after planned changes, and develops a psychological
model of the practice of job design which he then places in an
organisational context by tracing the effects in other
functions, stressing the lateral as well as vertical relationships. Mike Fitter concentrates on the ways in which the
redesign project necessitated changes to the information and
control systems. He then uses a socio-technical analysis of
the local control systems as a medium for understanding both
the changes within the department, and the implications of
those changes for other organisational practices and systems.

In the concluding chapter, Frank Blackler considers the
future of job redesign through examination of the pioneering
work of Emery and Trist and of other emancipatory psychologies,
concluding that job redesign theorists have made a major
contribution in their day, linking social psychology with
social policy. He argues that whilst there are factors such
as unemployment mitigating against the significance of job
redesign, there are also changes underlining its importance
(such as developments in microprocessor technology). His
conclusion is that job redesign should be explored as one
approach towards employee emancipation at work and that social
scientific endeavour should be invested in studying general
psycho-social problems and in searching for localised
solutions to issues.

Two final points are worth making. In the first place it
is clear there are real differences in the perspectives adopted
by the contributors. For example, job redesign, to some, is
worthy of critical evaluation in its own right, whilst to
others it remains inconsequential or trivial unless it
impinges upon the current distribution of power and control in
organisations. But having admitted to inevitable differences,

there is much in this book to suggest that collaboration
between, let us say, managers, trade unionists, psychologists,
sociologists and economists, would be enormously fruitful if
directed towards long-term empirical evaluations of practical
job redesign initiatives. Whilst multi-disciplinary work may
be difficult to coordinate, it surely provides an exciting
opportunity for furthering our understanding of the meaning,
relevance and impact of job redesign at all levels in
organisations. As editors we are encouraged to feel that
social scientific endeavours, concepts and methods, do have a
definite contribution to make in a future of social, economic
and technological change, as organisations and trade unions
perforce continue to redesign people's jobs.

                                              John Kelly
                                              Chris Clegg

Chapter 1

PERSPECTIVES ON JOB REDESIGN

Toby D. Wall

INTRODUCTION

The concept of job redesign has become a topic of
considerable contemporary interest and controversy in
Western societies. It has led to initiatives at a political
level, has been the focus of enquiry among social scientists,
and in a relatively few but widely publicised instances, has
been translated into direct action.

        This chapter considers the nature and development of
this interest, and is addressed to the question of why it
has emerged. The discussion is divided into four parts. In
order to draw some boundaries around the subject matter, the
scene is set by a brief outline of what is meant by the
term job redesign, and this is followed by an account of
current interest in the concept where the emphasis is on
recent political initiatives. These initiatives are in
part attributable to an emergent body of knowledge concerning
job redesign. The next and major section of the chapter
consequently examines some of the evidence on the effects of
alternative ways of organising work. The concluding section
considers factors affecting the diffusion of job redesign.

        It will be appreciated that any account at this level
of generality is to some extent a caricature. Nevertheless,
like any caricature, whilst prey to the criticism of
exaggeration and over-simplification, its purpose is to
highlight the distinctive features of the subject.

THE TERM JOB REDESIGN

The term job redesign is used here to describe a family of
concepts which are also sometimes referred to under the
titles of work reorganisation or work restructuring. Thus it
subsumes such notions as job rotation, job extension, job
enlargement (both 'horizontal' and 'vertical'), job enrichment and autonomous work groups, each of which is considered
separately later.

1

The essential feature of job redesign, and equally of the more specialised notions it encompasses, is that it is a relative concept. It represents a reaction against traditional ways of organising jobs, which are seen as having resulted in a trend towards increasing work simplification. Developments in industrial societies in the shape of the division of labour, technological advance and the evolution of systems for work measurement and specification, are argued to have coalesced in such a way that they have inexorably led to fragmented and repetitive jobs involving the exercise of little initiative, control or intellectual skills on the part of their incumbents. This is held to be the case not only in manufacturing industry, where the most obvious example is the assembly line, but also to have spread to most other areas of work. Whether one accepts the work simplification thesis (which is considered in greater detail in part three), and there are those who argue that with advancing technology and a movement of labour from manufacturing towards service industries, it is now being reversed, it does provide the evolutionary perspective against which the concept of job redesign is to be understood. In essence job redesign refers to the deliberate attempt to reverse this trend, to organise the work of individuals or groups in such a way as to provide greater complexity with respect to one or more of the following characteristics: variety, autonomy, and completeness of task (carrying out a whole and identifiable piece of work).

The value basis which underlies job redesign is readily apparent in the literature. Thus with respect to work simplification, Braverman (1974) refers to "the degradation of work in the twentieth century". Marx (1867) comparing the factory worker with the craftsman, describes the former as alienated because of the skill loss, and also as a result of his lack of ownership of his work. Similarly, Hackman (1977) states that job redesign "in the long term, can result in organisations that rehumanize rather than dehumanize the people who work in them" (p.102). Sometimes less explicit in the writings of proponents of job redesign, however, is the belief that it provides a means of meeting both the individual's and the organisation's goals of improved wellbeing and work performance. This unitarist notion is evident in the idea of joint optimisation which is central to the socio-technical approach. It is also clearly specified by Hackman (1977), who describes job redesign as "the alteration of specific jobs (or interdependent systems of jobs) with the intent of increasing both the quality of the employees' work experience and their on-the-job productivity" (p.98). Argyris (1964) expresses an equivalent view.

Thus the concept of job redesign can best be understood in terms of its historical context and its value basis. It is a reaction against the perceived trend towards work simplification, which has also come to incorporate a belief in the

2

possibility of joint optimisation.

CURRENT INTEREST IN JOB REDESIGN

One perspective on the current interest in job redesign is
provided by the fact that it has recently been recognised as
an issue for debate at national and international level. Thus
it has been included as a central element in the potentially
larger theme denoted by the term 'the quality of working life'.
As Butteriss states (1975), this term refers to "the idea that
a person should be treated as an entity in his own right, and
should be given autonomy over his work. The main conceptual
breakthrough is the belief that jobs and work organisations
can be arranged and designed to give the individual autonomy
so that his psychological needs and capabilities are met"
(p.1).

 Explicit international promotion of job redesign came to
the fore in the mid-nineteen seventies. In 1974, for example,
the Council of the European Economic Community passed a
resolution which recommended, "eliminating certain soul-
destroying forms of work", included the statement that the
assembly was "convinced that social progress will in future
depend on the interest workers take in jobs", and therefore
suggested that "parliamentary and governmental authorities,
as well as workers' and employers' organisations in member
states, actively promote the humanisation of working
conditions" (pp. 1-2). In the appendix to the resolution it
was further proposed that there was a need "to investigate
measures of job redesign to eliminate meaningless, repetitive
and fragmented work", "to institute special systems -job
enlargement, job rotations (sic), self-controlling groups -
for assembly-line and similar production line workers, subject
to the aim of future elimination of assembly-line work", and
"to increase individual responsibility and create an atmosphere favourable to team spirit and solidarity" (pp.2-3).
Similarly, as Butteriss(1975) reports, the Organisation for
Economic Co-operation and Development adopted a supportive
policy as illustrated by the following statement, "We
recommend affirmative action to secure improvement in the
quality of working life with emphasis on the goal of personal
fulfilment over and above the technical and economic requirements of production. We recognise that such development
depends on considerable changes in attitude on the part of
both employers and unions, and that more positive action by
Government is needed to facilitate this" (p.29).
 The emergence of bodies concerned to promote research
and disseminate information on job redesign, such as the
International Council for the Quality of Working Life
(registered in 1975), and the PIACT project of the
International Labour Organisation (Programme for the Improvement of Working Conditions and Environment, 1976) further
illustrate initiatives being taken internationally.

3

Support for the development and practice of job redesign is also evident at a national level. It is now the case that the governments of most Western countries have set up agencies concerned with the quality of working life. In the United Kingdom, the Department of Employment commissioned a report entitled, 'On the Quality of Working Life' (Wilson, 1973). In 1974, on the recommendation of a tripartite steering group of representatives from government, the Trades Union Congress and the Confederation of British Industry, the same government department instituted the Work Research Unit. The overall objective of this Unit is described as being to stimulate changes in the way in which work is organised in industry and commerce. The accomplishment of this was to be by the dissemination of information, devising training programmes, assisting organisations with initiating changes, and by financing specific research projects. Similarly, in 1979 the Social Science Research Council earmarked £250,000 to promote research into 'Work Organisation' (SSRC Newsletter, No. 40).

In West Germany a "Humanisation of Work Programme" was initiated in 1974 under the joint sponsorship of the trade unions and the Ministries of Labour and of Technology. In contrast with the few hundred thousand pounds of support which has been allocated by the British to these developments, some £66 million was provided in 1975 by the West German government to finance experimental projects over an initial five year period. This figure has now been raised to take account of inflation. These projects cover a wide range of factors including lighting, air pollution and noise, as well as being concerned with the psychological work environment and job redesign. They are unified, however, by their emphasis on the improvement of working life for shop-floor employees. As Jenkins (1978) reports this "is far larger and more ambitious than any other such programme" (p.1).

The above comment may be accurate with respect to financial support, but is less so in other terms. In Scandinavian countries since the early 1960's, there has existed government backing for the development of job redesign which is seen as part of a more general programme to promote the 'democratisation of the work place'. In Norway, for example, the Work Research Institute, originally set up in 1960, received government backing in 1965 at which time it came under the guidance of a secretariat representing university, government, trades union council and employers' federation interests. Much of the work undertaken has been in association with researchers from the Tavistock Institute of Human Relations. In Sweden and Denmark similar developments took place in the late 1960's and early 1970's, and are receiving continued support from all interested parties.

Initiatives on job redesign are also evident in Australia, Canada, France, Italy, Japan, Holland and the United States. In effect what is being witnessed is the integration of job redesign into the social policies of a wide range of countries.

4

Lafittes' (1962) description of social policy is particularly pertinent in this context. He depicts the concept in the following terms:

> Through collective action, particularly by imposing the state's directing power on the forces of the market, we seek to steer society along paths it would not naturally follow, towards accepted goals unattainable without public organisation - the great communal Super-ego, as it were, striving to marshall the drives of the great social Id. Through social policy we assert the primacy of non-economic values, our belief that the way of life matters more than the ways of getting a living . . . .
> Social policy could be seen as our determination to return to the old norm in a world transformed by industrialism (p.58).

For better or for worse, job redesign as a central ingredient in the striving towards improvements in the quality of working life, is currently a focus for social policy.

Whilst there may exist a continued growth in the volume of public, quasi-public and private interventions in social life, it is nevertheless more than coincidence that job redesign, rather than other ideas emerging from the social sciences, has been adopted. The reason for this lies in the values underlying job redesign which appear to many to match well on to those ideas gaining credence in a range of other contexts (see Davis, 1976; Den Hertog, 1976). In education for example, there has developed a move towards less authoritarian approaches in teaching with more emphasis on individualism and self expression. In society at large there has arisen criticism of bureaucracy and of the quality of the relationship between man and his work (e.g. Herrick and Maccoby, 1975). Job redesign is seen as a way of meeting this criticism. Klein (1976) makes the point in the following way when she argues that job redesign "should lead to a greater interpenetration between industry and the rest of society, lessening the split between values expressed in the working arrangements of society and the values expressed in other institutions" (p.70). The emergence of worker participation as a legitimate issue for debate and legislation is based on similar values, ones which emphasise the mature citizen's right to an influence over those decisions that affect him. Indeed the link between job redesign and industrial democracy has been carefully forged by a number of writers (e.g. Emery and Thorsrud, 1969 ; Bolweg, 1976) who see such innovation as a possible or necessary first step towards reaching the values of democracy within work organisations. Add to that the belief that job redesign can also be of benefit to productivity, then its attraction is evident. It is a way of marrying the old with the new. It should be recorded, however, that there are those who do not perceive job redesign in this way, arguing that it is too trivial to be worthy of consideration (see part 4 below). Nevertheless the surface characteristics of job redesign are such as to encourage adherence to the idea within political and academic circles.

Despite political promotion of job redesign, and similar support by a large body of social scientists active in teaching and intervening in work organisations, the interest of those closer to the work face is undoubtedly less strong and less unified. Whilst some organisations have taken substantial and well publicised initiatives in this area (for example Volvo, Saab, Philips, ICI, and FIAT), it could not be said to be a burning issue in the world of work as a whole. Precise evidence concerning the proportion of work organisations aware of developments in job redesign, considering change of this type, or undertaking innovations, is not available, but it is clearly only the few (see for example, surveys by Reif, Ferrazzi and Evans, 1974; and Taylor, 1979). And where job redesign has been tried, it has often neither spread nor indeed survived in the longer term. Indeed, paradoxically the very existence of social policy in this area implies there must be a high degree of apathy, resistance or lack of conviction within organisations otherwise there would be no need for action to 'steer society along the paths it would not naturally follow'. The causes for such lack of interest are considered later. First, however, we explore the existing evidence relating to the efficacy of job redesign.

EVIDENCE ON THE HUMAN AND ORGANISATIONAL CONSEQUENCES OF JOB DESIGN AND REDESIGN

The emergence of job redesign as a subject for social policy is not only a response to its value basis but also to a body of evidence. This contribution to the debate is considered by depicting the main characteristics of: (i) the 'conventional' approach to the design of jobs; (ii) research on the effects of simplified work to which the 'conventional' approach leads; (iii) proposals for redesigning jobs; and (iv) research on the effectiveness of alternative proposals for job redesign.

'Conventional' Job Design

The major influences on 'conventional' job design practices may be traced back to the writings of such theorists as Adam Smith (1776) and Charles Babbage (1835). A core concept in their arguments was the division of labour, which they saw as providing the means for greater material output per man hour worked. In the view of Babbage - "when each process, by which any article is produced, is the sole occupation of one individual, his whole attention being devoted to a very limited and simple operation, improvements in the form of his tools, or in

6

the mode of using them, are much more likely to occur in his mind, than if he were distracted by a greater variety of circumstances". He argued that such a division of labour would result in more 'economy of production' through reducing training times, reducing materials wasted in learning, avoiding the work time inevitably lost in more complex jobs in moving from one task to another and in changing tools, and increased levels of activity through the "skill acquired by frequent repetition of the same processes". This was further underlined by the principle that manufacturers, by such division of labour, could purchase the exact levels of skill or effort required, rather than adopting the more economically wasteful approach of requiring these to be present in all individuals and having the majority of skills unused at any one moment in time. In essence it was a doctrine of deskilling jobs by reducing their complexity - a fragmentation of work into its component tasks.

The writings and practical demonstrations offered by Taylor (1911) and Gilbreth (1911), elaborated upon this theme and provided the tactics to enable the general strategy to be implemented. An important aspect of Taylor's approach is that it made the design of jobs towards more effective methods based on the division of labour, a function of management and not, as implied by Babbage, as a natural evolution from the job incumbents' specialisation. As Taylor stated, "management must take over and perform much of the work which is now left to the men; almost every act of the workman should be preceded by one or more preparatory acts of the management which enable him to do his work better and quicker than he otherwise could". These "preparatory acts" concerned making work more efficient, to which end the following procedure was recommended. A number of individuals who were particularly able at the work in question were to be located, and the physical movements they used to be closely watched and carefully timed. From these the most rapid, as well as the slowest and redundant movements, were to be identified. Finally, a new method of working was to be developed which capitalised on the rapid movements and eliminated the unnecessary ones. The equipment and technical layout associated with the jobs were to be similarly treated. Having decided on the 'best method', it was to be put rigidly into practice by training individuals in its use.

With a number of routine manual jobs, Taylor's approach was put into effect with spectacular results in terms of increased output. On a more complex level, the principles of the division of labour and closely controlled fragmentation of jobs, were shown to be a practical proposition of enormous economic benefit by the establishment in 1914, of a car assembly-line by Henry Ford at Highland Park in Michigan.

Many contemporary commentators see these influences as critical factors underlying a disjunction in the evolution of jobs (e.g. Davis and Taylor, 1972). The earlier order of

skilled and composite work in which individuals practised all
the skills involved in making a complete product, was halted.
Subsequently, through the principle of the division of labour
and Taylor's 'scientific management', as expressed in the work
of managers, production engineers, work study practitioners
and others involved in designing the content of jobs, it is
argued jobs have become increasingly simplified. As Klein
(1976) describes,

> the choices made in the design and organisation
> of work have tended to be in the direction of
> rationalisation, specialisation and the sub-
> division of tasks, and the minimising and
> standardising of skills . . . . first in
> manufacture and later in administration, the
> knowledge and methods of the natural sciences
> have been put to the task of discovering methods
> of working and organising which would give
> economical and predictable results (p. 14).

That work simplification has spread from manufacturing to most
other areas of work is an argument offered by many commentators (e.g. Braverman, 1974; Cherns and Davis, 1975; Kraft,
1977).

The degree of absorption of these principles into contemporary job design practices has been explored by a number
of researchers. Davis, Canter and Hoffman (1955) undertook a
survey to obtain information on the manner in which American
organisations designed jobs. This revealed that of fifteen
factors considered, the most important were: minimising the
time required to perform the operation; obtaining the highest
quality possible; minimising skill requirements; using
equipment or tools presently on hand; minimising floor-space
requirements; achieving specialisation of skills; and minimising learning or training times. Providing for operator
satisfaction was subordinate to all these (ranked 10), as was
safety (ranked 15). This study is far from adequate scienti-
fically since it is based on a mere five percent response rate.
Nevertheless the characteristics it revealed matched sufficiently closely onto the experience of observers and practitioners to attain credibility and few have denied the authors'
generalisation that "the majority of companies believed in
limiting the content of individual jobs as much as possible.
This means limiting the number of tasks within jobs and
limiting the variations permitted in tasks or jobs" (p. 7).

More recent studies by Hedberg and Mumford (1975) on
British and Swedish systems analysts, and by Taylor (1979) on
American engineers and American, United Kingdom and Swedish
systems analysts, reveal a similar pattern of results. Taylor
concludes that

twenty years of technological progress and
innovation have had little corresponding effect
on the professional values of design practitioners
. . . . production engineers and systems analysts
select job design criteria remarkably similar to
those chosen by their predecessors in the 1950's.
They still prefer to minimize the immediate costs
of production rather than to emphasize a long-term
approach to job design which recognizes the economic
cost of worker frustration and acknowledges employee
satisfaction and motivation   (p. 61).

It is against this perceived reality, which is driven by
an economic imperative, that certain political initiatives are
beginning to be taken. The kind of evidence which supports
such opposition is the subject of the following section.

Research on the Effects of Simplified Work

Concern for the human costs of simplified work is not a new
theme. Early research focussed particularly on the lack of
variety in and the repetitiveness of jobs rather than on the
elements of autonomy and responsibility. The Industrial
Fatigue Research Board enquiries in the 1920's , showed that
in such work as soap wrapping, tobacco-weighing, cigarette
making, cartridge-case assembly and bicycle chain assembly,
the deliberate introduction of greater variety could improve
output and was preferred by operators (Wyatt, Fraser and
Stock, 1928). More telling was a subsequent Industrial
Health Board inquiry (Fraser, 1947) which looked at the
incidence of neurotic illness among more than 3,000 male and
female employees in British light and medium engineering
factories. This revealed that such illness was most common
amongst those who found work boring, held a job offering
little variety, were engaged in assembly, bench inspection or
toolroom work, or performed jobs requiring constant attention.
The results led Fraser to conclude, "It may be less important
to make jobs 'foolproof' than to design them so that they will
not be disliked . . . . More variety and scope for initiative
and interest could be introduced without fundamental alteration to production programmes" (p. 10).
Walker and Guest (1952) examined the relationship between
repetitiveness in assembly-line work and job attitudes among
American car workers. Of those performing more than five
operations, they found 64% reported their jobs to be fairly
or very interesting. Of those carrying out two to five
operations, 44% gave the same response; whilst only 33% of
those whose jobs involved a single operation expressed the
same views. Kornhauser (1965) explored the relationship
between mental health and job characteristics with a sample
of more than 400 American male blue-collar car workers. His

9

data showed that differences in recorded mental health varied systematically with skill level - being lowest for those engaged in repetitive, routine, machine-paced work. He concluded with respect to mental health, that "by far the most influential attribute (of jobs) is the opportunity work offers - or fails to offer - for use of workers' abilities and for associated feelings of interest, sense of accomplishment, personal growth and self respect" (p. 363).

More recent work in this area shows two points of divergence from that described above. First, it has (somewhat unaccountably) failed to pursue directly, issues associated with mental health, relying more on measures of job attitudes and performance as the 'dependent' variables. Secondly, it has expanded the range of job characteristics considered, to include explicitly the discretionary elements of jobs in addition to that of variety or repetitiveness. The work of Hackman and Lawler (1971) is illustrative of this. They found among employees in a telephone company, that the degree of variety, autonomy, task identity and feedback that characterised their jobs, was positively associated with their levels of job satisfaction, job involvement and feelings of accomplishment. A large number of other cross-sectional and analytical investigations revealed broadly similar results (e.g. Blauner, 1964; Turner and Lawrence, 1965; Shepard, 1969; Susman, 1973; and Hackman and Oldham, 1976). From the point of view of psychological well-being, a reasonably strong case has emerged against simplified work. Even though individual studies are far from definitive, the consistency of the findings using a wide variety of populations and research methods, implies the existence of a relatively general phenomenon. Some would deny the direction of causality implied in this research, arguing that the more alienated or dissatisfied individuals with lower commitment seek out jobs that require little involvement in terms of skill or responsibility. Goldthorpe's thesis (1966) is an example here. Nevertheless, the most common interpretation is that job characteristics are determinants of psychological reactions, and it is this view which has predominated and found its way into the political arena.

Proposals for Job Redesign

Proposals for redesigning jobs have predictably paralleled findings on the effects of simplified work, starting with a concern to counteract repetitiveness and moving on to encompass the provision of autonomy and discretion. One of the earliest suggestions was for job rotation, in which individuals are allowed, or required, to move from one job to another at specified intervals. This leaves unchanged the basic divisions of labour (thus retaining the essential benefits therefrom) whilst at the same time ensuring an increase in the range of activities experienced by the

individual. The cost to the employer is in the need to train individuals in more than one job; his potential gain is a consequential increase in the flexibility of labour.
Horizontal job enlargement is similarly a 'one-factor' proposal for job redesign, aimed at increasing variety. In this case, the content of jobs is specified so as to cover a wider range of component tasks of different kinds. It is to be distinguished from job extension which may be defined as the addition of very similar tasks to an existing job which increases the number but not greatly the variety of operations performed by the individual.

Other more recent proposals focus more explicitly on the discretionary elements of work. Vertical job enlargement refers to a deliberate increase in the degree to which an individual can control the planning and execution of his work. It involves such changes as increasing the discretion of the job holder over how to carry out the tasks, how to schedule them and how to organise his time. Job enrichment is essentially an alternative term for vertical job enlargement, the separate expressions reflecting a difference in theoretical origins. While vertical job enlargement evolved as a consequence of Herzberg's (1966) Two-Factor Theory of Work Motivation, the characteristics of job enrichment are illustrated by Paul and Robertson's (1970) definition, which is "building into people's jobs, quite specifically, greater scope for personal achievement and recognition, more challenging and responsible work, and more opportunity for advancement and growth" (p. 17).

The notion of autonomous work groups (or more accurately, semi-autonomous work groups) has a very different heritage from the above proposals. It has its roots in socio-technical 'theory', which in turn has been developed in association with open systems theory as applied to social sciences (e.g. Katz and Kahn, 1966, 1978). As a form of job redesign the notion of autonomous work groups differs from the others considered in two important respects. First, the emphasis is on organising work for groups rather than individuals; secondly, attention is given to a range of contextual variables, which the other approaches tend to ignore. This latter characteristic undoubtedly reflects the different background of this proposal. Whereas the concept of autonomous work groups evolved from detailed and extended studies of organisational change (e.g. Trist and Bamforth, 1951; Rice, 1958), the other forms originated principally from cross-sectional or comparative investigations. Nevertheless, the central elements of autonomous work groups map directly on to those which characterise the other forms of job redesign which include the discretionary perspective. As Kelly (1978) observes, the notion of the autonomous work group which emerged was of "a group of multiskilled workers which possessed all the skills essential for the performance of a particular, 'whole' task, and which decided on its own

11

allocation of labour, and sometimes on other matters such as internal leadership" (p. 1071). "Variety","responsibility for a meaningful or whole task", "involvement in co-ordination and decision-making" and "perceptible relations between the job and the outside world" (pp. 1076-1077) are central elements in the design of work for such groups. These elements bear a remarkable resemblance to those of "task variety", "autonomy" and "task significance" which are at the heart of the 'theory' behind vertical job enlargement (Hackman and Lawler, 1971, Hackman and Oldham, 1976) and job enrichment (Herzberg, 1966). It is also interesting to note that a development emerging from production engineering, that of group technology, in practice results in jobs of a very similar nature to semi-autonomous work groups (see Edwards, 1972; Burbidge, 1975; and Blackler and Brown, 1978; for more detailed accounts of this particular form of job redesign).

In summary, proposals for job redesign fall into two categories. The first, represented by job rotation, horizontal job enlargement and job extension, is focussed exclusively on the provision of greater variety of task experience for the job holder. The second, represented by vertical job enlargement, job enrichment and autonomous work groups has a broader base. It allows for greater variety but its essential characteristic is the provision of greater discretion or self-determination for the job incumbent. It is a proposal for more fundamental change since in principle it cuts across traditional demarcation lines of authority and control, at least those at the lower levels within organisations. It is on this second category that most contemporary interest is focussed since, as the following section reveals, this appears to have the greater potential for affecting the quality of working life.

The Effects of Redesigning Jobs

In principle it should be a relatively simple exercise to evaluate alternative proposals for job redesign. Each form could be implemented and its impact upon employee performance and well-being determined. A comparison across the alternative forms would then reveal the most powerful of the proposals, and those which have less merit. In practice however, this is not feasible for a variety of reasons. First, there is considerable overlap between alternatives with respect to the changes they require in jobs. For example, job enrichment and semi-autonomous work groups both provide greater discretion for the employee in carrying out his or her work, and as a consequence the individuals are free to vary their activities within the agreed limits and may consequently be instituting job rotation. In implementing one form of job redesign, changes are also often necessary or occur 'naturally', which correspond to those emphasised by an alternative form, and the conceptual distinctions between

12

them become blurred.

A second problem results from the fact that job redesign, particularly those forms emphasising increased discretion, requires simultaneous modification to a wide range of work characteristics and procedures. Increasing an employee's autonomy for example, will often require alterations to the role played by immediate supervision, managerial style more generally, the level of pay for which the job holder is eligible, the technology, and a variety of other factors. In short, in any one case, it is possible that one, a limited number, or all the changes implemented in pursuit of job redesign, may be the determinant of any observed effects.

A third problem concerns the way in which changes are introduced. In laboratory conditions it has been shown that the mode of introduction can be at least as important as the nature of the change effected (e.g. Seeborg, 1978). In practice the method of implementation will vary from situation to situation, and can be expected to affect the results obtained. Similarly other contextual factors will play a part. No two organisations, or departments within organisations, are identical, and the process of translating the general principles of job redesign into specific practice, results in a wide variety of different changes in different circumstances, by differing means. In other words, to some extent each instance of job redesign is unique.

Finally, in field settings, there are considerable methodological problems in designing a study in such a way as to limit the number of available interpretations of the findings. Traditional experimental methods are rarely appropriate. 'True' experiments involving random allocation of subjects between experimental and control conditions are typically not feasible. Randomisation cuts across established relationships, attitudes, skill-interdependencies, behaviours and practices that are critical aspects of working life. Such a practice may therefore be unacceptable to job holders and, should it be accepted, would introduce a strong element of artificiality. Moreover, technical considerations often make it impossible to divide a sample into two since the processes of production cannot cater for alternative forms of work organisation in the same environment.

In summary, because of the conceptual overlap between the various proposals for job redesign, the fact that job redesign is a systemic or multivariate change, that the method as well as the content of change may affect the outcomes obtained, that all such change is in some senses unique, and because practical constraints inhibit the methodological rigour which can be (and has been) achieved in field settings, empirical studies of job redesign necessarily entail difficulties of interpretation. Moreover, other weaknesses in the evidence not inherent in the subject matter are prevalent in the literature. Thus, only a small number of investigations report the use of measures of known reliability and provide statistical evaluation of the changes recorded, and many accounts give but a general description of the change introduced. There are therefore problems associated with the adequacy of the data when considering the area as a whole. Nevertheless, if job redesign is a powerful contributor to employee well-being and performance, its effects should transcend these exigencies even though disentangling the finer structure of the causal relationships will be less than straightforward.

Several authors have attempted such an overall evaluation, and whilst emphasising the interpretational difficulties they face, have discerned consistent patterns in the data. In relation to job rotation the picture is not too promising. Although in some instances benefits have been recorded (e.g. Rosen, 1963), in general little positive effect on employees' attitudes or performance has been established (see Swedish Employers' Confederation, 1975). However in combination with other changes, where arising spontaneously, or where it provides relief from physical fatigue, job rotation has been found to have a role to play. Very similar findings have emerged in relation to horizontal job enlargement and job extension. Thus these 'one-factor' proposals for job redesign, focussed on the provision of greater variety, have shown themselves to be relatively weak vehicles for substantially improving the quality of working life.

A more encouraging picture arises from accounts of vertical job enlargement, job enrichment and autonomous work groups. Several reviews of these initiatives have been published (e.g. Argyris, 1973; Birchall and Wild, 1973; Srivastva et al, 1975; Cummings and Salipante, 1976; Taylor 1977a, and 1977b; Cummings and Molloy, 1977). With respect to the first two forms, Cummings and Molloy's (1977) conclusions are representative. Their analysis of 28 projects revealed "that job restructuring produces improvements to performance and the quality of working life" (p. 93). They warned, however, that "careful scrutiny of the experimental designs, and the inferences made from the data, point to the need for caution in interpreting the claims made, especially regarding attitude improvements" (p. 93). Similarly, from a consideration of sixteen studies of semi-autonomous work groups, these authors concluded:

> although the efficacy of these results is less
> than ideal, evidence supports the positive
> effects attributed to autonomous work groups.
> Specifically the implementation of certain action
> levers - autonomy/discretion, interpersonal/group
> process, information/feedback, task variety,
> technical/physical and pay reward systems - appears
> to lead to improved performance and human satisfac-
> tion (p. 48).

What exists in fact is a body of evidence which is far
from definitive. Not only are there the methodological
weaknesses and other inadequacies considered above, but there
also exists some suggestion of bias both in respect of the
reporting of individual studies and in the selection of which
studies are reported (see Birchall and Wild, 1973; Srivastva
et al, 1975). For those who wish to take an alternative view
there is plenty of ammunition and room for reinterpretation.
Nevertheless, it is a body of evidence consistent with the
view that forms of job redesign which emphasise increased
discretion and autonomy for job holders, typically enhance
performance and/or satisfaction at work. The evaluation made
by the Secretary of Health, Education and Welfare in the USA,
in response to the findings of the government commissioned
study, "Work in America" (1973 - US Department of Health,
Education and Welfare) is appropriate more generally both with
respect to the status of current evidence and its political
significance. Commenting on the support this report gave for
job redesign, he stated - "its conclusions may not be fully
supported by its data and may in fact be off by quite a bit,
but if it is anywhere near the truth we had better start
thinking about its implications" (New York Times, 22nd
December, 1972).

FACTORS AFFECTING THE DIFFUSION OF JOB REDESIGN

There is of course a yawning gap between policy statements
and actual practice. Whilst social policy may provide an
important impetus it has to be espoused at all levels within
organisations before it becomes a reality. At present job
redesign, despite governmental support and generally
favourable field trials, has shown greater diffusion at the
level of principle than of practice. Some might argue that
this reflects a normal 'culture lag'. This argument, however
is weakened by a consideration of other innovations affecting
work organisations which have been more readily and rapidly
adopted. 'Scientific management' is a most obvious example!
One must look more closely therefore at the properties of job
redesign to understand its current lack of impact on the
practice of work in Western societies. Three sets of issues
are pertinent in this context. The first concerns the
centrality of job redesign within value positions concerning
reform in work organisations as a whole; the second concerns
conflicts between job redesign and existing practices and
interests within organisations; and the third focusses on
problems inherent in existing knowledge about job redesign
which limit its applicability. Each of these is considered
in turn.

Job Redesign and Work Reform

Though many have argued in favour of job redesign on the basis that it reflects prevailing societal values with respect to needed reform, to others it has opposite characteristics. In particular those adopting a particular form of Marxist analysis oppose such change on principle. Any development taking place within a basically capitalist system is suspect. The French Confederation Generale du Travail (CGT) for example, states, "As long as the capitalistic system exists, organisation of work, whatever form it takes, will remain subordinate to the goal of maximum profit" (see Delamotte, 1975). From this point of view the historical trend towards work simplification and increasing managerial control, stems both from the separation between labour and capital, and from the division of labour (see Braverman, 1974). Given this economic determinism, job redesign would at best be regarded as a partial solution to the problem, or but a trivial innovation. At worst it would be seen as a cosmetic exercise which might serve the purpose of maintaining managerial control or as a means of covering up the cracks. A rather more general version of such opposition comes from a conflict between priorities. For those who hold the view that an important objective is to achieve greater power equalisation within work organisations, or ultimately workers' control or a classless society, job redesign is sometimes seen as a threat. The reasoning is that it may be successful in creating more satisfying work and thus undermine the level of grass-roots support for the more important struggle and its accepted champions, the trade unions. Such weakening of trade union support is in itself a cause of concern. As Cherns and Davis (1975) point out, "The notion of democracy at the workplace with sharing of power, autonomous groups and so on, involving the worker in decisions about his own work, can appear as devices for undermining the loyalties of union members" (p. 34). At least one clearly management orientated author has recognised this, when he entitled his book on job enrichment, "Managing Without Unions" (Myers, 1977).

But not all trade unions, even those with equivalent Marxist leanings to the French CGT, reach the same conclusion. Thus the Italian unions see job redesign as a viable alternative to traditional job design, as long as the initiative comes from the workers (Delamotte, 1975). Moreover, they believe that if initiated in this way, job redesign will provide a first step towards 'social control' by workers of the production processes. This line of interpretation is also evident amongst those who see in job redesign a threat to managerial prerogatives. As Cherns and Davis (1975) observe, employers "are conscious that a process of this kind, once begun, is hard to control, that the appetite grows on what it feeds" (p. 34).

It is clear from the above discussion that widely divergent interpretations of the implications of job redesign can and have been made. And, because of these contradictions, considerable uncertainty exists among both union and management representatives as to whether or not job redesign is worthy of support or is a threat to their basic objectives. Such uncertainty is not conducive to positive reaction and has no doubt played its part in preventing a rapid diffusion, or rejection, of job redesign within organisations. (For a fuller discussion of these issues, see chapters 2, 3 and 4 in particular).

Job Redesign and Existing Practices

The more general concerns over the impact of job redesign considered above, find expression in a more focussed manner when such change is planned within organisations. A particular concern is with the threat job redesign poses for the position and status of supervisory personnel. Forms of job redesign based on discretion require much of the decision-making activities which traditionally are the responsibility of the supervisor or foreman, to be given to the individual worker or the work group. This can either fundamentally change the supervisor's role and generate a need for a new form of authority structure, or indeed, as experience has shown, remove the supervisory role altogether (see Klein, 1976; Hughes and Gregory, 1978). It is understandable that people in such positions, and the unions which represent their interests, would adopt an antagonistic stance.

A wide range of other interest groups and practices also often become affected. Thus job redesign involves the amalgamation of previously separate tasks into the roles of individual employees, and this can run counter to existing principles of skill categorization and agreed areas of demarcation which have evolved from years of negotiation or from the formalisation of custom and practice. Similarly, it often has implications for the role of production engineers who may be required to take more explicit account of ill-defined 'human needs' when creating work systems. Information systems within organisations, personnel selection, managerial style and practice at all levels, training, and a wide variety of other areas can be affected. Personnel employed within these functions may quite understandably see job redesign as representing an invasion into their own areas of autonomy and as such resist the move. A particularly important issue is that of pay. A fundamental element in most job evaluation systems on which pay rates are based, is the notion of discretion. Since the better supported forms of redesign are based on the principle of increased discretion for shop floor employees, they have implications not only for basic wages, but also for that sensitive and volatile area of differentials between groups of employees.

In short, job redesign can cut across a wide variety of areas within organisations, and to be effective, often needs to do so. From the point of view of its acceptability, this pervasiveness can be a threat to those directly involved with these different ancillary functions, and as a consequence the prospect of job redesign attracts a great deal of resistance. It is these kinds of consideration and reaction that in practice have often prevented the adoption of job redesign within organisations. Whilst the existence of seemingly successful experiments suggests they are not insurmountable, they certainly are deterrents. (See chapters 5, 6 and 7).

Existing Knowledge on Job Redesign

The final impediment to the diffusion of job redesign to be considered here, relates to the nature of knowledge on the subject. It has already been noted that evidence concerning the efficacy of various forms of job redesign is less than satisfactory. The concern here, however, is with the systematisation of this knowledge and its relevance to practice.

Alexander (1978) reminds us that "the purpose of theory is to explain so that experimentation and change can be given direction and a better chance of succeeding" (p. vii). Many commentators conclude that, with respect to job redesign, social science has been inadequate in this respect. This stems in part from the terminology used. The point is made forcibly by Cherns and Davis (1975) when they note the absence of "a common language among researchers and practitioners" and "the fact that none of the different languages used is easily understood, thus requiring a number of non-existent dictionaries" (p. 9). McLean and Sims (1978) similarly point to shortcomings in the existing research among which are the following:

1 A lack of precision in the use of key terms
2 Weakness in the theoretical foundations
3 Tenuous links between practice and theories
   underlying practice (p. 9).

In fact there is no single theoretical foundation to job redesign, but rather a number of models with different characteristics. With respect to the discretionary forms of job redesign, namely - job enrichment, vertical job enlarge- ment and semi-autonomous work groups, the respective theoreti- cal bases are reflected by Herzberg's (1966) Two-Factor Theory of Job Motivation; Hackman and Oldham's (1976) Job Characteristics Model; and socio-technical systems theory (illustrated in the work of Davis, 1957; Emery, 1959; and Trist et al, 1963). Each of these models has been partly successful as shown by the fact that they have all fostered a number of empirical studies. However they have proved to have important weaknesses, particularly from an applied standpoint.

Considering first the Two-Factor Theory and the Job Characteristics Model, each might be seen as possessing commendable specificity with respect to salient job variables, and the causal relationships of these with job attitudes and behaviour. Their main weakness however is that they leave out of account a range of contextual variables of evident significance, in particular those concerned with technology, supervisory roles and managerial practices, and include only simple uni-directional causal relationships. In contrast, the socio-technical systems approach accomodates a broader range of variables and causal relationships, recognising many factors in the context of work organisations. In spreading its net so wide, however, this approach leaves largely undefined the factors to be included or excluded and the nature of the relationships amongst them. It is such observations that led Clark (1975) to conclude that "sociotechnical analysis probably is one of the best known, highly relevant, least understood, and rarely applied perspectives. The author feels that its application is far beyond the area of comprehension of many executives and policy makers . . . ." (p. 184). This theme is reiterated by Hill (1972) who calls for a further simplification of socio-technical systems analysis to make it appropriate for more general use, and by Klein (1976) who notes that "it is easy to agree that the enterprise is an open socio-technical system; it is a little hard to know what to do next, if one's own learning and experience have not been within this tradition" (p. 76).

In short, the Two-Factor Theory and Job Characteristics Model do not have the requisite breadth to map convincingly onto the problem area, and socio-technical systems analysis has to date provided insufficient structure. What is required is development in the middle ground (see den Hertog and Wester, 1979; Wall, 1980), of conceptualisations providing breadth of coverage without sacrificing specificity with respect to the salient elements and the relationships amongst them. These require two further properties not explicit in existing approaches. First, specification of the time bases of change (see Wall, 1980), and secondly, consideration of the process of change (see Clegg, 1980).

THE POINT OF ADVANCE OR RETREAT

Opinions differ widely as to the future of job redesign as a concept or set of principles of relevance to work organisations. To some, work and social change in this area is in its infancy, and the best is yet to come. Others argue that since substantial resources have already been deployed to mine this particular seam, the lack of advance to date suggests the investment is not worthwhile. They foresee a rapid demise. The coming of other more obvious changes, for example, the development of micro-processors, and increased unemployment,

are seen by yet others as likely to supercede the interest in
job redesign. The existence of such divergent views is, of
course, a natural product of an area of enquiry which is
founded on great uncertainties and divergencies of evidence,
of theory and of value. The future will decide how job
redesign fares in the role of a tool to be used by man to
organise his own way of life. For the moment however, the
most constructive approach seems to be to keep an open mind,
to avoid making dichotomies which in practice may not
represent choices that have to be made. Micro-processor
technology for example could be, and in one instance known to
the author already has been, used to help make complex production systems more flexible so as to allow the principles of
job redesign to be implemented. Similarly we must distinguish
between how job redesign is used in the context of other more
important objectives, and how it might be used. Thus the
argument as to whether job redesign undermines or supports
existing authority structures for example, may not be one of
principle, but one of practice. Just as advances in knowledge
of energy generation and medicine can be used for different
purposes, so may information on how to design work.

Chapter 2

ECONOMIC AND STRUCTURAL ANALYSIS OF
JOB REDESIGN

John E. Kelly

INTRODUCTION

For a period in the late 1960's and early 1970's innovations
in the design of jobs in manufacturing and service industries
were widely and favourably reported and popularised in
management periodicals, magazines and seminars, and at workshops and conferences (Davis & Taylor, 1972; Davis & Cherns,
1975; Weir, 1976). Reorganisation of assembly line work at
Volvo's Swedish car plants received considerable publicity and
acclaim and was seen by some as heralding new prospects for
the humanisation of work in an industry better known for its
monotonous, repetitive and highly paced jobs. Not only car
plants, but other sectors of manufacturing as well as
clerical work also experienced strategies of job enlargement,
job enrichment, and the creation of autonomous groups (Wild
& Birchall, 1973). A myriad of outcomes was seen to flow
from these strategies ranging from the conventional changes in
'job satisfaction' through to the inauguration of the post-
industrial society and the supersession of alienation. Work,
in short, was destined for a dramatic and far reaching transformation.

These practices have been associated with job redesign
theory, an umbrella term which embraces a number of similar
approaches to the design of jobs within the enterprise
division of labour (see chapter 1). The aim of the present
chapter is to explore simultaneously the major assumptions and
limitations of what I shall call classical job redesign theory
as well as some of the consequences of taking an alternative,
economic and structural approach.

The next section describes job redesign theory in terms
of its core propositions, and their empirical support.
Following this the perspectives on the employment relationship
of Marx, Taylor and Baldamus are briefly outlined, and in the
light of this discussion a number of other critical approaches
to job redesign are commented on.

The ensuing section then brings these two perspectives, the classical and the alternative, to bear on a series of assumptions underlying job redesign theory and practice. The perspectives are next evaluated in the light of statistical evidence and secondary case study material. The penultimate section of the chapter applies both perspectives to two detailed case studies in order to assess their relative utility and validity; the final section looks at the neglected economic costs of job redesign.

THE CORE OF JOB REDESIGN THEORY

Job redesign theory belongs to a classic and longstanding tradition in industrial psychology centred on the explanation of two key variables often thought to be associated, namely job satisfaction and job performance (Tiffin and McCormick, 1975). According to the theory the creation of fragmented jobs lacking variety, autonomy and similar characteristics, engenders feelings of boredom and dissatisfaction in their occupants. In addition such jobs often fail to motivate employees to high levels of performance, and may indeed contribute to such phenomena as absenteeism and turnover (Herzberg et al., 1959; Friedmann, 1961; Argyris, 1964; Hackman and Lawler, 1971). The solution to these problems follows directly from the analysis: jobs should be redesigned so they possess the properties of variety, and wholeness, and so their incumbents can exercise autonomy and responsibility.

The general theory is slightly difficult to describe since it is in fact an amalgam of three specific theories - job enlargement (Guest, 1957), job enrichment (Herzberg et al., 1959; Herzberg, 1968), and sociotechnical systems (Trist et al., 1963). Nevertheless, the essence of the theory can be depicted as follows:

FIGURE 2.1

Job Redesign Theory

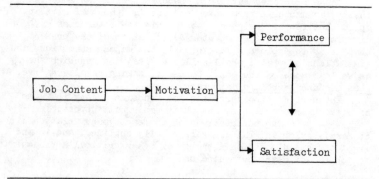

Naturally the specific theories of job redesign differ in particular ways. Herzberg et al. (1959) were initially concerned with the psychological properties of jobs, such as the degree to which they facilitated 'achievement' and 'responsibility' (although they later adumbrated actual job characteristics), and worked at the level of individual jobs, job performance and accountability. Sociotechnical systems theory, by contrast, has emphasised interconnections between jobs, or work roles, and has focussed attention on the relations between social and technical systems at work. Job enlargement (and other theories of job dimensions) have emphasised the careful specification and measurement of job features such as variety and feedback. The theories also differ in the posited relationship between job performance level and satisfaction: Herzberg et al. (1959) tended to treat satisfaction and motivation to perform as separate outcomes of job content (although they also on occasion conflated the concepts), whilst Hackman and Lawler (1971) considered satisfaction to be an outcome of job performance.

All of the theories share a similar perspective on the outcomes of job redesign. If one and the same set of changes in job content can simultaneously raise performance levels, and thereby meet the employer's interests, as well as raise job satisfaction, which meets the employee's interests, then we have in job redesign a powerful technique for the provision of mutual benefits for the parties involved.

EMPIRICAL SUPPORT FOR JOB REDESIGN THEORY

The theory is often thought to possess a narrow empirical base, derived from case studies and experiments of varying though usually weak methodological rigour. The evidence reported in such cases often consists of vaguely described measures of productivity changes, and tests of job satisfaction, whose psychometric and conceptual properties are rarely known (Cummings et al., 1977). The well known cases and experiments have undoubtedly played an influential role as demonstration projects in putting over the idea of a strong link between job content and job performance. The studies at Volvo, ICI, AT and T, Philips and elsewhere seemed to show that if job content was altered in the theory-specified direction, improvements ensued in performance levels and reported satisfaction, and the Conant and Kilbridge (1965) study is a good example of such exercises.

In this case, a conventional 6-man assembly line produced domestic appliances, and each worker's job cycle time was approximately 20 seconds. The management of this American company was dissatisfied with output and product quality, and was anxious to realise cost savings. It was decided (whether with worker or union involvement is unclear) to abolish the assembly line and create individual work stations at which each worker would assemble the entire product previously assembled by the whole line. Workers then exercised more control over the pace of their work, enjoyed a greater variety of tasks (their new roles included quality checking), completed a whole product, and had responsibility for their work. An attitude survey revealed a strong liking, though not a clear cut preference, for the new assembly method, and productivity and product quality both showed improvements.

Cross-sectional studies have provided support of a different kind for job redesign. It has been established in several countries that although the reported incidence of 'job satisfaction' among an occupationally heterogeneous sample can be as high as 88%, such findings conceal predictable occupational differences. Blue collar manual workers tend to report themselves as satisfied with their jobs less frequently than their white-collar managerial or technical counterparts, a difference attributed in part to the constraints surrounding manual work, particularly in industries such as vehicle manufacture (Blauner, 1960; Centers and Bugenthal, 1966; Quin et al., 1974).

Post-war studies of the car industry, by Walker and Guest (1952) and Chinoy (1955), were interpreted as showing the deleterious consequences for job satisfaction of the repetition, pacing and monotony of assembly line work. Narrowly prescribed and externally controlled tasks were not of course the monopoly of the car industry and the classic inter-industry survey by Davis et al., (1955)[1], uncovered a continuing adherence to principles of job design which resulted in considerable fragmentation of jobs, or what more recently has been labelled 'deskilling' (Braverman, 1974). Many of these principles were attributed (incorrectly in several cases) to the theory and practice of scientific management. The difficulty with Taylor's work, it was said, was that whatever its validity in its own time, it was rapidly ceasing to deliver its intended benefits for social and technological reasons. These reasons will be considered when I survey the key assumptions underlying job redesign theory, but before doing that I turn to consider a radically different approach to work and employment.

THE CAPITALIST EMPLOYMENT RELATIONSHIP: MARX, TAYLOR, BALDAMUS

For Marx the employment relationship under capitalism was an economic exchange between the owners of means of production-factories, mines, machinery, etc., on the one hand, and sellers of the capacity to labour on the other (Marx, 1965)[2]. The necessity for the exchange arose from the workers' standpoint because, owning no means for producing the goods and services required for their own existence, they were compelled to place their capacity for work at the disposal of an employer. From the employer's standpoint, the employment of workers was vital to the production of goods which could be sold in product markets and thereby realise a profit, a determinate rate of return on capital invested. For _both_ parties the act of producing goods was fundamentally instrumental in character, and subordinate to the production of wages and profits respectively. But what is the relationship between profits and wages within this 'cash nexus'? According to Marx profits derive from unpaid labour within the working day. Workers receive, directly and indirectly, only part of the value of the goods they produce: the remaining portion - surplus value - is expropriated by the employer and appears in a variety of forms among different sections of the capitalist class, such as profit, rent, interest, etc.. The expropriation of this surplus value is based on the legal and economic power of the employer as owner of the means of production. From this necessarily brief analysis it follows that the employer has a direct economic interest in reducing the price of labour in order to maintain or increase the rate or volume of profits, whilst conversely, the worker has an equally direct interest in raising the price of labour, but thereby eating into profits.

The employment relationship therefore contains an inherent, structural antagonism derived from the exploitation of labour which is central to the capitalist mode of production. This is not to deny that both parties have an interest in co-operating to produce the goods whose sale is essential for their economic gains, and this distinction between spheres of conflict and co-operation has been reproduced in, for example, surveys of employee attitudes towards participation (Ramsay, 1976). Nor does it follow that this structural, economic antagonism will necessarily be expressed in overt conflict: the relation between structure and behaviour is considerably more complex and mediated by many factors.

More generally, the analysis suggests that employers are inevitably confronted with two problems in the achievement of their goals (Braverman, 1974). First, because in the employment relationship (often nowadays embodied legally in a contract) workers agree to sell their _capacity_ to work for so many hours daily and not a fixed quantity of labour, the employer is faced with the task of securing and maintaining particular levels of performance. This problem appears variously as the problem of _control_ and/or _motivation_. Second, the employer is faced with the necessity to minimise the cost of labour in order to maintain or increase profitability, an imperative which in Braverman's view issues in a secular tendency to deskilling.

What follows from this is an analysis of the employer's concern with productivity. In Marxist terms an increase in productivity, i.e. an increase in physical output per man hour, will enable workers to produce goods equivalent to the value of their wages in a shorter period of time, and hence increase the period of working time available for surplus value production. Work under capitalism therefore has an alienated character evidenced in the facts: " . . . . that labour is external to the worker . . . . Hence the worker feels himself only when he is not working; . . . . His labour is therefore not voluntary but forced . . . . It is, therefore, not the satisfaction of a need but a mere means to satisfy needs outside itself" (Marx and Engels, 1975, p. 274). Thus, once again, we arrive at the necessity for controls over labour - to secure, maintain and improve levels of performance. And since labour has a fundamentally instrumental character it follows therefore that manipulation of wage levels and systems is likely to constitute the most powerful lever for influencing worker performance.

Such indeed (although for different reasons) was the conclusion reached by Frederick Taylor (1903, 1911, 1919, 1947; see also Kelly, 1981)[3], whose model of job performance is depicted below:

FIGURE 2.2

Taylor's Model of Job Performance

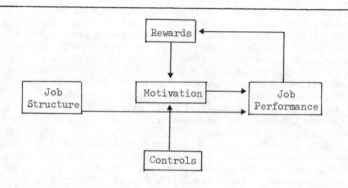

Where job redesign theory locates job performance determinants within the worker-task nexus (narrowly defined), Taylorism located this same nexus within a much wider context comprising extrinsic rewards (principally pay), organisational controls, such as performance standards or supervision, and job structure. The latter was described as efficient according to the proportion of "unnecessary and superfluous" motions which had been eliminated from the prescribed method of job performance.

The sources of this model are to be found both in Taylor's philosophical assumptions and in his analysis of industrial conflict. He took for granted the idea that workers were motivated by individual, economic self-interest. Within prevailing employment relationships, employers therefore frequently operated incentive or piecework pay systems, and in

order to reduce labour costs and raise productivity they
resorted to rate cutting whenever there was a transitory,
upward drift in job performance levels. Workers, in turn,
therefore, learned to regulate their output at fixed levels to
avoid rate cutting, and thus obstructed the employers' efforts
to raise productivity. The necessity for rate cutting and its
associated antagonism arose from the inability of employers to
raise productivity by altering methods of work performance, or
job structure. Yet, if this were done, argued Taylor,
productivity could be improved, work made easier and more
'efficient', and wages and profits could rise simultaneously
(though the latter he thought, might increase proportionately
faster). Taylor's analysis of output regulation and economic
antagonism was adopted in part, by Baldamus (1961). The in-
determinancy within the employment relationship (identified
by Marx) provides ample scope for bargaining between the
parties over the constitution of an appropriate amount of
labour in return for any given sum of wages or earnings and it
is this bargaining (in the broad sense of the word) which
occupies the centrepiece of Baldamus' analysis of the
employment relationship, or the wage-effort bargain. Indeed,
"the organisation of industry . . . .", according to Baldamus,
" . . . . ultimately revolves on a single process: the
administrative process through which the employee's effort is
controlled by the employer" (1961, p. 1).

According to this perspective, worker-employer conflict
is an enduring feature of employment since each party
constantly strives to increase the wage-effort ratio in their
own favour. The notion of a fair ratio mutually acceptable to
the parties, which thus eliminates conflict,would be considered unrealisable in view of the inherent vagueness of 'fairness'
(Hyman and Brough, 1975), and the constantly changing
conditions of production.

Baladmus' analysis is certainly consistent with Marx's,
as Eldridge (1975) has observed[4], although unlike Marx (but
like Taylor) he does not locate his conclusions in the context
of a mode of production driven by profit. By analysing the
determinants of boom-slump cycles within capitalist economies,
Marx's view allows us to recognise and analyse concomitant
variations in managerial and worker behaviour. It is more
difficult to see how, within their respective frameworks, one
avoids the 'stoic pessimistic' vision of unending conflict
painted by Baldamus, or the tempered optimism of Taylor based
on the prospect of continuous economic growth.

It should also be noticed that each of these theorists
endeavoured in different ways, to describe and analyse worker
responses to jobs. Marx's account of alienated labour has
already been presented. Taylor's (1919) early view of work
was close to that of Marx insofar as he concentrated on the
cash nexus and considered work itself to possess little
intrinsic value, but later in his career his view gradually
shifted to embrace elements of satisfaction derived from work

27

performance and co-operation with employers in a 'joint venture' (Taylor, 1947). The tension between these positions was never successfuly resolved, or indeed acknowledged. For Baldamus, the satisfactions available in work such as traction and contentment, were strictly relative: industrial work itself was fundamentally instrumental and unsatisfying in character.

For each of these writers economic and structural analysis of work was the most powerful entry point for examining work performance, and psychological considerations were strictly secondary (see also Gouldner, 1955; Ackroyd, 1974; Kelly, 1978). In order to understand changes in worker behaviour and attitudes, it was, therefore, imperative to begin with a study of corresponding developments in systems and levels of wages; in job structure; and in other organisational controls over employees, and this perspective will be adopted through- out the remainder of this chapter. However simplistic this view may appear, it is in fact consistent with much of the evidence on phenomena such as strikes, affluence, and absenteeism widely interpreted by job redesign theorists as vindicating their own analyses. But before examining these phenomena, it will be useful to comment briefly at this stage on a number of other critical approaches to job redesign advanced over the past few years, and their relation to the approach outlined above.

CRITICISMS AND CRITIQUES OF JOB REDESIGN THEORY

Some critics, such as Cummings et al. (1977) have serious reservations about the methodological rigour of many of the allegedly corroborative studies, and have suggested the available evidence is not as convincing as many would like to believe. Within their self-imposed limitations (which are rarely made explicit) such criticisms are undoubtedly valid, but the more fundamental issue of the theoretical plausibility of job redesign and its coherence with other perspectives and evidence, has been overlooked. One might have legitimately expected more sceptical writers to have matched their attitudes with a corresponding degree of incisiveness in their criticism, but this has not been the case. 'Radical criticism' of job redesign falls into two main classes, concerned respectively with the essence and the significance of job redesign.5

Under the first heading can be found two main arguments, both of which contrast the appearance of the phenomenon with its reality, either economic or political. According to the economic variant, despite the rhetoric about job satisfaction, human growth, alienation, work humanisation and so on, in reality job redesign is concerned with such mundane and hard- headed matters as profitability, productivity and cost reduction (Banks, 1974; Hales, 1974; Rasmus, 1974; Hughes and Gregory, 1978; Rosenhead, n.d.). Job redesign, in short, is a "con" and seeks to improve managerial interests whilst ignoring those of workers. This line of attack (labelled liberal-radical by Nichols, 1980), is extremely problematic, for it is virtually impossible to find any statements in the literature advertising job redesign solely or largely as a means to promote job satisfaction or similar goals. On the contrary, one of its main strengths has always been its claim to satisfy the mutual interests, economic and psychological, of employers and workers respectively. And the argument adducing weaker and less frequently reported data on job satisfaction, alienation, etc. as evidence for the neglect of workers' interests in comparison with their employers, actually succeeds in reproducing the extremely dubious view of job redesign theorists that employers' interests belong to the economic sphere, whilst workers' interests are located mainly in the psychological sphere (Blackler and Brown, 1978). Absent from this argument is any sustained analysis of workers' economic, or material interests, as outlined above.

The political variant of the argument asserts that job redesign is in fact an instance of a wider and more continuous system of managerial control over labour, and this feature overrides any micro-level changes in 'autonomy' (Gorz, 1976; Friedman, 1977). One of the difficulties with this argument is that it comes dangerously close to elevating control over labour to a position of pre-eminence, as an end in its own right, rather than analysing it in relation to other objectives such as surplus value production. And the argument has an abstract character from which it is difficult to see how one could produce more concrete analyses of specific job redesign practices.

On the significance of job redesign we can discern two diametrically opposed views: there are those who declare the significance of the phenomenon has been over-estimated because it is either trivial or limited in its sphere of application. Conversely there are writers who argue the opposite, either for economic or political reasons. The triviality argument asserts that the alterations in division of labour arising from job redesign are insignificant compared with some (usually unspecified) concept of significant change (Braverman, 1974; Zimbalist, 1975; Nichols and Beynon, 1977). Alternatively, or in addition, it is alleged that the circumstances under which job redesign can be initiated are socially, economically and/or technologically limited (Gomberg, 1973; Levitan and Johnston, 1973). The first argument begs the question as to what would constitute 'significant' change and whether this is an appropriate standard by which to evaluate job redesign, whilst the second variant appears to lead in the direction of dismissing job redesign as unworthy of analysis.

Economic reassessments of job redesign have drawn attention to the often neglected, economic consequences of the phenomenon, such as threats to: promotion prospects, manning levels, workloads, labour markets, pay levels, skills, job security and union organisation (Delamotte and Walker, 1973;

Tchobanian, 1975; Hull, 1978). Some of these consequences can
be shown empirically to have occurred but others such as
weakening or inhibition of union organisation are very much
less salient in the UK than the USA. Whilst this approach to
job redesign is potentially very promising, its proponents have
not located their observations within a coherent theoretical
framework that would permit their understanding and explanation, and that would allow us to discover the degree to which
they were necessary or contingent features of job redesign.

The political variant of this argument has been advanced
by writers such as Bosquet (1972), Gorz (1976), and Zimbalist
(1975), and posits an inherent radical dynamic within the
process of conceding elements of autonomy or control to shop
floor workers. By a cumulative process shop floor control
escalates to the point where it threatens or undermines
capitalist imperatives and structures. No evidence has
actually been adduced in favour of this view, a fact that is
not altogether surprising because of its conflation of the
concepts of autonomy and control.

The most striking feature of all these criticisms is
their failure to engage in a <u>theoretical</u> confrontation with
the theory and practice of job redesign. Some critics have
deprecated its methodology, others have sought to dismiss it,
others to unmask its ideological content, or to subsume it
under a more abstract category. None of these approaches
seems likely in itself, to advance our understanding of the
theoretical <u>and</u> ideological significance of job redesign, or
to provide tenable grounds for modifying or rejecting the
current theory of specific practices.

ASSUMPTIONS UNDERLYING THE THEORY

Job redesign has certainly cohered around a narrow conception
of worker-task relations, to the theoretical exclusion of
wider features of organisations and their environments. But
this is <u>not</u> to say that the theory has lacked a bedrock of
auxiliary propositions and assumptions which tie it in with
similar developments in other spheres of intellectual work.
On the contrary, it is important for the present argument to
recognise that the 'core' theory both derives from and
reinforces a body of semi-theorised assumptions whose
implications are rarely elucidated. This recognition both
legitimates and necessitates a far more comprehensive
theoretical examination of job redesign than has hitherto
been advanced. At the same time it provides the only means
for understanding the persistence of the theory over a period
of almost thirty years.

In the following sections the major assumptions of
classical job redesign theory are articulated and for each
area or topic in question the utility of the alternative
perspective is also considered. It is worth noting here that
these discussions are reconstructions of sets of ideas, rather

than simple presentations, as different forms of job redesign theory have attended differentially to different themes. Sociotechnical systems theory has analysed changes in technology in more detail than job enrichment, to give but one instance. Nevertheless, each of the assumptions articulated can be found to a greater or lesser degree underpinning each of the main theories of job redesign.

Social Trends

One of the major elements contributing to changing forms of job design was thought to be rising levels of education which in turn generated rising aspirations centred around job content. Equally, moves towards less authoritarian teaching methods were seen by some writers as having underwritten the increasing trend for employees not to submit automatically to authority (Davis, 1966, 1972; Thorsrud, 1972; Ginzberg, 1975; Herrick and Maccoby, 1975). Higher demands of work were thought to be reflected in such diverse phenomena as demands for participation in decision-making, and in job quitting and absenteeism (see below). Apart from its conflation of years of schooling (which has increased since the 1940's) with education (which may or may not have 'improved'), there is actually very little strong evidence for such inter-linked processes, except in countries like Sweden, where a degree of labour market segmentation has created the recruitment difficulties experienced by some Swedish employers (Berglind, 1975; Meidner, 1975). The rising aspirations thesis also fails to analyse countervailing mechanisms. Even if it is the case that educational levels have risen over the past 20 years or so, the process has not occurred against a static backcloth of jobs and qualifications. Rather, as the supply of qualifications has increased, so too have the demands of employers (Berg, 1970). Jobs once open to holders of 'CSE's' are increasingly being occupied by 'O' level entrants. Developments in employment practices then can be seen to have exerted a downward pressure on aspirations. And if we consider more direct attitudinal evidence on the job aspirations of school leavers, there is no clear suggestion of a secular upward trend (Paul, 1977). This is not to say that such a trend has not occurred, but only to note that the evidence adduced in its favour is couched in such general terms as to make any evaluation of its meaning extremely difficult.

Technological Trends

The social trends identified above happily coincided, it was argued, with the growth of automated and semi-automated technologies in which the dissatisfying jobs engineered by 'scientific managers' were being gradually eliminated, to be replaced by the more challenging tasks of machine maintenance, process supervision, etc. (see Hales, 1974; Kelly, 1978

for reviews; Blauner, 1964; Gallie, 1978). The argument will
doubtless be familiar to those acquainted with post-industrial
society and Second Industrial Revolution writings (for a
critique, see Kumar, 1978). For some theorists such processes
of job upgrading were seen as more or less inevitable, whereas
others argued they were contingent on managerial choices which
themselves reflected either traditional, scientific management-
type values, or the more enlightened neo-human relations
values of trust and co-operation (Theories X and Y in
McGregor's (1960) terms: see also Davis and Taylor, 1975).
The rise of new technologies was also to usher in or be
associated with both higher skill levels of jobs, as well as
new social values. Where the mass production technologies of
the Industrial Revolution were associated with competition and
conflicting objectives, the new technologies are more likely
to be associated with collaboration around linked objectives,
i.e. with increased social integration (Davis, 1966). Although
Blauner's (1964) work has often been used to support such
arguments, both his data and his interpretations of it have
been subjected to serious questioning and criticism (Eldridge,
1971). His conception of the chemical industry as a site of
highly skilled and responsible work overlooked the continuing,
high proportion of semi-skilled and labouring jobs found there
(Nichols and Beynon, 1977), even though data on these latter
categories of labour was available in Blauner's own work
(Table 26). More recent work has discovered significant
variations in both worker attitudes and social integration
within the same technology, and the study by Gallie (1978)
suggested cultural traditions and industrial relations systems
were more salient influences on both social integration and
alienation than the structure of technology per se.

This structure must therefore be understood within the
context of particular sets of social relations, an observation
which leads us to question the argument that technological
developments per se will necessarily generate an average
rising level of skill in manufacturing and service employment.
Braverman (1974) has argued that discussion of skill levels
in terms of average shifts, or trends across whole populations
conceals the actual dynamics of movements in skill (but see
Elger, 1979). On the one hand he accepts that new occupations
and branches of employment, such as micro-electronics,
computers etc. may indeed initially, or even for a sustained
period, create new and highly skilled jobs such as systems
analysis, or programme writing in the computer field, or an
increase in maintenance posts for automated technologies.
But he proceeds to argue that the logic of capital accumulation
compels the adoption of a systematic division of labour in
order to drive down labour costs and augment the rate of
exploitation. Thus in the programming field, Kraft (1977)
has shown that fragmentation of jobs, and cheapening of labour
power, has already become widespread. Less skilled work is
being removed from programmers, routinised and standardised,

and executed by cheaper and less qualified employees. The
proportion of skilled work thus diminishes.

Division of Labour and Economic Incentives

Both social and technological trends were thought to conflict
with and express the inadequacy of, traditional principles of
job design, embodied in Taylor's insistence on the fragmentation of manual and supervisory jobs, and the rigid separation
of conception and execution. The short-cycle, repetitive and
regulated jobs thus produced had yielded and were continuing
to yield, considerable economic benefits but they were also
subject to diminishing returns, revealed for example by output
'restriction' and absenteeism (Herzberg, 1968; Hackman and
Lawler, 1971; Daniel and McIntosh, 1972; Birchall, 1975;
Herrick and Maccoby, 1975; Trist, 1976). Traditional methods
of performance control involving supervision, financial
incentives and work and method study, were becoming less
effective. The objection to these methods was partly moral
and partly theoretical, the latter argument being grounded in
the 'affluent society' theses circulating in the 1950's, which
penetrated many job redesign writings (Galbraith, 1958).
Herzberg et al. prefaced 'The Motivation to Work' (1959),one
of the key texts in the genesis of job redesign, with the
assertion: "There was the feeling that in a world in which
there was a surfeit of material things man was losing zest for
work, that man and his work had become distant and alienated"
(p.ix). A similar assumption underlay Maslow's (1943, 1970)
emphasis on the increased motive power of higher order needs,
such as self-actualisation, as compared with lower-order needs,
such as material well-being. Indeed for Herzberg, writing in
1966, the worker continually concerned with material or
hygiene needs, the persistent 'hygiene seeker', was afflicted
with a 'sickness' of motivation (p. 81). The shift of
emphasis away from organisational rewards and controls, such
as pay levels and systems and disciplinary procedures, is
characteristic of large segments of post-war industrial
psychology (Blackler and Williams, 1971). It was undoubtedly
the case that many other people were reviewing theories of
financial incentives, and their corollaries such as output
regulation and 'loss of management control' (Brown, 1962), but
how far this reflected changing patterns of employee needs,
and how far tighter labour markets under 'full employment',is
a difficult problem. Nevertheless, the Introduction to a
recent collection of readings entitled 'Management and
Motivation' (Vroom and Deci, 1970) observed that, "This
approach to motivation rests on a rather substantial foundation of psychological research and theory" (p. 13). A
similar point was reiterated in two recent reviews of the
literature on pay incentives, written by psychologists.
According to Lawler (1971), ". . . .Individual (incentive)
plans typically lead to substantial increases in productivity"
(p.128). Whilst Marriott (1968) noted that despite its many

deficiencies the available evidence served to " . . . . reinforce the large body of opinion that human beings, given the right conditions, are stimulated to produce more if a pecuniary inducement is directly linked to the effort they make" (p. 174). And a study of changes in payment systems in Sweden found similar, and predictable, effects in a survey of 73 plants (Lindholm, 1972). Of those which replaced piecework with flat rates, i.e. abolished financial incentives, productivity fell on average by 15-25%. Those companies which introduced an incentive where none had previously existed, experienced productivity increases averaging 25-35%. On the other hand small increases in productivity (5-10%) were also elicited by the transition from piecework to flat rates plus incentives.

More pervasive effects of pay incentives have been documented by writers such as Roy (1952), Klein (1964), Lupton (1963) and Cunnison (1966) in their studies of output regulation and worker attitudes. And on fragmentation of jobs both Drucker (1970) and Barnes (1968) have argued that the enthusiasm for this principle has carried its application beyond the point where it is economically viable, or optimal. The problem with extensive division of labour was not the principle per se but its over-zealous application.

Industrial Conflict

But, of course, if economic problems were due for elimination, then presumably the kind of industrial class conflict fuelled by such problems, and evidenced throughout the inter-war years in massive strikes, would also decline, a thesis adumbrated by Ross and Hartman (1960). And associated with declining class conflict would be a withering away of class ideology and consciousness, a view encapsulated in the embourgoisiement and end of ideology theses (see Goldthorpe et al., 1969). Classical job redesign theory grew and matured in this intellectual and economic climate and as such bears the hallmark of its origins (as undoubtedly will the perspective advanced in this chapter).

Evidence relating job discontent to collective industrial action is extremely sparse and generally speculative or ambiguous. Certainly a recent review was unable to reach any conclusion on the salience of such discontent (Kelly and Nicholson, 1980), but if we consider analyses of industrial conflict, from varying sources, we discover not a declining concern with material issues, as job redesign theorists posit, but a continuing and recently increasing, concern. In statistics collected by the U.K. Department of Employment, some two-thirds of officially recorded industrial stoppages were assigned a principal cause either of wages or workloads throughout the period 1950-76 (Smith et al., 1978). The notion of a principal cause is open to serious conceptual and methodological objections - how does one distinguish principal

34

from other causes? Is the notion of 'cause' synonomous with
that of an issue or demand? Could there not be several
principal causes for any single dispute? Nevertheless, the
idea that material or economic issues have declined in significance, for workers and for industrial conflict, appears to
be contradicted not only by admittedly questionable facts, but
by the theory of relative deprivation and reference groups.
According to this conception the provision of economic goods
(or services for that matter) is not judged by recipients
solely or largely by reference to its need-satisfying
properties, which, given a static conception of need suggests
the possibility of need-fulfilment, but is evaluated in
relation to the provision, and the inputs (work, abilities,
requirements, etc.) of other, relevant groups (Runciman, 1966).
Economic or material needs are therefore likely to continue to
play a prominent role in industrial conflict, especially under
conditions of high inflation.

Such conditions, particularly since the late 1960's in
the U.S.A. and the U.K. have served to slow down and for short
periods actually reverse, increases in living standards, and
with inflation running at between 10% and 20% per annum over
the past few years, there seems good reason to be sceptical
of claims that the motive power of material needs is being
eroded by affluence.

Theory and evidence on the determinants of absenteeism
and turnover (sometimes conceptualised as unorganised action)
offer little more support for the notion that both phenomena
reflect job-centred discontents. A recent review concluded
that the link between absenteeism and job satisfaction was at
best tenuous, at worst, nonexistent, and that the occasional
findings of an inverse relationship were probably specific to
certain types of organisation (Nicholson et al., 1976).
Equally, labour turnover has been shown to be only weakly
related to job satisfaction (Lyons, 1972). Both phenomena
would appear to be far more responsive to external pull from
factors outside the employing organisation, such as domestic
circumstances, or alternative employment opportunities, than
to internal push from job dissatisfaction. In addition, there
is evidence to suggest that variations in absence rates
between organisations may reflect concomitant variations in
'absence cultures', or socially sanctioned norms regulating
and legitimating particular levels of absence (Nicholson, 1977).

The Prospect of Industrial Harmony

If conflict within organisations originates in job dissatisfaction and reflects a mismatch between organisational goals
and individual needs (see for instance Argyris, 1957), it can
be argued that the strategy of job redesign ought to impinge
directly on this sort of conflict. Improvements in job
content would be expected to reduce such conflict, and since
its various manifestations, absenteeism, go-slows, etc. are

dysfunctional for the organisation, if not for the individual, then job redesign also assumes a moral value.

The crux of this positive assessment of prospects for industrial peace lies in an asymmetrical characterisation of the interests of the parties in employment. Employers are primarily concerned with goals such as profitability and productivity, employees are chiefly interested in, or will respond positively to 'improvements' in job content. These same improvements in jobs will simultaneously provide satisfaction for employees, and increased performance (via higher motivation) for employers. Again, several writers in the sociotechnical tradition have tried to link a decline in competitive values and the emergence of 'co-operation' to the more integrated structures of new, or advanced technologies (Trist, 1976).

The alternative view of employment advanced would question this vision on two key points. The first is the managerialism entailed in the notion of conflict as a dysfunctional phenomenon: from the employee's standpoint, absenteeism for instance, may well be a very functional activity in terms of coping with domestic problems. Secondly, it would challenge the neglect of the economic interests of employees, in terms of wages, and the conditions of work implicated in the wage-effort exchange and would suggest the investigation of such features before generalising about future trends in industrial peace.

PROBLEMATIC EMPIRICAL FINDINGS IN JOB REDESIGN CASES

The emphasis placed on the consistency and coherence of job redesign theory serves to demonstrate the embeddedness of the theory as such in a wider and deeper nexus of propositions which are rarely described and analysed. It is not intended to suggest the absence of contradictions or inconsistencies. Indeed, if we examine the cases in the literature, we can discern a number of facts which it would seem difficult to accommodate within the confines of classical job redesign theory.

Whilst many cases have reported simultaneous improvements in job attitudes and job performance, a significant minority have departed from this pattern of results. Locke et al., (1976), Kuriloff (1963), Ford (1969), Paul and Robertson (1970), Penzer (1973), and Anon (1975), have all reported conventional initiatives in job redesign which, as the theory predicts, resulted in improvements in job performance measured usually in terms of productivity, i.e. physical output per man-hour. But the studies failed to report corresponding changes in job satisfaction, and in a number of cases, motivation. However one interprets job redesign theory these findings are difficult to explain. If job satisfaction is a function of the performance of redesigned or enriched jobs, the prediction has clearly failed in these cases.

Alternatively, one could argue job satisfaction is a function of job content, but independent of job performance, but that viewpoint won't explain the discrepant findings either. And the only (conceptual) alternative, that job performance derives from job satisfaction is clearly and equally untenable. There are methodological alternatives, which would suggest that the measuring instruments were inadequate, or insufficient time elapsed to detect attitudinal changes and so on. But these arguments are essentially ad hoc, since they cannot explain why other studies using equally poor measuring instruments or equally short-time periods <u>have</u> detected attitudinal changes. Their function (which is not to deny their validity in all cases) is to sustain hypotheses contradicted by pertinent facts.

Conversely, there are cases where job redesign has culminated in attitudinal improvement but performance has been unaffected, e.g. the studies by Emery and Thorsrud (1975), Rush (1971), and Powell and Schlacter (1971). Such findings are contrary to the view that job satisfaction derives from effective job performance, but on the reverse hypothesis, it is unclear why performance improvements failed to materialise given the redesigned jobs. And if one posits the independence of satisfaction and performance it is equally unclear why improved job content should generate measured changes in satisfaction (a variable difficult to conceptualise and measure in any case) but not in performance. There may, of course, have been technical barriers to performance, although such an account seems unpromising in the particular cases under consideration. More generally, it has been argued that such findings could merely signify the inappropriateness of a <u>universalistic</u> theory of job redesign which imputes similar motives to all employees. Some employees may be reconciled or adapted to short cycle, repetitive work and hence resist job redesign because it is not perceived as rewarding, or may indeed be considered psychologically threatening (Turner and Miclette, 1962). The individual difference hypothesis is, in principle, quite plausible. In practice it has proved difficult to discover general psychological correlates of responses to job redesign, and the attempts centred around the Protestant work ethic, growth need strength, and urban-rural differences, have all encountered empirical objections in the form of contradictory evidence (Stone, 1976).

In addition to these 'anomalous' findings, there are a number of 'facts' about job redesign exercises which the classical theories have never systematically tried to explain. In many cases of job redesign, changes have been introduced in levels and systems of pay; in workloads and manning levels; and in work methods and workplace design, as the following table shows (from Kelly, 1979, chapts. 6-8).

TABLE 2.1

Incidence of Economic and Structural Mechanisms of Job
Performance in Cases of Job Redesign (as percentage of
total number of cases)

Item	Incidence	Number of Cases
Pay rises	65%	93
Incentive pay systems	59%	46
Labour elimination	68%	121
Flowline re-organisation	28%	55

These figures were obtained from a detailed examination of
almost 300 cases of job redesign reported in academic journals,
management and business periodicals, technical journals, books,
and internal or unpublished reports. Cases where relevant
information was not reported have been excluded from the table.
Thus in all those cases where definite information was
supplied on payment systems, 59% (N=46) of such cases reported
the use of an incentive system (including piecework).

Of course, job redesign theorists could argue that pay
rises were provided after productivity improvements; that
incentive systems have been shown to be of limited utility and
to generate contradictory outcomes, such as output regulation
or reduced labour mobility; that labour elimination results
from job performance improvements; and that flowline re-organisation - a structural change in job design - is only effective
to the extent that it generates internal motivation. None of
these interpretations, as we shall see, is actually tenable in
these forms, but before proceeding to a more detailed examination of particular cases of job redesign, let us conclude
this section.

The arguments and evidence adduced hitherto do not point
unambiguously to the superiority of either the classical or
the alternative approach to job redesign. The strengths of
the classical approach are well known: its theoretical
statements are relatively clear and testable; there is a not
inconsiderable body of evidence consistent with them; its
proponents have endeavoured, in some instances, to deploy
experimental methodologies and to use sophisticated quantitative techniques; and the theory is, on the whole, easily
communicable. Nevertheless the above discussions have
clarified a number of grounds for taking seriously an
alternative approach:

(a) many of the assumptions underlying job redesign
theory, especially in the area of industrial conflict, have

been seriously questioned and such phenomena shown to be <u>more</u>
amenable to economic and structural analysis;

    (b) the relative neglect of contextual factors in job
redesign theory and cases would suggest the possible utility
of the alternative approach with its emphasis on the employment relationship as the context of job performance;

    (c) there exist anomalous findings within job redesign
cases, such as attitude - behaviour discrepancies;

    (d) the types of variable predicted by the alternative
approach to be more salient determinants of job performance,
such as pay rises and incentive pay systems, are in fact
frequently found in cases of job redesign.

In the next section the respective utility and validity
of the classical and alternative approaches are assessed in
two detailed case studies.

CASE STUDIES

The two cases chosen for detailed description are typical
instances of job redesign in the sense that the changes
introduced in job content conform to the prescriptions of the
conventional theories, and both were described and recognised
as bona fide instances of job redesign. They will therefore
enable us to compare the explanatory power of classical job
redesign theories with that of economic and structural analysis
of the employment relationship and work performance. Furthermore the cases represent two of the most common forms of job
redesign: reorganisation of flow lines and creation of
autonomous groups. Information is available in the literature
on almost 200 similar exercises (Kelly, 1979, 1981). The
cases chosen here are atypical only in the degree of information
they provide on aspects of work organisation constituted as
significant by the two theoretical perspectives examined in
this chapter.

The Meccano Case[6]

The Meccano factory in question is based in a large North
Western city and its sole product is toy cars. The product
range is large, over 100 lines, and the plant employed, in
1971, approximately 1200 employees of whom some 75% were union
members. The main unions were the GMWU, for the mainly female
assembly workers, and the AUEW for the skilled and semi-
skilled male workers. Production was highly labour intensive,
especially in the assembly and sub-assembly areas, and
workers were paid on flat rates plus group or individual
incentives according to the mode of work organisation. All
of the manual work in the plant had been subjected to Work
Study, and indeed job timings were regular occurrences on the
shop floor.

The local management had been experiencing a number of
difficulties for several years, which had gradually assumed

even greater significance. The problems were variously located in the inflexible structure of the assembly lines and in the predominantly female labour force with its rapid labour turnover, but the chief problem can be analysed in terms of a growing contradiction between production and distribution. Meccano produces toy cars at the upper (price) end of the market which removes it from competition with many other manufacturers. During recessions however, some consumer spending is diverted lower down the price scale, and the company usually fares badly under these more competitive conditions. Distribution is also geared up for a very short product life: new models yield high initial sales but these fall off rapidly, and manufacturers subsequently issue further models. With the regular introduction of new products, sales are thus maintained at a higher level than would otherwise be the case, but this continual transformation of the product is a phenomenon which has considerable repercussions on the production process within the plant. Apart from a small amount of on-site manufacture, the Liverpool plant is basically an assembly unit using unpaced flow lines of up to a dozen workers, i.e. it is a mass production system. As the product range expanded however, product runs became shorter and shorter as the diversity of orders grew in line with the product range. This meant that the proportion of 'idle time' during product changeover also grew, and hence labour productivity was being reduced. In more abstract terms, the management was operating a <u>mass</u> production system under conditions where it was increasingly producing its goods only in large (or indeed sometimes even small) <u>batches</u>. Efforts to improve distribution via rationalisation of the system for incoming orders having failed to solve the problems, the management turned its attention to the production system itself, and in 1971 called in a firm of consultants to report.

The consultants advanced a series of proposals, the four major ones being:

(a) abolition of assembly lines and their replacement by individual work stations at each of which an entire product would be assembled;

(b) introduction of a new, and more standardised system of work study;

(c) an increased accountability of the workforce to management (i.e. increased managerial control);

(d) an increase in basic wage rates of 8% and the replacement of all group-based incentives by individual incentives.

Following negotiations with the unions involved, implementation occurred in two phases, the differences between which are crucial in understanding the ensuing costs and benefits.

Phase 1. In this first phase a small experimental unit of
twelve workers was created on a separate part of the factory
floor. Each worker sat at an individual work station in front
of a set of containers holding all of the parts necessary for
product assembly. Each was systematically trained in the
assembly process to use work methods prescribed by time and
motion analysis. Earnings received were equal to their own
average earnings for the previous two months on conventional
assembly lines, regardless of the new levels of performance,
i.e. the incentive component of the pay system was temporarily
eliminated. After two months the group's productivity showed
an increase of 35% over their performance on a conventional
assembly line immediately prior to the experimental period.
   In order to understand this result we must consider the
various components of total unit production time, as shown in
Table 2.2.

TABLE 2.2

Job Redesign at Meccano : Production Results, Phase 1

	Assembly Line	Unit Assembly (UA)
Actual unit production time*	4.44	4.13
Non-productive time	1.97	0.68
Balance-delay time	0.43	0.27
Total unit production time	6.84	5.08

* All times in minutes

Increase in productivity = $\dfrac{6.84 - 5.08}{5.08}$ x 100% = 35%

Interpretation of these results in terms of classical job
redesign theory would tend to focus on the increased motivation derived from the greater variety, challenge and
responsibility inherent in the new tasks, an explanation that
appears to be reinforced by the elimination of financial
incentives which might otherwise have been invoked in an
explanatory capacity. But another, and more structural
explanation is possible. The biggest reduction in unit
production time stemmed from a fall in non-productive time.
On the assembly line workers were not directly responsible

for product quality, and their bonus earnings were tied only to product quantity. With high production pressure, the result was a fall off in quality, and the stationing of supervisory personnel at the end of the line to check finished products. On unit assembly workers were directly responsible for quality, and because assembled products could easily be traced to the individual responsible, time spent on quality checking decreased. Actual unit production time was also cut by encouraging workers to use two-handed assembly methods, and by virtue of the fact that the product handling involved in passing products along the assembly line had disappeared in unit assembly. Finally, waiting time (enforced non-working on the line arising from unequal workloads and poor materials supply) was also reduced as individuals no longer worked interdependently. Thus, job structure, in the Taylorist sense, was rendered more efficient, and employer control over workers was increased because defective work quantity or quality could readily be traced to its author. At the same time, of course, job content was improved in the directions specified by job redesign theory.

However, despite these improvements, the proportion of the working day in which workers actually engaged in production remained constant at 60%. Any increased motivation resulting from the changed content of jobs appeared not to have issued in increased levels of effort, as measured by working time. Rather it appeared that the period of working time was being used more efficiently.

Phase 2. In the second phase of the experiment, the Unit Assembly method of production was extended into other sections of the shopfloor, involving a total of 36 employees. The employees new to UA were trained in the same way as the Phase 1 group, and their job content was also the same. The only difference between Phase 1 and Phase 2 appeared in pay levels and the pay system. Basic rates were increased by 8%, and all UA workers went onto an individual incentive scheme. The effect of renewed incentives for the Phase 1 experimental group, and the transformation of group to individual incentives for the remainder of the Phase 2 group,was to further increase productivity after a period of twelve months, by 35%. Explanations based on improved job content would be unable to account for this further increase since jobs had undergone no further changes between Phases 1 and 2. The only change which could account for the new level of productivity was the combined reintroduction of incentives, and fresh introduction of individual incentives which tied pay more closely to performance. The proportion of the working day spent in production rose from 60% to over 80%.

Overall then it would appear that improvements in job content could have been responsible at most for only a small percentage of the total, observed increase in productivity. The more salient determinants of performance were centred around job structure, pay levels and incentives, and increased organisational controls, mechanisms identified long ago in Taylor's writings, and which are also consistent with the perspectives of Marx and Baldamus.

The Ahmedabad Textiles Mills Case

This case study has been described elsewhere by Rice (1958), and re-analysed by the author (Kelly, 1978), and the present account draws heavily on this re-analysis. The textile mills were organised on an extensive and detailed division of labour involving twelve grades of worker. The site of the experiment - the automatic loom shed - was manned by 29 workers. In grades such as sweeper, and fitter, there was only one man, and he was therefore responsible for all 244 looms. Each jobber was assigned 112 looms; each smash-hand 60-80; and each weaver 24-32 looms. These differences rendered horizontal communication between grades extremely difficult, and in practice communications would travel upwards to supervisory levels, and then return downwards to their targets, thus placing a heavy and difficult workload on supervisors.

The experiment emerged from managerial disappointment with the productivity gains from the introduction of automatic looms. In addition product quality, measured by the percentage of cloth damaged, was variable and tending to be unacceptably low.

In line with the sociotechnical systems orientation, Rice attributed the problems of the weaving shed to a mismatch between the social and technical systems. Whilst the latter required considerable co-ordination and inter-dependence, the former was organised around independent work roles. The solution therefore followed clearly, and the workers were re-organised into teams of seven men, with each team possessing all of the skills needed for production which had previously been distributed among twelve occupational grades. Over and above the amalgamation of skills required by this re-organisation, workers were also to be 'flexible', i.e. to be willing to move from job to job as production demands required. Thus the workers' new jobs entailed more variety, autonomy and responsibility, and each team was responsible for a whole task. Simultaneously basic rates of pay were increased for different grades, by up to 44%. Generally speaking, the results were impressive, from the standpoint of management: productivity and product quality both showed significant improvements.

But these indices nevertheless showed variations that were quite independent of job content, but which did correlate with changes in pay levels and systems, and supervisory controls. Before re-organisation only one third of the workers were on piece wages (8 weavers and 2 jobbers per group of 29 workers) whilst the remaining ten occupational groups

were paid time wages. At 85% loom efficiency a certain sum
was paid to the weavers and jobbers, and variations around
this figure resulted in proportionate gains and losses in pay.
After re-organisation, all workers were transferred to an
incentive payment system, and on achievement of the 85% norm,
all would receive a "small rise in pay" (Rice, 1958, p. 68).
The effects of these incentives on performance were predictable without reference to changed work methods and work
organisation: average loom efficiency rose from below 80%
to almost 90% as workers sought to increase their earnings
(Rice, 1958, p. 76; see also Roy, 1969).

Despite their 'intuitive' acceptance of the re-organisation they did unfortunately neglect loom maintenance, and
achieved higher efficiency at the price of increased damage
to the raw materials. Supervision was therefore tightened in
the 'second phase' of the re-organisation, and quality
improved whilst efficiency fell to a new low of 72%, climbing
rapidly then to 78%. It should also be noted that the group
of seven workers was assigned an additional worker for half of
each day during this phase. After three days, supervision was
relaxed, and efficiency continued to climb back towards 90%
whilst damage stabilised at 20%. The explanation for the
efficiency gain is that the looms were run during meal breaks
by the supervisors until the yarn broke - previously this had
not been done (Rice, 1958, p. 74).

The re-organisation was followed up for six months,
during which time efficiency was mostly stable, at about 90-
93%, and damage at 24%. Eight months after the start of the
experiment, efficiency began to fall, reaching 77%. The
workers protested that the quality of the yarn was poor and
thus giving rise to more stoppages, too many in fact for them
to cope with. They first requested extra help, and when this
was turned down, asked for compensation for loss of earnings.
According to Rice, the first request signified a 'task-centred'
orientation on the part of the workers, but we are asked to
believe that when the request failed, the workers then
'produced' a cash-orientation. Was their acceptance of the
re-organisation not so thorough-going after all? Or were
their attitudes contradictory, a mixture of 'intrinsic' and
'extrinsic' orientations? Rice bends over backwards to
preserve his original hypotheses about the workers' behaviour
- after all he says, they had to contend with absenteeism,
machine breakdown, lack of training, etc., from which he
concludes it is surprising that efficiency didn't fall even
sooner and to a much greater extent (Rice, 1958, pp. 88-95).
A far more parsimonious interpretation is available: the
workers' requests for extra help, and extra cash, were not
'separate' requests but two sides of the same coin, that coin
being the wage-effort bargain (Baldamus, 1961). Perceiving
an upward drift in effort relative to pay, they first tried to
realign the two through effort reduction, that is, by asking
for higher manning. When this failed, they approached the

problem from the other end and asked for more pay.

There was a second experiment involving non-automatic looms, in which the changes introduced were rather similar. The pre-change situation was very different, with a group of 22 workers for 40 looms. Unlike the automatic shed, in which there were twelve grades of worker, here there were only three (jobber, weaver and ancillary) and many duties performed by ancillaries in the automatic shed were carried out by weavers in the non-automatic shed. The changes consisted of the creation of a group of workers (eleven instead of twenty-two) responsible for 40 looms, in which the weavers' duties were now divided up among front, back and smash-tent workers. All workers (instead of just the weavers) went onto piece rates, and bonuses were paid on a composite output and quality index. Efficiency was raised from between 40 and 60% to 85%, 70% being the level beyond which bonus was paid, whilst damage fell from 20% to 5%. In explaining these results Rice (1958) entirely abandoned any notions of the importance of individual job content, for although

> . . . . the weavers performed an integrated 'whole' task - the conversion of yarn to cloth. (p. 163) The amount of time they spent outside the shed suggested that the workers derived no more than a very moderate satisfaction from the efficient performance of their tasks. (p. 121)

Therefore,

> The immediate practical result of the experiment has been to demonstrate that . . . . the break-down of the 'whole' task of weaving into component operations, each performed by a different worker, and the reintegration of the workers into an internally structured work-group that performs the whole task on a group of looms, can be accomplished in one process . . . . (p. 166)

This is a very clear statement of the Durkheimian analysis of division of labour. Many of the results of this case, for example reduced costs, derive quite directly from the 50% reduction of manning levels, and more significantly, from the furtherance of the division of labour, and the introduction of output and quality bonuses for all workers.

COSTS OF JOB REDESIGN [7]

In both of these case studies a number of costs were incurred by workers which would call into question the "mutual benefits" thesis in job redesign writings. In order to consider this thesis more systematically, a total of over 200 cases and experiments in job redesign was examined. Data was

collected on predicted costs, such as job losses, labour
intensification, non-provision of pay rises, and increased
managerial control, to consider the extent to which the
antagonisms inherent in the employment relationship manifested
themselves in these ways. A total of 57 cases was discovered
in which information was provided on the numbers of jobs
redesigned and eliminated respectively.

TABLE 2.3

Job Losses in Cases of Job Redesign

Jobs Redesigned	Jobs Lost	Total Cases
1958	528	53

The fate of the <u>workers</u> occupying these jobs is difficult to
determine: some were redeployed, or retired, but it is
difficult to believe there were not some redundancies with the
associated problems (which naturally vary according to local
labour markets).

Whilst the phenomenon of job loss may be seen as
expressive of the structure of the employment relationship, it
cannot be explained quite as simply. It has been demonstrated
elsewhere that the incidence of job loss varies both with the
<u>form</u> of job redesign - being much higher with autonomous group
creation than with flow line re-organisation - as well as
between national economies - being considerably higher in the
U.S.A. than the U.K. (Kelly, 1980).

The provision of pay rises reveals an equally complex
picture:

TABLE 2.4

Pay Rises in Cases of Job Redesign*

Pay Rises Awarded	Pay Rises Not Awarded
38	29

* Figures refer to numbers of cases

On the one hand employers' economic benefits are increased to the degree that wage rises are not awarded, and the incidence of non-provision is highest in the U.S.A., where union density is the lowest amongst countries using job redesign. On the other hand the provision of wage rises and incentives has been analysed as an essential mechanism for raising job performance in cases of job redesign, which accounts for its relatively high incidence.

Managerial control over labour is a less tangible phenomenon and hence more difficult to assess quantitatively but reports of its augmentation are readily available. It was described as a feature of the Meccano case (above) and indeed it is particularly characteristic of this form of job redesign, as Sirota (1973), a work study engineer recognised, " . . . . management found it was much easier to identify the source of quality problems when they occurred because they knew which employee had built which mechanism" (p.13). Again, the incidence of such increased control varies with the form of redesign, and it should be noted in any case that it need not accompany a reduction in worker control over immediate aspects of production since control is not a zero-sum phenomenon.

Finally, labour intensification is a characteristic feature of several forms of job redesign. Where a series of discrete work roles are amalgamated (e.g. machine set-up, simple maintenance and operation) the effect on the worker is a simple increase in workload. Equally, in many cases of autonomous groups it has been shown theoretically that labour intensification is a necessity if productivity is to be raised (Kelly, 1978). Employee perceptions and responses to such intensification are likely to vary considerably and some may welcome additional duties as a way of alleviating boredom, whilst others may carry them out only when satisfactory readjustments have been made to pay levels.

CONCLUSIONS

A fresh analysis of job redesign cannot be expected to stand solely on the basis of two case studies, in neither of which was attitudinal data, for instance, collected and presented. The cases, however, are atypical only in the amount of material available, and a longer study of job redesign has demonstrated the applicability of economic analyses to many more similar cases and experiments in the literature (Kelly, 1979, 1980).

We have seen in the present chapter that many of the assumptions and premises associated and connected with job redesign theory are open to serious question and criticism. The idea that dissatisfaction with job content, specifically with monotonous, repetitive and fragmented work, fuelled such diverse phenomena as absenteeism, low productivity, turnover, and strikes, was shown to be empirically weak and theoretically untenable.

The substitution of the 'individual vs the organisation' as the central, organising motif for the analysis of conflict within economic enterprises was shown to be unable to provide a satisfactory account of continued, and growing economic strife, and to constitute in toto a far less useful approach than traditional notions of collective, sectional and conflicting economic interests. And finally, the analyses of rising aspirations, skill levels, and technological requirements in jobs have all (in different ways) encountered serious difficulties. Rising levels of education do not necessarily generate rising aspirations since employers also respond to changes in educational systems by raising entry requirements, thereby providing a countervailing and depressing force on job aspirations. Demands for increased influence and participation at work, sometimes conceptualised as democratisation, have taken both more radical and more conventional forms in Europe, by comparison with job redesign. The more radical forms embrace demands for supervisory boards and worker directors; the more traditional forms centre on the extension of collective bargaining. Common to both forms and absent from job redesign writings, is the concept of power. Yet, even these demands, such as they were, have receded in the face of the perceived threat to jobs posed by 'the new technologies'. The focus, in the 1950's debates on automation and mechanisation, on job content and skill levels, has hitherto been displaced in the 1970's and 1980's by a more basic concern with jobs per se.

The second approach taken here to job redesign theory was the identification of a set of empirical problems whose explanation posed a serious challenge to the content and limits of the theory. There were dissociations found in numerous cases between attitude and behaviour changes, e.g. cases where 'job satisfaction' improved but productivity remained constant. Further, and more seriously, there was a high incidence of pay rises, incentive pay systems and labour elimination in job redesign cases which the classical theories could not account for. And these same mechanisms, in addition to changes in job structure and supervisory control, offered more plausible and valid accounts of two detailed case studies than any of the classical theories.

These theoretical difficulties are not separate, but interlinked, and derive from the same fundamental source, namely the inadequate conceptualisation of the employment relationship. The failure of job redesign theory to describe and analyse the structural antagonisms inherent in employment relationships permits the theory to 'overlook' economic determinants of conflict and alienation, to underestimate the significance of economic and structural determinants of job performance, and to over-estimate the possibility of reconciling the interests of workers and employers via job redesign.

We saw in two case studies that the mechanisms identified by Taylor - changes in pay levels and systems, in supervisory controls, and in job structure, as well as in manning levels — and linked with the Marxist analysis of the antagonistic employment relationship, were able to offer more plausible accounts of changes in employee behaviour than any of the conventional job redesign theories. In turn it was seen that a series of economic costs for workers, neglected by the classical theories, were also evident in a wide range of cases. Economic and structural analysis of job redesign outcomes is both more plausible and more powerful than conventional approaches centred on job content and 'intrinsic' motivation, and is more consistent with our knowledge of related phenomena such as industrial conflict.

It is also worth noting that although Braverman dismissed job redesign as an insignificant trend in relation to deskilling, it can in fact be accounted for within terms very similar to his own, as has been shown here. The same imperatives which tend to generate deskilling can also, under specific circumstances, result in the reverse phenomenon, job redesign.

This is not to say that classical theories of job redesign are wrong in toto and that the type of analysis offered here is necessarily superior. Rather it is to argue for the superiority in general of the present approach. There may well be cases of job redesign where explanations employing concepts such as 'intrinsic motivation' are likely to be of greater validity. The literature on individual differences in 'needs' and preferences has been used to suggest that the majority of workers are 'instrumentally' orientated to work and unlikely to respond to job redesign. Only a minority therefore may behave in the predicted manner. An alternative interpretation of these attitudinal differences would argue that such differences influence not the presence of a response to job redesign but the mode of response. The behaviour of instrumentally oriented workers in job redesign exercises is best explained in terms of the general theory outlined above, whilst the minority of workers with strong intrinsic, or moral attachments to their jobs and organisations, more easily fall into the mould of conventional job redesign theory. Equally, whilst the alternative approach above may offer a more plausible account, in general, of job performance, it may be that conventional job redesign theory could more usefully account for job attitudes, in particular job satisfaction.[8] The alternative approach recognises that the association between job attitudes and job performance is weak and declines to offer a general theory accounting for both phenomena.

A further implication of the present analysis concerns the ideological significance of job redesign. If ideology is understood as partial and distorted social thought reflecting the interests of a particular class or class fraction in society (cf. Larrain, 1979), job redesign appears to fit readily into this rubric by virtue of its exclusion of economically driven conflict and the possibility it holds

49

out of considerable interest reconciliation within employment relationships. Again, psychological studies of job content and division of labour have focussed almost exclusively for the past twenty years on upgrading of jobs, when many jobs have in fact passed through the reverse process. The concentration of such research efforts on what is almost certainly a minority phenomenon may be seen to constitute a systematic distortion of the general trends in division of labour, as discussed by Braverman (1974).

NOTES

1. The effective response rate in this survey was however very low - 5% - and the results should be interpreted with caution.

2. The following discussion is based largely on Chapters 6, 7 and 9 of Capital, vol. 1.

3. F.W. Taylor's most popular work was The Principles of Scientific Management, but his Shop Management,Testimony before the House Committee, and A Piece Rate System in F.W. Taylor, Two Papers on Scientific Management ,were more detailed and instructive. A fuller analysis of these writings is available in J.E. Kelly (1981). See also Littler (1978).

4. J.E.T. Eldridge, 'Industrial relations and industrial capitalism', in G. Esland et al., (1975). This consistency should not be overstated, and is certainly not predicated on the idea that the categories 'economic' and 'structural' are unambiguous and homogeneous. The emphasis on consistency here is intended only to generate an alternative pole of reference in a specific debate.

5. This chapter, incidentally, will not discuss the small amount of French work analysing job redesign as a form of Taylorism because the material is not easily accessible, and because it is pitched at an overly high level of abstraction. See for example M. de Montmollin (1974).

6. This description is a shortened version of that contained in J.E. Kelly (1979), Chap. 9. The factory, incidentally, was suddenly closed by the management in 1979 and then occupied by the workforce. The management has subsequently obtained repossession with a Court order.

7. This section is a considerably shortened version of Kelly (1980).

8. W.W. Daniel (1970) has offered a rather different extrinsic-intrinsic dualism to account for shifts in employee attitudes. Initially, and in the bargaining context, questions of wages and workloads were in the foreground of workers' concerns about a job enrichment exercise: some months later their expressed concerns and interests centred on job content.

Chapter 3

JOB REDESIGN AND TRADE UNION RESPONSES : PAST PROBLEMS
AND FUTURE PROSPECTS

Denis Gregory

INTRODUCTION

As the title suggests, this chapter splits fundamentally into
two parts. Firstly, it examines what may be identified as the
traditional trade union response to the issue and practice of
job redesign. Secondly, and perhaps of more current interest,
in reviewing the implications of micro-technology, it attempts
to evaluate the critical pressures and options for job redesign
which trade unions must face as a result of the increased
application of such technology.

In the first part of the chapter the commonly levelled
charge that trade unions are typically defensive or disinterested in job redesign will be examined. It is strongly
contended that such postures have to be assessed in the wider
context of the political economy if these apparently negative
reactions are to be fully understood. Equally, it will be
suggested that unless some serious consideration is given to
broadening the conceptual framework within which the majority
of job redesign theories appear to be located, the practitioners of these theories will remain firmly and unproductively
stuck between the needs and aspirations of capital on the one
hand and those of labour on the other.

This criticism of job redesign is taken up and amplified
in the second part of the chapter which argues that the
dysfunctions between theoretical prescription and the real
needs of the clientele (whether the owners of capital or
labour) are further exacerbated by the potential consequences
of microprocessor-based technology. By way of conclusion
here, it is suggested that adherence to the typically narrow
contextual framework will almost certainly minimise the
effectiveness of the practice of job redesign as a tool which
might help to smooth the management of change in the capital/
labour mix of given sectors of the economy.

SOME DEFINITIONAL PROBLEMS - 'CALLING A SPADE AN IMPLEMENT FOR SOIL DISPLACEMENT'

In order to understand one part of the traditional trade union response to job redesign theory, we should consider the effect on trade unionists of the stream of socio-psychological refinements and developments which have emerged in the post-war period. It is not impossible, for example, for a shop steward or full time official located in the Engineering sector to have been confronted at various times by management inspired solutions (to whatever difficulty that was currently bedevilling production) which have been labelled 'job enlargement', 'job enrichment', 'autonomous work groups' and 'participative job design' to name but four. Despite the sometimes overtly humane tone introduced into this labelling process, no examples can be found of a job redesign technique which does not have improved production efficiency as its first priority. Given this, the established shop steward can be forgiven a certain scepticism that 'plus ca change, plus ca la meme chose'; when the reality underneath the label is perceived, that once again it boils down to 'them' trying to screw more work out of 'us', a defensive reaction sets in. It should then come as no surprise to hear the latest derivation of job redesign discussed by trade unions locally as 'just another management con' or 'a productivity deal in disguise'. Clearly neither changing the labels, nor naively complaining about obstructive trade unions, offers any solution; but what can be done to bring forward a constructive joint approach?

First and foremost the theorists and practitioners should look into their own corner - if job redesign is concerned with increasing productivity then this must be clearly stated; if the consequences of work organisation changes are reduced manning levels, then that too must be faced 'up front'; if increased autonomy only refers to decisions as to how given workloads will be handled by a particular group, why dress this up as the end of management control?

Secondly, behavioural scientists at the point of contact with a workforce would be well advised to minimise their use of jargon. Terms like 'sociotechnical systems' and 'participative job design' have very little currency on the shop floor. Moreover, if either term provides a cover for attempts to either increase the tempo or intensity of workloading, then credibility will suffer. Far better for the practitioner to re-label his or her theory and prescriptions with terms well understood on the shop floor, even if in some circumstances this does lead to the use of words like 'productivity' and 'efficiency'. This should not be interpreted as an anti-academic bias (a charge frequently levelled - although less frequently justified - at trade unions) but rather as a pre-condition for the establishment of an effective means of communication. Indeed, it would be somewhat ironic if the average behavioural scientist, whose training has traditionally placed a heavy emphasis on the importance of communication, did not accept this point.

DETERMINANTS OF THE 'TRADITIONAL' RESPONSE

In a recent and comparatively rare piece of empirical research (Hull, 1978), the following beliefs were found to help form trade union responses to new work organisation initiatives. Firstly, scepticism borne out of experience in dealing with management proposals which alleged benefits for the workforce. Secondly, that such initiatives were essentially the management's prerogative whilst the union's role was essentially reactive in these circumstances. Lastly, that proposals to change the established form of work organisation, were recognised as being important only insofar as they were translatable into traditional collective bargaining priorities and practices.

The second point noted above represents something of an oversimplification. For whilst Hull showed that the work organisation changes he studied all flowed from management proposals, it is not the case that trade unions adopt a purely passive role with regard to the generality of changes in work organisation. To understand this point it is necessary to distinguish between 'formal' and 'informal' changes. Hull referred exclusively to formal (i.e. management sponsored) changes and in this context his conclusions are supported. At an informal level, however, individual workers and their groups have persistently demonstrated both a talent and an inclination for making changes to the organisation of the work in which they are engaged. For example the practice of 'working up the line' (working for short periods well beyond the normal pace or demand) 'earns' informal breaks for production workers in many industries. Similarly, unofficial systems of manpower 'cover' bring about major social benefits for the workers concerned, with little or no negative consequences for the overall utilisation of labour.

In these instances unions are cast in a tacit role insofar as the acceptance of such practices are concerned and are active in defending them against management encroachment.

Whilst these attitudinal postures are of critical importance in conditioning what is widely interpreted as a negative response to progressive ideas, they only provide half a picture and commentators who have delved no further have tended to conclude that unions are by and large entirely disinterested in new forms of work organisation, job redesign, job enrichment and so on. In fact, nothing could be further from the truth. Trade unions from their inception have been continually engaged in shaping the organisational forms of work and in struggling for the genuine enrichment of jobs.

Collective bargaining objectives have developed beyond the maintenance of money wages to include related items such

as pensions, sick pay, holiday schemes and adjustments to the
duration of working time. These, together with the successful
procurement of progressive legislation in the fields of
redundancy, dismissal and health and safety would all be seen
by trade unionists as contributing towards a 'genuine enrichment' of jobs. Additionally, the ways in which particularly
craft unions have strongly influenced the hiring and training
of new workers, together with the persistent attempts of all
unions to moderate and contain the effects of increasing
capital intensity on working practices, can hardly be said to
have had no bearing whatsoever on the forms of work organisation that have subsequently evolved.

The point of departure between the type of job redesign
and work organisation favoured by trade unionists and that
embraced in the theories which populate management and
behavioural sciences, centres around the issue of control. We
use the word 'control' here in its wider, more political sense
to describe the power to influence the key decisions which in
any company will determine how many and what type of jobs will
be required. Only sociotechnical systems theory with its
promulgation of autonomous and semi-autonomous groups comes
anywhere near to creating a shift in control towards the
workforce which could be identified by a trade unionist as
worthwhile. Yet even in the most advanced examples of
autonomous group working, the boundaries within which decisions
are taken by the workers concerned, are strictly limited and
have little or no influence on the critical decision-making
process concerned with capital investment, product development
and so on. These remain firmly embedded in whichever corporate
boardroom ultimately wields the financial 'stick'.

By comparison, consider the management response to
situations where considerable influence over the organisation
of work resides in the hands of the shop stewards. Piecework
payment systems provide a good example of the ability of shop
stewards to control the pace of work and the manning levels of
given work groups. Until comparatively recently this practice
dominated large sections of the British motor industry. In
contrast with measured day work (MDW), the system which has
largely replaced it, piecework provided incentives (and enrichment) in the sense that 'job and finish'[1] practices afforded
real opportunities for shorter working time, whereas manning
levels were self policed to ensure that individual earnings
were optimised. MDW, which it was argued during its negotiated
introduction at British Leyland in the early '70's, offered a
much more humane approach to the effort/reward relationship -
smoothing out the former whilst stabilising the latter - has
come under considerable scrutiny recently in an attempt to
restore incentives and trim back on what is seen
(particularly at British Leyland) as a tendency to overman.
Yet, piecework, crude a system though it undoubtedly was and is,
has always avoided these pitfalls.

Why then change? In fact members of British Leyland's

management have openly admitted that they had to 'buy out' piecework to re-establish management control over the flow of production and the frequency of disputes (Gregory, 1978). As subsequent events have shown, the advent of MDW has made little difference to managerial efficiency in either of these aspects, but the point remains: control was the real issue. Again, as recent experience at British Leyland amply demonstrates, the question of 'Who controls?', continues to dominate the company's industrial relations. It was therefore not surprising that the strongest reaction to the management's imposed pay agreement was sponsored not by the proposed low wage increase (in real terms a wage cut), but by the changes in working practices and manning levels which formed a vital part of the overall package.

Consider also management responses to attempts by the organised workforce to offer constructive alternatives to existing forms of production organisation, resource allocation and corporate goals. In the last five years a number of alternative corporate plans have been formulated by groups of shop stewards operating at company level. The most notable, that of the Lucas Aerospace Combine Committee, ranges widely, cogently and in well researched detail over the need for, and ability of their company to produce 'socially useful products' which would generate both income and employment. A central thrust of the Combine's argument is that the revenue and employment so created would be far more acceptable and stimulating than that currently derived from the company's production of weaponry. Given the considerable time and expertise which went into the formulation of the plan, and the specific attention paid to suggesting commercially viable products, the almost total disregard for either the concept or detail of the proposal shown to date by Lucas management, provides one of the better examples of organised capital's refusal to yield any real commitment towards meeting the non-traditional demands of organised labour.

Moreover, since this alternative worker-sponsored corporate plan moved well beyond a simple defence of jobs, into areas of work organisation, individual job design, participation and energy conservation, the action of Lucas management in refusing to consider the alternative strategy because it stemmed from the 'unofficial' Combine Committee rather than the 'official' Confederation of Shipbuilding and Engineering Unions (CSEU), reveals precisely how important ultimate corporate control is to them, and the lengths (the mere fact that the plan came from an 'unofficial' group of Lucas employees is a pathetic excuse) to which they will go to preserve it.

Yet it could be argued that the Lucas Aerospace alternative corporate plan in effect represents the highest form of 'job redesign' yet to emerge, taking as it does the totality of the capital/labour production relationship and suggesting a radical (but viable) re-shaping. Given the management response to this and other worker plans, e.g. at C. and A. Parsons and Vickers, (to say nothing of the dismissive contempt shown to worker initiatives put forward to save doomed steel plants at Corby, Consett, Ebbw Vale, East Moors and Shotton, even though these came from official trade union organisations) who can say that the trade unions have the sole franchise on defensive behaviour?

What these alternative plans also do is pose the most coherent challenge yet formulated to traditional corporate prerogatives and control boundaries (George, 1979). At a lower level it is evident that the owners of capital are prepared to allow a certain incremental erosion of <u>management</u> functions through any one of a variety of 'participation' options from the genuinely progressive to the paternalist. This usually provides a convenient blind alley along which the demands of organised labour can be shunted and allowed to be played out well away from the crucial decision-making arenas.[2]

In this context job redesign, insofar as it confines itself to improving the efficiency of a particular process and either consolidating or increasing management control, is a perfectly acceptable management tool. Once job redesign reaches beyond these boundaries to challenge traditional control relationships and posit efficiency in <u>use</u>-value (e.g. building cars which have a much longer life expectancy, are easy to maintain, minimise environmental damage and have a maximal fuel efficiency) rather than purely <u>exchange</u>-value (e.g. building cars which deteriorate rapidly beyond a life expectancy of around 5 years, are increasingly difficult to maintain, are neither fuel nor resource efficient and are major polluters of the environment), then it becomes a revolutionary threat and is treated as such.

It is hardly surprising that this polarity ultimately finds its way into the collective bargaining process (assuming the existence of recognised trade unions), since this provides the only sustainable means by which the relative strengths and aspirations of capital and labour can be controlled and balanced. Proponents of 'alternative' methods of introducing change to the workplace, either through some form of joint consultation or via the more recently emerged style of an imposed 'consensus' a la Michael Edwardes, would do well to study the course of British industrial relations in the post-war period. Our system of collective bargaining has easily absorbed and outlasted any alternatives posed by 'consultation' or 'participation'. Indeed the coverage of bargaining has extended significantly to embrace a range of terms and conditions beyond the traditional settlement of cash remuneration. It is this very 'elasticity' of the bargaining framework which offers, in the author's view, the most fruitful ground for the joint exploration of job redesign possibilities.

Two critical questions should be raised here: firstly whether or not management and unions are prepared to seriously

bargain about the design of jobs, since our experience of
productivity bargaining in the 1960's suggests that the control
and efficiency benefits accruing to management easily out-
weighed any residual 'enrichment' of the workforce concerned.
Indeed, many workers and unionists remember productivity
bargaining as being a process of wholesale impoverishment of
what Herzberg (1966) would term intrinsic factors. Of
arguably greater importance, given the twin challenges posed
by the shift in the world's economic power relationships and
the accelerating implementation of high technology, the second
question is whether our collective bargaining power structures
are sufficiently flexible and bold enough to pick up and
hammer out a new set of production relationships incorporating
the more radical vision of say, the Lucas Combine Committee's
alternative corporate plan?

I return to the crucial second question in the last part
of this chapter, but will confine my remarks here to the
relatively short run issues raised by the first question.

With respect to placing the design of jobs formally on
the collective bargaining agenda, in addition to the legacy
of scepticism from previous attempts at productivity
bargaining, we should remember that many of the 'hygiene'
factors offered by British industry fall well below average
European standards (Gardner, 1979), hence the purchasing
power of the British worker is significantly below that of the
majority of his/her European counterparts whilst hours of work
in most British industries remain in excess of what is normal
in Europe. The importance of satisfying these basics prior to
engendering any meaningful workforce interest in intrinsic
improvements in job content, has been repeatedly stressed by
job redesign theorists but seemingly ignored in the British
context. Yet the deterioration of our economic performance
post-1974, has generally added a further twist to the already
narrowly defined bargaining priorities of pay and job security.

This is not to say that these bargaining priorities cannot be opened up, even in the midst of our worst post-war
recession, to confront major job redesign issues. Current
union attempts to bargain for shorter working time in part as
a response to unemployment and in part as a genuine attempt
to improve the work/leisure trade off, are a case in point.

Recent empirical research carried out by the Trade Union
Research Unit at Ruskin College, has shown that jointly
bargained changes in work organisation can significantly
reduce actual hours of work at plant level (TURU, 1980).
Alongside of this has to be contrasted the negative attitudes
shown by employers generally, amply illustrated by the 1979
Engineering dispute, to the notion of reducing working time.
This tends to increase trade union scepticism with regard to
the sincerity of employers' commitment to any meaningful
improvement to the quality of working life. The demand for
reduced working time once again points to the gulf between
what is an acceptable re-organisation of work to the unions,

and what is seen as a threat to control and competitiveness by the employer.

The same could be said of union attempts to improve health and safety conditions at work. It should be beyond dispute that improvements in this sphere make a material contribution to the quality of life of both the individual (through reducing accidents and disease contracted at the workplace), and that of society as a whole (minimising the risk of major accidents such as Flixborough and controlling the spread of pollution). However, the passage of the Health and Safety at Work Act (1974), was bitterly opposed by major employers' associations, whilst the subsequent delay in introducing the safety representatives' regulations, owed a great deal to the orchestration of implacable employer hostility by the CBI (Gregory, 1979). In so doing employers were signalling in no uncertain terms their dislike of any extension of industrial democracy (one of the main reasons for the regulations had been to fulfill the Labour Party's pledge to extend industrial democracy into key areas of the workplace) and any encroachment on traditional areas of management prerogative - in this case the control of health and safety at work. The benefits, both theoretical and actual, of spreading control through the medium of trade union based safety representatives, were ignored in a far more primal desire to retain power and control in management hands.

To date, behavioural scientists, at least in the U.K., appear to have avoided straying into these particular battle grounds. Indeed, it is hardly a fertile environment for the preservation of traditional academic neutrality. However, since the majority of work organisation/job redesign experts have, in the past, operated at management behest and to the requirements of organised capital within the 'micro' fields of individual job analysis and small group working, a bolder venture of worker consultants in Sweden, working with the trade unions whilst drawing their salaries from a fund levied on employers, is worthy of study. Some recent work (Kjellen 1980a, b) suggests that the compromises so feared by U.K. academics are neither as pressing or painful as may be feared.

Moreover, it seems highly likely that collective bargaining in order to cope with industrial restructuring, will move into a lengthy period of productivity or (using the more recently coined phrase) efficiency bargaining. The involvement of behavioural scientists as a resource for both sides would be of value in the joint management of future change, if only in terms of clarifying the options for job redesign which may arise.

FUTURE PROSPECTS : FACING UP TO TECHNOLOGICAL
CHANGE

To return to a point made at the outset, to contend that
unions are or have been disinterested in job redesign, is to
ignore the entire evidence of union involvement in the implementation of technological change in the post war period.
Tackling the widespread fear that automation would destroy
hundreds of thousands of jobs, a memorandum issued by the TUC
in 1955 argued:- "Within a fully employed economy its
increased application may not create problems significantly
greater than those caused by other forms of industrial
development" (TUC, 1955). The key to this was seen as
maintaining the tempo and consequences of technical change
within a collective bargaining framework. Hence the memorandum concluded:- "The major job of the trade unions will be to
keep automation within the field of industrial relations;
countering assumptions that working conditions, earning
opportunities, pace of working and other matters affecting
work people can or should be arbitrarily fixed by machines or
technicians" (TUC, 1955). More recently, the TUC have
spelled out their objectives with regard to 'new' technology.
Len Murray in April, 1979 argued:- "It is not just a
question of accepting the new technology or of fighting it.
The issue is how we can maximise its benefits and minimise
its costs, and ensure that its benefits are equitably shared"
(TUC 1979, p. 5). This line is echoed in other recent material
issued by individual unions, notably that of the T & GWU,
APEX, and AUEW (TASS). Explicit job redesign issues are
identified for example by APEX who identify the problems
associated with micro-processor based office equipment as
including:

> - lower job interest due to a reduction in the
> variety of office duties, contact with other
> staff, and career and promotion prospects;
> - restructuring of the office environment in
> line with the technical requirements of the
> equipment and associated health and safety
> implications. (APEX, 1979).

Both the T & GWU and AUEW (TASS) express their concern at the
increased, non-accountable manipulative power which the advent
of cheap, ultra-flexible micro-technology has placed in the
hands of multi-national companies: further evidence, if it
were needed, that unions will not be reacting to new technology
solely in terms of its impact on the specific workplace.
    At workplace level, however, the initial union response
has taken shape in the form of new technology agreements. As
a means of defending existing employment opportunities whilst
advancing the quality of working life, the TUC identify the
following as crucial to any such agreement:

- full agreement on the range of negotiating
issues should be a precondition of technological
change;
- joint management and union teams should be
formed to consider, assess, implement and monitor
technological change. As part of this joint
process a plan for change should be produced to
fit individual circumstances;
- wherever possible, full job security should be
guaranteed for the existing workforce. Displace-
ment effects should be offset by redeployment,
retraining and/or the re-organisation of working
time. (TUC, 1979, p. 32).

The TUC explicitly recognise that:- "negotiators must be ready
to take the lead in pressing for a joint assessment of the
opportunities for using new technological processes . . . ."
and that: "Unions will often need to take the initiative in
pressing for change so as to avoid a belated and inadequate man
-agement decision which will have more damaging effects on the
workforce" (TUC, 1979, p.32). This can hardly be construed
as a wholly defensive response to the introduction of new
technology. The preconditions outlined by the TUC are by no
means unrealistic in the context of rising unemployment and
failing economic performance. However, the most encouraging
aspect for the perceptive behavioural scientist is surely the
TUC's advocacy of individual unions initiating change. This
would appear to offer very real opportunities for the
proponents of job redesign to leave their narrowly determined
frameworks and move into the critical labour/technology
interface.

In regard to the second question raised at the end of the
previous section, it is not unreasonable to suggest that the
TUC by its guidance, and one or two individual unions by
example, notably the POEU, have shown a distinct awareness of
the need to "hammer out a new set of production relationships"
in collectively bargaining about the implementation of new
technology. For example, Clive Jenkins the general secretary
of ASTMS has certainly outlined the boldness required. In the
introduction to his recent book "The Collapse of Work" he
argues:

No longer is it good enough to repeat the old
cliches and slogans about work and unemployment
any more than it is sufficient to rely upon the
traditional short term palliatives. We shall
have to fundamentally question why we work, how
we take our leisure and whether work itself is
a positive activity. (Jenkins and Sherman,
1979, p. viii).

The questions which Jenkins in turn poses are equally formidable whether addressed to employers, government or academics. How many employers or government ministers would be prepared to accept that the "traditional short term palliatives" of economic growth can no longer be relied upon to create additional employment opportunities?

Certainly, the conventional wisdom from the Treasury, Department of Industry and the Department of Employment, argues that the application of micro-technology will create as many jobs as it displaces in our economy as a result of the beneficial productivity effects which will accrue. This testament of faith is taken in defiance of recent econometric work carried out by researchers in the Department of Employment (Wragg and Robertson, 1978) which shows that the old assumptions of a "virtuous circle" relationship between growth of productivity and growth of employment are not sustainable for the major components of the manufacturing sector of our economy over the period 1954-1973.

Neither is the historical evidence quoted by the government departments a realistic guide (Sleigh et al., 1979). To argue that micro-processor based technology will have the same job creational effects as the development of the computer did, is to ignore the vast differences and advantages in cost and flexibility which the new technology offers.

Similarly, how many job redesign proponents have addressed the question, "Why do we work?", before they begin to unroll their theoretical frameworks? If it does no more than force this question into the open, the advent of cheap, flexible technology will have achieved something. Once confronted, the choices are plain enough: we either continue our downward spiral of de-industrialisation with rising unemployment, price instability and increasing social tension, or we accept a post-industrial society where work and leisure (not unemployment) are radically reconstructed on a high technology base, and where the long eschewed questions relating to the attainment of sustainable growth in a world of finite resources can (hopefully) be confronted.

The challenge to the behavioural scientist, as to the trade unionist, must lie in the timely formation of an accountable and jointly managed path to the second option. The signs are, that in their rejection of de-industrialisation (not new technology per se) the trade union movement is prepared to advance to an altogether higher plane. The question remains: can the same be said of the behavioural scientist, the employer and the politician?

NOTES

1. The practice whereby on completion of a given
production target, the worker or workgroup carried the right
to leave work before the official finishing time.

2. For all the talk of increased worker participation in
the last decade, concrete examples are hard to find. Moreover,
only the recently ended experiment at the Post Office provided
anywhere near adequate representation for unions at Board
level.

Chapter 4

COLLECTIVE BARGAINING AND JOB REDESIGN

Ceridwen Roberts and Stephen Wood

INTRODUCTION

This chapter is concerned primarily with the sociological
approach to job redesign. We particularly consider recent
theories which attempt to criticise both the ideology and
practice of job redesign as associated with modern human
relations theory and psychology.

We begin by outlining these theories and then proceed to
examine a case study in a fairly strongly unionised
situation.[1] In so doing we point to some inadequacies in
these views and the way in which future work might proceed.

For many writers, social science in industry equals
behavioural science techniques and especially job redesign.
Certainly job design is one of the few problem areas in which
social scientists have had great impact; the others are
probably industrial relations and business accounting and
economics. Blackler and Brown (nd) thus argue that with the
increasing interest being shown by external groups in socio-
technical ideas about job design, it may appear that social
science has "come of age". They are certainly right to imply
that this kind of view has underlain the recent work of the
job design theorists, as there is widespread acceptance that
social science has 'a lot to offer and that the basic problem
now is how a rapid diffusion and acceptance of such ideas
throughout the modern world, may be encouraged'. The
implication in much of this programme is that both the theory
and the tools are now available for an applied social science
approach to change in industry. For despite differences of
viewpoint about the precise theories and tools which
constitute this approach, the overall unity is provided by its
orientation and fundamental philosophy. This may be briefly
characterised (as others in this book show) by its focus on
the application of theories of motivation and satisfaction to
industry, and particularly through changing the nature of work
and the division of labour. Underlying the programme is a
view that through allying the demands of production more

closely to the needs of individual producers, both the
productivity and the 'quality of working life' will improve.
The achievement of this unity will amount to radical change, a
humanisation of work, as some put it.

This work has been founded on models of human needs and
thus it is not surprising that psychologists rather than
sociologists have dominated its development. Within the
human relations movement the two disciplines were closely
related, but since the war they have developed their studies
of industry in diverse and largely unrelated ways. Perhaps
one of the basic differences between the two has been their
attitude towards the human relations movement. Psychologists
have not been totally uncritical towards it, and for example,
it is not always readily acknowledged that Herzberg et al.,
(1959) built their self-actualisation approach in opposition to
many of the assumptions of Mayo and his followers (see, for
example, Mayo, 1946). But they have not been as critical of it
as have many sociologists. The basic fear of sociologists is
the managerialism and manipulation that they perceive as
inherent in the human relations tradition. Much sociology has
been motivated by this fear, to the extent that at times it
might be so excessive as to represent a kind of paralysis.
Less excessive responses have taken two broad paths. First,
some such as Lupton (1969), have sought to broaden organisational and managerial studies away from human relations and
psychology through the use of sociological insights. Second,
and particularly in the seventies, there have been attempts
to develop a more critical study of industry, which is not
simply concerned to 'expose' past theories for their
managerialism, but also to study such theories in practice
and relocate industrial sociology within the more general and
classical tradition of macro-sociology (e.g. Eldridge 1971;
Esland et al., 1974; Nichols, 1980).

The first of these avenues is the less important for our
present concerns. But it should be noted that it is amongst
those who have taken this line that the most contact between
sociology and psychology occurs. Job redesign has come
increasingly into the centre of, for example, Lupton's work,
although overall it remains a 'contingency approach', in which
each technique and change programme is seen as potentially
and equally important but is not necessarily relevant to all
situations (Lupton and Tanner, 1979). Thus human relations
theory is not ruled out as incorrect, irrelevant, or even
inadequate, but simply as inappropriate to particular contexts,
its utility thus being contingent on certain configurations of
situational factors (see Wood, 1979). It is interesting to
note that those who have taken the second direction have
equally not been dismissive of the potential relevance of the
human relations movement. Many of the packaged versions of
industrial sociology have, in the past, presented the field
as a linear progression from Taylorism through human relations
to modern theories, in a way that implies they have been

superseded by more contemporary work because of the intellectual inadequacies of previous approaches. In contrast, the
recent work of Nichols (1975, 1976), Braverman (1974) and
Blackler and Brown (1978), does not make this assumption. One
of its strengths is that it acknowledges that human relations
and Taylorism are not theories of management but are also
practices. Thus, whilst their theoretical underpinnings may
seem outmoded to academic social scientists, they may remain
extremely relevant to industrialists and may indeed dominate
the way in which managers structure not only their thinking,
but also the work systems they manage.

Perhaps the most explicit statement of this position has
been made by Braverman (1974):

> It is impossible to overestimate the importance
> of the scientific management movement in the
> shaping of the modern corporation and indeed all
> institutions of capitalist society which carry
> on labour processes. The popular notion that
> Taylorism has been "superseded" by later schools
> of industrial psychology or "human relations",
> that it failed - because of Taylor's amateurish
> and naive views of human motivation or because
> it brought about a storm of labour opposition or
> because Taylor and various successors antagonised
> workers and sometimes management as well - or
> that it is "outmoded" because certain Taylorian
> specifics like functional foremanship or his
> incentive-pay schemes, have been discarded for
> more sophisticated methods: all these represent
> a woeful misreading of the actual dynamics of the
> development of management. (pp. 86-7).

Furthermore, Taylorism operates in tandem with human relations
for, in Braverman's terms: "Taylorism dominates the world of
production; the practitioners of "human relations" . . . .
are the maintenance crew for the human machinery" (p. 87).
Job enrichment programmes and the like, according to Braverman,
are the modern human relations 'remedies'. The introduction
and propagation of them by consultants is motivated thus:
"Whatever their phraseology, (they) have only one function:
cutting costs, improving 'efficiency', raising productivity"
(p. 38). The recent origin and popularity of such 'reforms'
as job enlargement or enrichment, participation and removal of
time clocks, reflects, according to Braverman, the increasing
dissatisfaction of workers in the 1970's. Or to be more
accurate it reflects management's attempt to arrest the effects
of this 'apparent increase in active dissatisfaction', to
reduce labour turnover, absenteeism, apathetic working and
wild-cat strikes.

Given the motivation for such changes, it is argued by
Braverman that it is perhaps not surprising that many of the

65

changes have been trivial, minimal and 'cosmetic', and that
there is a 'gulf' between the rhetoric and reality of job
design, 'a certain air of hollow unreality'. Above all else
Braverman concludes, such modern methods "represent a style of
management rather than a genuine change in the position of the
worker" (p.39). Moreover it is a change which can be compared
"with the marketing strategy followed by those who having
discovered that housewives resent prepared baking mixes and
feel guilty when using them, arrange for the removal of the
powdered eggs and restore to the customer the thrill of
breaking a fresh egg into the mix, thereby creating an "image"
of skilled baking" (Braverman, 1974 p. 39).

Similar views have been developed by writers other than
Braverman. The implication of the work of, for example,
Nichols and Beynon (1977) and Blackler and Brown (1978) is
that job enrichment programmes are essentially a 'con'.
Blackler and Brown (1978) argue that:

> attempts to improve the quality of working life by
> job redesign alone are likely to amount to little
> more than a modern version of "human relations"
> management. On this view, notwithstanding the
> language of self-fulfilment and personal develop-
> ment characteristic of job redesign writings, the
> use of such ideas may serve as little more than an
> unobtrusive device to control others' behaviour.
> (p.12).

In the Braverman-type argument it is not always clear
whether the new human relations has any real impact on work
systems. The argument that it is totally cosmetic implies
there are really no changes, and hence its significance is
solely, but perhaps importantly, ideological. The associated
assumption that workers will be conned by it, implies that the
recipients of such schemes are passive, or even bovine, as
management is assumed to be by adopting what its critics call
a 'cow' sociology. Those who accuse job enrichment of being
trivial and marginal may indeed acknowledge that it may
involve, however slight, changes in the system of working.
But, and this is the important point, they are applying some
absolute or at least external standard in order to judge the
triviality and marginality of such changes. In Braverman's
case, for example, he works with a romanticised view of the
craft worker as representative of unalienated and meaningful
work, a view which is not dissimilar to the historical
characterisation of man in much of the psychology which has
spawned 'neo-human relations'. As Kelly (see chapter 2) has
argued, this procedure discourages any further analysis of
the phenomenon of redesign. Indeed Braverman relies almost
totally on statements about management techniques made by
those promulgating their usage.[2]

This leads both him and others to assume particular negative effects of job redesign, such as the individualisation of the whole participation issue, as well as the atomisation of the workforce. Thus they do not explore the possible contingent nature of such effects and features of job redesign, for example, the anti-unionism inherent in Herzberg's position. Furthermore, they impute a greater naivety on the part of proponents of job enrichment than in fact exists. Herzberg (1959, p. ix), for example, is quite aware that job enrichment is not simply a question of job satisfaction or applying theoretical psychology, but is a technique designed to benefit both workers and employers, and furthermore, that it is, as his critics stress, limited, since individuals at lower levels in an organisation, according to Herzberg, cannot realistically expect to exercise influence over the establishment of, for example, its overall goals. The result of such inadequacies in the characterisation of the new human relations, is that the critiques have not produced any fresh theory of job design, and that key questions remain unexplored and perhaps not even identified. Again, as Kelly suggests, one of the central questions which is not confronted is "does job redesign benefit both workers and employers and, if so, how?" i.e. what are the actual effects of such practices (1979, p. 189).

Bosquet (1972) is one writer who does attempt an answer to this question. He is optimistic about its benefits for workers. He does not, at least explicitly, deny its possible manipulative side, for he recognises that its introduction by management is aimed at increasing morale, inducing a cheerful obedience on the part of the worker, resulting in efficient prosecution of the work at hand, as judged by management. Job enrichment, according to Bosquet, "spells the end of authority and despotic power for bosses great and small. . . . It replaces the order and discipline of the barracks with the voluntary co-operation of workers whose autonomy and power extends to his work". In so doing it will lead workers to question the whole nature of the productive system; they will question the necessity of particular products, alleged technical and scientific necessities, and the whole basis of subordinate-superordinate relations. In short, job enrichment will lead to "workers liberated from brutalisation, oppression and boredom to struggle for their total emancipation" (p.33). Accordingly, job redesign contains an inherent dynamic towards increased autonomy and participation, and thus management's attempt to increase the meaning men find in their work, will almost inevitably 'boomerang against capital', as it is a matter of logic that questions about the nature of domination and control will spring from any extension of job enrichment. Whilst perhaps a useful corrective to the extreme defeatism of Braverman, this argument nevertheless appears to go too far in the other direction. Bosquet's excessively positive evaluation arises at least partly from his starting point, which involves an unnecessarily negative description of the factory as a prison or barracks, based on despotic power, prior to the new human relations. Furthermore, he works with a unilinear view of participation such that he equates, as Kelly (1978) stresses, the notion of autonomy with an embryonic form of workers' control, and does not adequately distinguish participation from job redesign, nor see the latter as concerned simply with granting workers some autonomy over certain decisions involving their immediate work.

Despite these weaknesses Bosquet's work does serve to point to the need in any overall and complete evaluation of managerial initiatives, to consider workers' reactions to them. In the evaluation of Braverman and others, as we have seen, there may be implicit assumptions about reactions, and furthermore assumptions which imply a greater degree of acquiescence and naivety on the part of the workers than is either fruitful or justified. How workers react to the new human relations is important both because they may turn it to their own advantage as Bosquet implies, and because work methods are ultimately jointly determined. Even the most instrumental and economistic workers, with no overt concern for so called intrinsic aspects of the job, can and do decisively influence the way in which production is actually achieved. The final effect of job redesign on the structure of work systems cannot be judged in abstract of such influence, and indeed it must be treated as only one, amongst many influences on the process of work structuring.

In the remainder of this paper we shall explore the intermediate ground between the Braverman and Bosquet positions; and in particular through a case study of a multiplant British firm, which concentrates on the differential reactions from the workforces in four sites, to what was ostensibly the same management initiative. For, as Nichols (1975) has rightly argued, even if our 'gut reaction' is towards the Braverman view, detailed concrete analysis is necessary in order to answer important questions concerning the current popularity of the new human relations and the likely consequences, intended or otherwise.

THE CASE STUDY : THE INTRODUCTION OF THE NEW WORKING RELATIONSHIP AGREEMENT

The case concerned a multi-divisional company (MDC) with an extensive range of products and technologies in a large number of plants. These are spread nationally at different sized sites in varying labour markets. The company however is run very much as a whole and major policies are centrally determined. This is true of its industrial relations and personnel policies and the company has long had a central negotiating system and a National Joint Negotiating Committee with its manual unions.[3]

Over the years MDC has acquired a reputation for being a "good" if "paternalistic" employer with above average wages and fringe benefits. Its paternalism was reflected, amongst other things, by its Works Council now existing alongside the Unions. Union membership levels amongst the manual workers, which varied from site to site, had been steadily rising and the long tradition of relative labour/management "harmony" had begun to be challenged in the 1960's by increasing unrest and short strikes particularly in the North East. It was against this background that over a period of years a major change programme was planned and implemented of which an important component, for management at least, was "job enrichment".

In this case study we examine the problems management was trying to solve in the programme of job and pay changes, and assess how far job redesign was a central feature of the programme. We compare the experiences of trade unionists at different sites and, by examining the variations in their reactions, attempt to assess the consequences of this type of behavioural science initiative in a unionised situation.

The case is concerned specifically with the following questions:

(1) What was meant by "job enrichment" in the context of this agreement and how extensively was it introduced? Was it company wide? Did it affect all manual workers? What re-organisation of the work task occurred and how radical was this? Did it involve the blurring of craft/non-craft demarcations or affect the role of supervisors?

(2) Why was it introduced? Was it to make work "more interesting", to combat absenteeism or labour turnover, or was it part of a managerial drive to re-establish control over the wage structure and to increase productivity?

(3) What role did the trade unions play, at what stage and at what levels were they involved in negotiations? Were they able to alter initial proposals significantly?

(4) What were the trade unions' attitudes to and experience of these proposals? What importance did they attach to "making work more interesting" or was concern with the monetary outcomes paramount in determining their negotiating stance?

(5) What was the process of implementation? Were shop floor workers themselves involved in introducing the changes and if so, how? What were their attitudes towards job redesign and the introduction of the new proposals? Was there training to help with implementation or the consequences of the "redesigned jobs", and for whom was such training available?

(6) What were the issues that arose during implementation and the early years of the agreement? What effect did it have on manning levels and did it lead to redundancy? If so, how and where? What was the effect on the wage structure and promotion opportunities?

The change programme took about eight years to complete, and we did not begin our research until it had been implemented virtually throughout the Company. So our study of the agreement's introduction was retrospective, although our assessment of its consequences was not.[4] We decided to concentrate on the experience of the three largest unions[5] at four sites. We selected the AUEW because it was the largest craft union at each site, and the TGWU and NUGMW because between them they organised the general workers though only one general worker union was represented at each site.

The four sites were chosen to illustrate particular problems which both the Company and Unions identified as important.[6] So:

"Traditional" Had experienced large scale redundancies shortly after the agreement (1972); it was characterised by comparatively labour intensive machine-tending technology, and a local labour market where unemployment was above the national average (TGWU).

"Militant" One of the Company's largest, most complex sites, characterised by several separate works belonging to different divisions of the Company, covering a wide range of products and technologies. Opposition to the agreement had been prolonged and bitter (TGWU).

"Greenfields" Acceptance of the agreement was generally held to have been relatively easy and successful. The process technology also provided examples of some highly skilled jobs (NUGMW).

"Dosy" Differed from the others in being the only site in the South and was in an entirely different labour market. The technology covered an extensive range of unskilled and skilled jobs (TGWU).

We collected our data in two ways. Much of the information about the background to the agreement and history of its introduction, came from extensive use of documentary material, in particular the minutes and papers of the National Joint Negotiating Committee. The rest of the data came from interviews with national[7] and local officials, and shop stewards of the three unions[8], and discussions with selected shop floor workers and managers at both local and national level[9].

ORIGINS OF THE WORK RE-ORGANISATION

This case is of interest because it illustrates the dynamic nature of bargaining about work re-organisation. Through our retrospective study of the implementation of MDC's final agreement - the New Working Relationship Agreement (NWRA) - we were able to identify at what point and why job enrichment became important, and to see to whom it was important. We were not able to look at the content of jobs pre- and post-NWRA and "measure" the degree of job enrichment which had occurred. Rather our assessment is based on an analysis of the agreement and the perceptions of trade unionists and some managers as to the importance and nature of job enrichment.

We began by tracing how interest in job enrichment originated and developed in central management's and national officials' thinking during the eight years it took to finalise and implement the agreement, which may be seen as having two stages. The first, the "Productivity and Pay Scheme" (PPS), effectively floundered on union opposition and the second (NWRA), while reflecting basic continuity differed from it in some important respects. [10] One of the more important of these, certainly ideologically, was the greater importance attached to "job enrichment" and "involvement" and "communication" in NWRA as compared with PPS.

Various factors led to PPS. Externally the Company was facing increasingly competitive world markets and had become pre-occupied with improving its productivity and efficiency. Internally it was undergoing technological change and mechanisation of some of its processes, experiencing industrial 'militancy' in certain sites[11] and finding that its payment system was increasingly inappropriate.[12] In particular, local control of the bonus and other pay elements had allowed 'wage drift', and it was also felt that the existing schemes did not adequately reward the mental effort increasingly required in some jobs. In the early sixties central management began to rethink its managerial theories and practices, and by the mid-sixties, decided to examine changes at shop floor level.[13] At management's initiative, a small joint management/union consultative committee was set up and considered various 'issues' papers, which identified current practices and problems and areas for change.[14]

Whilst the senior management believed that changing educational and living standards were leading to greater aspirations in work on the part of employees which would lead to dissatisfaction if not met, there seems little doubt that the main pre-occupation was with the efficiency and profitability of the Company. Concern with tapping individual potential through job enlargement or enrichment was seen as both a necessary long-term response to change in the general social environment, as well as likely to have a short-term pay-off. But of more crucial importance, was the degree of inter-union flexibility that could be achieved so as to improve productivity. PPS was based on the concept of "examining a job in its totality". This meant that tradesmen would be expected to operate plant where necessary, and general workers could "use tools to carry out the less skilled craft tasks which form only a subsidiary part of their work". (Quotations are from our interviews).

It was argued this greater flexibility, through the reallocation of aspects of a job as between, for example, general and craft workers, would increase job satisfaction, as it both gave the general worker a wider range of tasks and more control over his job, and eliminated menial tasks for the craftsmen. But it is apparent that for management and national unions, this would be a "spin-off" from reducing

demarcations, rather than something to be achieved for its
own sake through serious consideration of the principles of
redesigning a job to provide enrichment. The degree of
flexibility that could be achieved and the setting up of a
common job assessment scheme and pay structure for craft and
general workers to reflect this greater flexibility, was the
main aim of PPS. And it was on these traditional areas that
PPS floundered. Four years separate the signing of PPS and
NWRA at national level. During this time the Company
experienced sustained opposition to the agreement on two of
the three trial sites and only managed to get trials of PPS
at certain "more favourable and carefully chosen sites".[15]
The experience of stalemate and arguments against flexibility
led the Company and national unions to approach NWRA in quite
a different way.

The differences between PPS and NWRA were both substantive
and procedural, for NWRA represented a concession to the
workers' opposition to flexibility, the job appraisement
scheme and pay levels, and their fears about redundancy. It
was agreed that 'flexibility' did not mean that non-craft
workers should use tools which were normally the sole
prerogative of craftsmen, and that flexibility changes would
be formally recorded. This latter point was not welcomed by
management as it was felt to be contrary to the spirit of
flexibility. NWRA gave higher wage scales, a guarantee of no
enforced redundancy, and reaffirmed 100% unionisation as a
condition of employment for new staff. In procedural terms,
the unions went along with management in giving a much
greater emphasis to employee "involvement". This was to work
at two levels - firstly involvement in job assessments and the
implementation of NWRA, and secondly through the newly set up
hierarchy of joint management/union consultative committees
which replaced Works Councils. Employee involvement in job
assessment was the key aspect of implementation. Firstly
because detailed knowledge of the job was essential for a
real assessment of it, and secondly, it was felt, involvement
in changing it would lead to greater commitment to the change.
On management's side too, this involvement was seen as the
embodiment of certain aspects of job enrichment, for it was
felt that increasing involvement in the job, and increasing
the range of responsibility and challenge contained in it,
would lead to greater satisfaction with, and participation
in, work. So workers in each shop analysed what they actually
did, identified inefficient practices and tried to minimise
these either by improving flexibility amongst themselves or
across craft/non-craft lines, and where possible, tried to
extend their jobs and responsibilities. Every improvement or
addition was supposed to count in marks awarded to their job,
which thereby determined their grade and so their pay. That
was "the bait" or the incentive to co-operate. The consensus
of shop opinion determined the new job description: suitable
manning levels had to be agreed by the unions and tnen by

management. Once the job description had been agreed with
local management, it was presented by either some of the men,
or the shop steward on their behalf, to a panel of visiting
inter-divisional assessors drawn from management. This was an
important part of the exercise in so far as the assessors set
the grade for the job, and a great deal of emphasis was put on
the impartiality of the procedure. In a sense then, as far as
job enrichment was concerned, the process of change was as
important, if not more important, than the substantive
changes.

As we have seen, MDC's interest in job enrichment was
marginal rather than central; the "humanisation" of work was
not as important as re-establishing control over the wage
structure and increasing productivity, for MDC was not worried
by high absenteeism or turnover. Whilst MDC involved the
national unions from the beginning and negotiated about change,
the change programme was heavily influenced by the American
management theorists who had been consultants to the Company,
and who worked within a unitary framework for viewing an
enterprise. This above all else accounts for the overall
emphasis on the ideological, as opposed to the structural,
changes. Thus if it were to have major impact it would be at
"the ideological level" as Bosquet implies, but in an
opposite direction to what he hypothesises, that is a movement
towards management values. However, in reality at the local
level, this did not occur. Both the structural and ideological
impact varied between national and local levels and between
sites. In short the meaning, effects, and very nature of the
scheme, varied according to the context in which it was
implemented.

THE EFFECTS OF NWRA

NWRA's effects at local level fall into two main categories:-
traditional issues such as manning levels and redundancy,
payment for change and new grading systems; and the effects
of the 'job enrichment' part of the agreement.

MANNING AND REDUNDANCY

These were important issues at all the sites we visited, for
all had experienced redundancy in one form or another, in the
sense that manpower had reduced. For "cutting or slimming
down" to management, meant job redundancy to stewards, which
in the context of rising national unemployment they were
increasingly concerned with. NWRA in fact had stipulated "no
enforced redundancy" which was very important in that "it sold
the agreement" for "the financially committed worker attracted
by the terms, felt any problems were dealt with by this
clause". Yet a period of economic stagnation and major crises
in markets made it difficult to lose labour through natural
wastage. This was only possible in the South at Dosy, where

local unemployment was low and where MDC's national wage rates meant the Company was only average in wage terms and normally had higher turnover. At Militant and Greenfields, natural wastage was supplemented by early retirement schemes, but even this was not enough at Militant where a Voluntary Severance Scheme was also introduced and the number of employees fell from 7,000 to 6,000 in two years. Traditional experienced most redundancy proportionately, and this affected the stewards' attitudes to all other aspects of the agreement quite significantly, as they felt NWRA redundancies were made for economic recession arguments, and men had little choice but "to volunteer" in a situation where the additional severance pay decreased as the target date for volunteers got nearer. 700 men went here despite a local unemployment rate of 6.8%. Quite obviously against this background, concern with manning levels was fairly high. Stewards argued that they were so tight that illnesses and absences of any kind strained resources and meant overtime was an essential and increasing feature of employment, though one aim of NWRA had been to provide a regular salary with no overtime. Stewards also argued that members had been too keen to enhance their job descriptions to get a higher grade and more money, and had initially accepted manning levels that were too tight.

PAYMENT FOR CHANGE AND THE GRADING STRUCTURE

This issue is linked very closely to the issue of whether or not a once and for all bargain had been struck on flexibility. MDC management had intended that the 'wide' grading of NWRA and regularity of guaranteed income, would allow ongoing change without constant negotiation about payment, because it would take substantial change to merit reassessment of the job. Different sites reacted differently to this. At Greenfields, where as we shall see, the unions had not been very strong before NWRA, the stewards took a sanguine view of the system as they felt the wide grading bands meant that "miracles won't drag you into the next one. So you have quietened the striving and dissatisfaction". Paradoxically it was at Greenfields that the stewards also argued that "provided you can enrich the job, the sky is the limit"; they had proved it "by having reached grade 8 for some process workers". Generally however the grading structure was felt to be a strait-jacket for members and stewards alike, as it offered no prospects of additional payment for more complicated jobs on new products, and consequently the stewards had less to do to show their members and management alike that they were needed. At both Traditional and Militant, stewards wanted half grades to be introduced, and at Traditional were already involved in disputes about re-gradings for new tasks. But as Dosy was to show, it was also possible to use the grade structure in some plants in a way which reflected a spirit of job enrichment.

THE GENERAL EFFECTS OF JOB ENRICHMENT

The overwhelming picture which emerged was that job enrichment
was a more minor aspect of the whole agreement for the shop
stewards and their members, than it was for some of the
management we met. One union official said, "it was not
something the shop stewards talk about as a major element in
the agreement". Other stewards suggested that the idea of
job enrichment had been "oversold". Stewards at Militant,
the most politically and trade union aware of all those we
talked to, were perhaps the most critical of the Company's
"exaggerated" emphasis on the increased sense of responsibility that would result. While the stewards' parody of the
company line on this must also be seen as an exaggeration, it
is indicative of the type of presentation generally given on
the introduction of job enrichment: "The Company said,
'You'll have more sense of responsibility. You'll come out in
the morning raring to go'. Well it's all drivel and nonsense
and we know it". Evidence from the sites suggests that any
notions of making the job more interesting or enriched were,
of necessity, of marginal interest to the rank and file,
because basic factors such as pay and security came first.
Stewards at Militant explained job enrichment had been
accepted as "an attempt to remove drudgery from the job as
well as provide financial and personal enrichment". Nevertheless it was the financial aspect which attracted most attention from the rank and file. Satisfaction from the work
itself, as opposed to the social relations with work mates,
when and if it occurred, was regarded as a "bonus".

DIFFERENCES OF INTERPRETATION

There were important differences between local management and
union members as to what job enrichment involved and how
important it really was. For example, the unions did not see
unlimited flexibility or willingness to accept every change in
working practices, as job enrichment, whereas local management
clearly did. Genuine job enrichment, which offered workers
opportunities to make decisions, or to plan their work, or to
be responsible for quality control, was seen as being a step
forward. But stewards were quick to point out that some
"enrichment" was spurious. Adding certain extra tasks to a
job cycle does not necessarily make it more interesting and
the stewards distinguished between 'vertical' enrichment-
when responsibility was taken from the supervision, and
'horizontal' enrichment, which means "increasing responsibility" in terms of increased work load. Certainly the vertical
definition falls within Herzberg's meaning of the term, while
the latter does not - it is better known as 'job enlargement'.
On one of our plant tours these definitions were hotly debated
between management and stewards. Stewards denied that jobs
had been enriched and made more responsible because, they said,

75

men were only working more machinery than before. Obviously both types of change were involved in the NWRA exercise. Some of the instrument artificers at Militant and general workers at Greenfields, felt that they now had more responsibility and were able to plan their jobs and to take more decisions about what to do. Other workers who had more routine machine-minding responsibilities felt that their jobs had changed very little; they had perhaps taken on more tasks or were doing their own quality control, but did not regard this as very substantial.

INTER-UNION EFFECTS

Attitudes to job enrichment also varied between unions. It was, for example, much less important for craftsmen, for some of whom "job enrichment" appeared as a threat, by increasing the interest of the jobs of process workers at their expense. The allocation of simple maintenance jobs to general workers has been a feature of many productivity agreements from Fawley onwards.[16] Whether such flexibility is seen as a 'threat' or an improvement, i.e. where the craftsmen are relieved of tedious routine work and required to concentrate upon tasks requiring their own particular skills, is very much influenced by external factors such as the presence or absence of the threat of redundancy. But in any case, NWRA did have the effect of improving some of the craftsmen's jobs by giving them freedom to plan their own work sequence, by assuming some of the responsibility previously carried by foremen, and also by eliminating some of the more menial aspects of their tasks, which in some cases craftsmen had held onto purely because they attracted a good bonus.

REACTIONS TO JOB ENRICHMENT

Attitudes to job enrichment were sometimes undermined by varying experiences of the job assessment scheme. Stewards at Greenfields pointed out that job enrichment "fell very flat when two job descriptions, one as 'enriched as possible, the other with the minimum written in' got the same grade". In some respects too, stewards queried whether management was implementing NWRA fully. They felt there were "golden opportunities built into these job descriptions for enriching both up and across", and suggested that upward enrichment was checked by the problem of supervisors. Certainly at every site, stewards mentioned how the foreman's position had changed, and how there had been a reduction of supervisors. At Dosy, for example, the numbers were reduced by about one-fifth in one year alone through early retirement and natural wastage. Supervisors knew that they were being phased out through non-replacement when they retired, and were "scared of proving they ain't necessary". They responded by being very resistant to change and unwilling to allow any passing

76

down of responsibility to the general workers. It is not without significance that staff membership of trade unions . became an issue in MDC over this period.

Paradoxically job enrichment and the move to increase general shop floor responsibility, posed another type of problem for shop stewards as it virtually eliminated the promotion ladder for the shop floor. Whilst this had always been limited, promotion to foreman was the only way up for the "above average man". The official at Greenfields thought such men would feel frustrated and might channel their energies into more destructive channels for the Company. Stewards found that they had to tread a careful path between demands for enrichment and making sure that there were possibilities for promotion: "we enrich the job of the rank and file to improve their status at the supposed expense of being self supervisory, at the same time you want to keep open lines of promotion . . . . you cannot keep everyone satisfied at one level". This had been jointly recognised as a problem at Dosy by management and unions, and an informal promotion ladder was devised using the grading system (see above, pp. 72-73).

SOME CONSEQUENCES OF THE IMPLEMENTATION

As for that aspect of enrichment which management had looked to come from "consultation and involvement", it is probably true to say that there was a considerable feeling of change generated in the course of implementation. But unless this is consciously maintained by a continuous search for new methods of co-operation and an ongoing programme of change on management's part, it cannot be sustained. Some of the stewards felt local management's attitudes had only lasted until the agreement was put in. They wondered how far management at local level was committed to, or interested in, the wider aims of NWRA, for since its initial implementation, NWRA had hardly moved at all, and the "various alibis" for this, such as lack of trained men to take on the enlarged/enriched jobs, didn't ring true, "as it was up to management to run training courses".

These examples illustrate how difficult it is to introduce change at one level in an organisation without examining the impact on the total environment, and preparing for this adequately. Certainly they show that job enrichment should not be considered in isolation. In this case it was intimately related to the issue of the grading structure; it had consequences for promotion prospects; and it eventually raised issues of training of operatives for more highly technically skilled jobs. It is therefore not a concept to be applied without setting it firmly in the total work situation and understanding possible repercussions. In many cases it seemed that local management were themselves ill-equipped to see the total situation. There are no simple rules to apply in order to enrich jobs. It was often easier for them to see

77

what they thought of as 'involvement' as providing job enrichment, when in fact, this 'involvement' amounted to little more than the provision of more information about the Company's activities, or an entry into some degree of consultation. Yet some expectations had been raised. We found some aspects of job enrichment were welcomed and seen as having long-term repercussions. As one official said at Traditional,"if we are talking long-term about worker control, then this could well be one small step towards this end. Let's get the man on the factory floor taking a greater interest in his job, accepting more responsibility for the job so that at the end of the day when we ultimately take over the factory, the man has already conditioned himself to this decision by accepting a degree of responsibility". Certainly there was an interest at rank and file level, especially among younger members, to consider job enrichment as a new area where demands should be made, and national officers of both general unions regarded it as an issue of growing importance. They linked it with the need for increased training and better promotion prospects for general workers in the industry, and saw "job enrichment" and the whole question of work organisation, as being an area of increasing importance for the shop steward to be involved in. That this was argued nationally, when as we have seen financial incentives were of paramount importance for most members, suggests a need to look at the changes which NWRA effected in the stewards' position and bargaining power, and to ask whether stewards felt job enrichment was, or could be, a salient issue for their members.

Stewards' power crucially depends on their degree of shop floor support and their ability to affect the pay and conditions of their members. This varied considerably in MDC from site to site prior to NWRA, and so the effects of NWRA also varied. Some sites benefited from the 100% unionisation; for others, NWRA merely legitimated de facto situations, and this affected stewards' perceptions of whether they had gained or lost by NWRA. At Greenfields and Dosy, the general workers had had low levels of unionisation prior to NWRA (25% and 35% respectively) and thus had benefited from NWRA both quantitatively and, they argued, qualitatively. Involvement in NWRA at Greenfields had made the membership "much more interested in what's going on" and the calibre of the stewards improved too. They were no longer "just collecting stewards". At Dosy, stewards also felt pressurised by a keener membership as higher rates under NWRA were attracting younger men, more active in union affairs. At both these sites, stewards also felt that NWRA had given them more stature in the eyes of management, though stewards at Dosy were more critical of management and the agreement than at Greenfields. In contrast stewards at both Traditional and Militant felt they had not gained anything from NWRA in this respect, and lost a lot of the unofficial control they had won over aspects of pay and conditions. The ending of the bonus system was crucial here,

for as the stewards at Dosy said, they now had "less to do on
a day-to-day basis for the members", and at all three sites,
stewards argued that bargaining about "conditions" and other
terms, was no substitute for affecting their members' pay
packets each week. Thus they saw NWRA as a successful challenge by management to stewards' control of the bonus scheme,
brought about because "MDC stewards were too good at the
system", and they felt considerably weakened by only being
able to bargain about "irrelevant" issues like conditions.
This was not only because stewards had lost control over local
pay, but because they judged this to be a strategic issue for
developing members' consciousness. They argued that at the
present stage of development of shop floor members' expectations, an ability to influence to a degree their own pay
packet, remained one of the most formative experiences in
which members could be involved.

It is impossible to know how far the stewards were
accurately reflecting their members here or justifying their
own opposition to their loss of control under NWRA. Certainly
at Militant, where stewards had probably had more day-to-day
control of wages than at any other of MDC's sites and had
waged fierce and long drawn out opposition to NWRA, they
accorded both the least significance of the four sites to
NWRA, wondering "what grand strategy still has to be revealed", and showed least interest in developing new bargaining
areas based on NWRA, such as job enrichment. At Traditional,
the stewards' traditional bargaining stance to NWRA - that
they approached all agreements expecting management moves to
be a "con" - was reinforced by their need to deal with
traditional issues like redundancies and recurrent disputes
over grading. In contrast stewards at Dosy already appeared
to be looking around for other issues to exploit, and were
using the Joint Consultative Committees and joint manning
discussions, pressing for more on-the-job training under NWRA,
so men could be trained for the more "skilled" and better paid
jobs in the general worker grades. That they were able to
conceive of doing this is attributable to several factors;
their stable product market, the very different Southern
labour market they were in, a different history and culture
of trade unionism in the plant and the locality, and a technology more conducive to building up a job and developing
"career ladders" for general workers. Their lack of success
in pushing forward as fast as they wanted, attributed to
management's lack of real interest in NWRA, partly explained
their frustration with the agreement.

Thus at these four sites, the impact of job enrichment
at the time we studied them, had been mainly restricted to the
implementation of the NWRA rather than affecting the subsequent bargaining strategy of the stewards. This seemed partly
because of the newness of the agreement and the stewards not
yet having equipped themselves to deal with this situation,
and partly because traditional problems of redundancy and pay

anomalies had greater immediacy for them and their members, particularly in a worsening economic climate. Sceptics may also argue that the workforce rightly shunned "job enrichment" because it was so small scale and essentially manipulative as the severe constraints of technology and organisational structure were unchanged. This is impossible to prove or disprove, though the evidence from the sites suggests that genuine job enrichment was welcomed as a bonus, but pay came first in bargaining terms.

What is interesting, is that the national officers felt it was time to move back the frontiers of bargaining. So at national level, where pay and conditions bargaining took place, national officials in the three post-NWRA years we studied, were pursuing a policy of pressing home the issue of job enrichment, arguing that management had legitimated it as a bargaining area by introducing it through NWRA. But their attempts to broaden bargaining in this way were not very successful. Against determined Company opposition to increasing enrichment, and whilst major concern on the trade union side focussed on the anomalies and dissatisfactions with job assessment and pay, it proved impossible to get a wider audience and backing for job enrichment demands from the ordinary members and the majority of stewards. Perhaps the steward at Traditional was right to argue that one of the unions' biggest problems was that "the Company is more successful than ourselves in controlling the minds of MDC's workers". Certainly at all the sites, stewards agreed that MDC was held to be a good local employer and its paternalism did not encourage a critical and demanding membership.

At the same time as pushing for more job enrichment, the Trade Unions were arguing for more involvement in decision-making at all levels and suggesting that these two demands were intimately interlinked. As we have shown, NWRA had been accompanied by the setting up of Joint Consultative Committees, and at some sites these were being used by stewards to push for training and improvements in conditions. The national officers felt it was both imperative to give local sites more opportunity for involvement and bargaining, and nationally "to increase our participative role . . . . in MDC's corporate planning", and so they asked for mutual access to certain information about manpower costs and efficiency and argued joint management/union discussion was vital. Overall then, in their bargaining strategy, the unions were suggesting greater participation in all aspects of planning in the Company, for it was a crucial theme of theirs that discussion about involvement in the task, which management had initiated, had to be accompanied by discussion at all levels of Company policies.

CONCLUSIONS

Regardless of whether or not this case is typical of Job
Enrichment for manual workers in Britain, it illustrates the
way industrial sociologists analyse job redesign.

Firstly they are concerned with the power structure of
the organisation and the way in which the struggle for control
occurs between management and labour over the organisation of
the task and the rewards for effort. Thus they ask the
crucial question of what place behavioural science initiatives
have in these contexts, i.e. why they are introduced, how, and
with what consequences for the organisation, its constituent
groups and the individual worker.

Sociologists have challenged the theories of motivation
underlying these behavioural science initiatives by referring
to the very much more complex debate about the nature of
orientations to work, and the relationship between orientation
and satisfaction. Thus the individual's response is not
divorced from the structure in which he/she is located, and a
range of factors is seen as affecting responses to job
enrichment initiatives. For the success or not (to whom?) of
any implementation, is contingent upon the organisation's
external environment of product and labour markets as much as
upon its internal balance of power, industrial relations
climate, the attitudes of the workforce to the unions, and the
constraints imposed upon change by technological, economic
or political considerations.

This then enables us to consider the respective claims
and counter claims advanced by critics and advocates alike,
and assess the variation possible in the intermediate areas
between Braverman and Bosquet. Braverman's starting point is
an assumed de-skilling of jobs dictated by the logic of capital
accumulation and the need for managerial control. As such any
job enrichment or non-Taylorist management tactic, can
neither alter the content of jobs, nor be anything other than
ideologically insignificant.

An exploration of the middle ground between Braverman and
Bosquet's domino theory of worker participation, might usefully begin from the critiques of Braverman which question his
de-skilling thesis, and his interpretation and use of
Taylorism.

The emphasis in much of this work is on the way in which
jobs are not simply designed by an omniscient and all-powerful
management (or their consultants), but are the product of the
struggles of contending groups. Emphasis is also placed on
the diversity of reasons and influences on management for
introducing changes in jobs. So the increasing attention
given to job redesign is shown to reflect neither a simple
desire to "con" workers into accepting de-skilled jobs, nor
just an attempt to take control of their jobs and so counter
recalcitrant workforces. Rather it is generated more directly
by economic and technological forces, in particular the need

to increase the flexibility of particular workforces and to change the nature of supervision. As such job enrichment may well involve real changes in the nature and content of jobs, and in effect may not be qualitatively different from other, more traditional, attempts to change jobs which are not described in these terms.

Job enrichment programmes may thus be defined as any changes in jobs in which the intrinsic content of jobs is accorded some explicit significance. They will be used by management as part of their weaponry in the attempt to re-negotiate the division of labour. This cannot, however, be used to argue that job enrichment programmes are manipulative or that job enrichment is inherently managerial and a "con".

For firstly, as the case study illustrates, they may well involve real changes, however small, in the content of jobs. Secondly, and more important, management is aware that its workforce will react and that implementation is rarely a matter of simply making changes, but involves persuading, negotiating, and compromising about the extent and nature of the changes. Furthermore, in many instances, especially in Europe and the United Kingdom, workers do not simply act as atomised individ-uals, but react collectively through their trade unions and are certainly not "conned" into anything, as this case study shows.

Aspects of the programme were effectively resisted, such as the encroachment of general workers into traditional craft areas of work, and higher payment for change was achieved. And as well as resisting the proposals, the workforce also challenged the spirit of the programme, its ideological framework, by the key act of resolutely bargaining about change. Moreover, as we have shown nationally and at certain local sites, the unions were going on the offensive and attempting to enlarge the domain of bargaining by pushing for further implementation of job enrichment. In particular by working on two frontiers of control at once, they showed very clearly the inter-relatedness of task or technical control with policy or managerial control. It is when management sees "job enrichment" and "participation" as limited to task decision-making, and when these change programmes are introduced into non-unionised workplaces, that the likeli-hood of them enhancing managerial control is greatest.

Bosquet does not make it clear that the potential he sees in job enrichment for the transformation of the division of labour, is dependent on a well-organised, politically aware workforce where the desire for participation is well established and institutionalised in the form of collective bargaining, and where people's orientations to work go beyond the subtle cash-nexus of instrumentalism, such that bargaining for more interesting work and more say in the organisation of production, is as much on the agenda as pay and conditions. But if the implementation of job redesign is a complex process so too is the managerial decision to use such a technique, a

fact which carries implications for the future of job redesign
during mass unemployment. It is true that management in the
present case was responding to a shift in bargaining power,
evidenced in wage drift, and to that extent mass unemployment
would eliminate the necessity for job redesign. On the other
hand it was also endeavouring to reorganise working practices
in order to improve flexibility, productivity and profitability in the face of world competition. Competitive pressures
on the British economy have continued to increase since the
1960's and one can   therefore discern a rationale for the
increased use of job redesign in the present period. For long-
desired changes in working practices can more easily be
introduced because of mass unemployment and weak union bargaining power. There is good reason then to expect, on balance, a
continued resort to job redesign as part of the process of
restructuring; and certainly one cannot assume that if the
employer's 'problem of motivation' is reduced by increasing
levels of unemployment that job redesign programmes will have
no relevance.[17]

NOTES

   1.   The case study material is based on a study undertaken by Ceridwen Roberts and Dorothy Wedderburn.
   2.   For a fuller statement of this and other criticisms
of Braverman, see chapters by Elger, Wood and Kelly, and Wood,
in S. Wood (ed.), The Degradation of Work? : Skill, Deskilling
and the Braverman Debate, London, Hutchinson, 1981.
   3.   During the implementation of the agreement and our
research, sections of the Company's white collar workers were
attempting to get union recognition but this case study
concerns only the manual workers.
   4.   Since our original focus was on the effects of job
enrichment initiatives on trade unions and collective bargaining, this was less of a problem than it might seem. Our
failure to gain access to other firms in the early stages of
job enrichment suggests it would have been impossible to have
studied the programme as it unfolded.
   5.   In terms of numbers of members in the Company as a
whole.
   6.   Our names are chosen partly to reflect the nature and
degree of the trade union activity at each site prior to the
programme's introduction. "Traditional" reflected a site
characterised by a high union involvement and traditional
bargaining stances. "Militant" was so called because it was
seen as the most militant of the sites by management and
indeed the unions. "Greenfields" was not a new site but
levels of unionisation were very low here and the stewards
little more than collecting stewards. "Dosy" was also
characterised by fairly low unionisation and an older workforce who had 'retired to the easier jobs of MDC and weren't
union minded'.

7. We met the National Officers of the TGWU and NUGMW and an Executive Councillor of the AUEW. For convenience we refer to them throughout as "National Officers".

8. Our discussions with shop stewards often included group discussions with stewards from all unions on the site.

9. Wherever possible we interviewed people who had held office at the time of the agreement's negotiation and implementation. Whilst the full-time officials and most of the convenors were the same, two of the national officials had taken office during implementation and spoke with this perspective.

10. One national officer rejected this view. He saw NWRA as an entirely new agreement.

11. This is a relative concept of course. Compared with many big employers MDC had little industrial unrest.

12. There was concern that as much as 25-30% of weekly take home pay was made up by the bonus which fluctuated depending on the availability of work: thus opportunities for bonus varied from site to site. Both the Company and National Unions felt there were advantages in stabilising weekly pay and also in minimising overtime.

13. Interest in behavioural science techniques and theories in MDC dates from the visit of a few senior managers to the U.S.A. in the early sixties. These ideas were disseminated gradually and several American consultants visited MDC, e.g. McGregor and Herzberg.

14. The issues included the payment structure, the job appraisement scheme, the efficient use of manpower, and benefits such as holidays, sickness pay, overtime and shift payments.

15. It is quite clear that the sites were "well chosen". Most were in rural areas with little union organisation or experience. One suggested site was expressly turned down because of "unfavourable local reaction". Two of these "PPS by the back door" sites were to become show sites for the Agreement.

16. See Flanders (1964).

17. Ceridwen Roberts writes in a personal capacity and the analysis and views expressed are not necessarily those of the Department of Employment.

Chapter 5

THE PROCESS OF CHANGE : PRACTICAL PARADIGMS FOR REDESIGNING JOBS

J. Friso den Hertog and Frans M. van Eijnatten

INTRODUCTION

The extensive literature on both job and organisation redesign
focusses predominantly on the content of change. This chapter
attempts to demonstrate, through analysis of case studies,
that there needs to be much more emphasis on the process of
change.
    The Philips Organisation has been active in the field of
job redesign since the beginning of the sixties when attracting and holding staff in a rapidly expanding industry became
a major problem (den Hertog, 1978). Job redesign is regarded
within the company as the basic element of organisation design,
aimed at: "The organisation of the work and work situation in
such a way, that efficiency is maintained or improved, and job
content accords as closely as possible with the capacities and
ambitions of the individual worker" (den Hertog, 1978, p.52).
    Of the sixty local job redesign experiments conducted in
the last 15 years, most started at local level, and were
successful in one way but unsuccessful in another. They were
successful because they usually demonstrated that the 'ideas
could be made to work in practice' and they offered alternatives for the classical and corroded structures of existing
production systems. They were unsuccessful in the sense that
few projects diffused spontaneously through the rest of the
organisation. Critical appraisals of these programmes within
the company made it clear that there was an urgent need to
develop a new orientation on the matter. Six years ago the
first author became involved in the evaluation of one of these
projects in a Dutch television-receiver factory. In many ways
this particular experiment is representative of others and we
elaborate on it here as it marks a turning point in our thinking about job design.

THE CHANGE PROCESS AS A BLACK BOX

In this instance a production manager and a personnel manager took the initiative to start an experiment in one particular department. In the course of two years they developed a practical alternative to the traditional television assembly line. They created two semi-autonomous working groups, each consisting of seven people who were collectively responsible for the pre-assembly, assembly, finishing and inspection (as well as any subsequent repair) of a complete television set. The experiment incorporated a mixture of job redesign elements, of which the lengthening of cycle-times (from 3 to 20 minutes), integration of direct and indirect tasks, shortening of the hierarchical structure, and the implementation of work consultation, were the most important (den Hertog, 1978).

Within the company and outside, this particular project was used for several years to illustrate what can be done to change the traditional paced assembly-line production process. Many visitors passed through the experimental area, which was widely publicised. An extensive report was produced, based upon analyses of production data, questionnaires, interviews and observations (see den Hertog and de Vries, 1977). The results were positive. The 'experimental' employees no longer considered the old situation acceptable, and were more satisfied with their work than employees in the control group, who were still working in the orthodox way. Those in the newly created semi-autonomous groups took a more favourable view of their work, and stressed that only the very first steps had been taken along a path leading to further participation and autonomy. People liked the changes that had taken place and wanted them to be extended. Furthermore, a detailed economic evaluation revealed that the actual factory cost price of television sets assembled by the experimental groups was slightly lower than those assembled on the orthodox lines.

These rigorous behavioural and economic procedures, however, considered only the <u>direct effects</u> of the new method of working. As a total evaluation process it was deficient in two crucially important ways:

1. It ignored the broader context within which the experiment took place, completely failing to consider the effects of the new working arrangements on other departments (and vice versa). For example, the evaluation excluded any reference to the fact that the experiment was eventually stopped for planning reasons.

2. It ignored the process by which the old systems of working were changed into the new. It described what had changed but not how it had been achieved, nor did it suggest how the ideas could be applied elsewhere. For example, the evaluation omitted any consideration of how carefully the experiment had been protected and 'coached' as well as the particular consequences of this 'intensive care' operation.

From an organisational learning point of view, these

deficiencies are critical and to a large degree explain why
the good ideas available in various parts of the organisation
have failed to diffuse more generally and to have a major
impact on it. The first deficiency, the wider organisational
impact of job redesign, is addressed in the context of other
experiences by Chris Clegg (in chapter 6) and by Mike Fitter
(in chapter 7). This chapter focusses on the lack of adequate
models of the process of change.

The literature bears out the view that the evaluation of
this particular project was not unusual in its emphasis on
quasi-rational thinking about organisational change. Typically,
problems are measured and diagnosed by outsiders; variables are
manipulated in experimental sites; and particular outcomes are
monitored to test the effects of the changes. The whole
approach is based upon a positivistic frame of reference within which problems are tackled using well-defined solutions and
effects are demonstrated using 'before and after' research
designs. The detail of what actually happens during the
process of the change programme remains within a <u>black box.</u>

In practice organisational change does not happen like
that. More usually it is made up of a chain of ill-structured
interventions aimed at broad goals (Weiss and Rein, 1970). For
example, specified objectives are often as general as 'improving the atmosphere or climate' in a department, and in pursuit
of such an aim, a number of changes and subsequent modifications are made to working practices. Our experience convinces
us that change is a process of gradual development and hence
that the quasi-rational approach is an inappropriate way of
learning from action. Organisational learning is better
furthered by explicit analysis of what happens during the
process of change. In fact, ignoring the dynamic nature of
the change process places the job design researcher and
consultant in a rather <u>contradictory situation</u> (Argyris, 1968).
Although his aim is to break through the existing bureaucratic
patterns, he is following a path that has exactly the same
bureaucratic features as the original situation which he is
trying to change.

PRACTICAL PARADIGMS FOR JOB DESIGN STRATEGY

Becoming aware of this blind spot on the process of change, the
management and staff in this example drew a second conclusion:
<u>there are no simple answers, no standard solutions.</u> The re-
design of a large and complex production system is itself a
complex problem. Standard procedures or intervention packages
such as the recipes for success formulated by representatives
of the Job Enrichment School (see for example, Herzberg, 1976),
are of no practical use in this situation. Although Ford
(1969) and Myers (1970), claim there is one best way to
implement job enrichment, their approaches are far too
simplistic to be adequate in the production environments to
which we are referring (although they may be effective in

87

small clerical organisations). As stated above, planned organisational change is best seen as a development towards broad aims, requiring many unstructured interventions. These interventions cannot be left in black boxes and cannot be taken from standard tool kits.

At this point the question arises: What is the alternative? Can we find integrated theoretical or practical models which can guarantee, or at any rate, increase the probability of the successful planning of interventions? A number of writers answer this question with a clear 'no'. (For example, see Lawrence and Lorsch, 1969; Clark, 1972; and Tiefenthal, 1976). They argue that interventions which are required in the redesign of production systems are so complex and situation-specific, that there is no one-way-to-do-it. We agree with this argument. Organisations themselves have to develop their own methods and models which fit their actual situation and their own circumstances. But, whilst there does not appear to be an all-embracing integrated theory of change, we have gradually learned, because of our experiences, to deal with a number of important strategic change issues. Twenty years of job design practice cannot be put aside.

In analysing past and current change efforts and relating the outcomes from local experiences to the available body of theory on organisational change (see Dunn and Swierczek, 1977; and den Hertog and Wester, 1979), we certainly believe that practical paradigms can be formulated which can act as heuristics to guide the management of the change process. Van Strien (1978) defines such paradigms as: ". . . . a circumscribed way of dealing with a set of problems in practical reality" (p. 291). He stresses that they are established on the basis of prior interventions 'which have worked'.

On the basis of action research we have conducted in this area (for example, see den Hertog and Wielinga, in press), we have formulated five practical paradigms which have proved to be useful in job design practice within the Philips organisation. These paradigms are related to: diagnosis; prevention; learning; participation; and conflict handling. They are illustrated below using examples from particular projects in which we have been involved.

PARADIGM ONE : DIAGNOSIS

One point of agreement in the literature on organisational change is that change efforts should be problem-centred. The diagnosis of particular problems is often seen as an essential springboard for action (for example, Lawrence and Lorsch, 1969). With regard to job redesign, Birchall (1975) states that the initial diagnosis of a situation should reveal the nature of any weaknesses in personnel, policies, and operating systems, as well as giving an indication of the possible relationships between these basic system variables.

The way problems are defined indeed determines to a large

extent which subsystem in the organisation is tackled. A comparative case analysis of six job design and job consultation projects illustrates this point. (For a fuller description of these cases, see den Hertog and Wester, 1979). The projects were started in separate engineering workshops which are very similar in terms of products, technology and organisational culture. Table 5.1 summarises the outcomes of an analysis of each of these projects with respect to: the stimulus for change, the diagnosis, and the principal changes which were actually achieved.

The analysis reveals that only one of the projects gave sufficiently detailed consideration to the issue of problem-definition. Only in project B was the diagnosis carried out thoroughly and focussed upon broad aspects of the organisation. Large numbers of employees from different levels and functions were involved in this effort. In other projects (C,D,F) most of the attention went to particular social aspects of the organisation. In cases A and E very little effort was invested in the diagnostic phase at all. As we shall see later, it is also relevant to observe which groups and individuals were involved in the diagnostic phase. (Participation of different groups and levels was most intensive in case B. Elsewhere the problem inventory was carried out by a single change agent or a small task force).

On the basis of this comparative study we would conclude that the way problems are itemised and defined, has a significant impact upon the development of a project. When attention at the start of the project is paid to social aspects of the organisation alone, we can observe that the solutions are prescribed in the same domain. A good example is case D: here the existing consultation and communication structure had failed to the extent that the participants had ceased to use it. The social science researcher was given the task of finding out why. In his investigations almost all his attention was given to examining the relationships between individuals and groups. The main characteristics of the organisation and its technology were ignored. This is in direct contrast to case B, in which the diagnostic phase incorporated almost every aspect of the organisation.

This analysis illustrates the danger of what Skinner (1971) calls 'the piecemeal syndrome'. By this he refers to a common organisational practice in which problems in one subsystem after another are tackled without consideration of the interrelations between them. According to Skinner this results in fighting the symptoms instead of curing the underlying disease. In most of the cases above, this fact was recognised much later in the course of the project, so that the researchers had to step backwards and start again.

In practice an initial diagnosis determines to a large extent the direction in which the change energy is invested. In order to develop solutions that are successful and enduring, the organisation has to be considered and analysed as a whole,

TABLE 5.1

Stimulus, Diagnosis and Principal Changes in 6 Shopfloor Projects

Project	Stimulus to Start Project	Diagnosis : How Problems Were Identified and By Whom	Principal Changes
A	Change in production arrangements such that fitters had to be re-trained to become operators.	Some discussions of general workshop problems were held at management level and were led by a local consultant.	Creation of 3 semi-autonomous groups in which 3 operations (drilling, milling and fitting) were integrated. 'Werkoverleg'* was instituted, some methods and control tasks were delegated to the groups and levels of management were reduced.
B	After a successful trial in one plant an attempt was made to renew the organisational structures and processes of a whole product division.	Working groups comprising elected representatives from all levels and departments were given the task of:- a) describing in detail the current situation in different departments in social, economic and technical terms; b) analysing critically each situation along the same dimensions.	Change-over from a process-oriented layout to groups with a product-oriented layout (i.e. as autonomous as possible). A number of specific changes were made:- a) fewer levels of management; b) decentralisation of other functions (especially quality control and methods departments); c) production groups responsible for own delivery times; d) 'Werkoverleg' instituted.

C	Accumulation of internal problems made personnel and production management aware that something had to be done.	Based on discussions with supervisors and craftsmen, a personnel manager diagnosed the problems. Primarily directed at issues such as, labour turnover, pay systems, and craftsmen/staff relations.	A consultation structure was set up at 2 levels; departmental manager/supervisors; and supervisors/craftsmen.
D	Elected members in a representative consultation committee withdrew from the process.	A social scientist from a local university made an analysis of the social system using questionnaires and interviews. Focus on communication processes.	Range of consultation mechanisms were implemented. Work consultation allowed for direct contact between foremen and craftsmen (on initiative of either). Group system allowed for contact between craftsmen (without foremen who could attend on request). Departmental mechanism allowed for contact between elected representatives and management.

91

TABLE 5.1 (cont'd)

Project	Stimulus to Start Project	Diagnosis : How Problems Were Identified and By Whom	Principal Changes
E	Awareness in factory management team that competitive position of plant was worsening as a result of internal weaknesses.	Discussions at management level of general workshop problems, with particular focus on supervisor/craftsmen relations. No detailed study.	Consultation structure set up to enable foremen to meet their craftsmen on a monthly basis.
F	The entire production arrangements were re-located on a single floor. The opportunity was taken to re-examine the organisation.	A personnel manager, after discussions with some supervisors and craftsmen, itemised the problems. Focus on communications and supervisor/craftsmen relations.	Change in layout and a more product-oriented structure implemented. Tool shop and engineering were made more autonomous and 'werkoverleg' was instituted.

* 'Werkoverleg' is a Dutch term for shopfloor democracy, defined by Koopman and Drenth (1979) as "a system of regular and formalised consultation between the supervisor and his subordinates as a group, aimed at participation in and influence upon decision-making, especially with respect to their own work situation". (p.1)

paying equal attention to the economic, social and technical aspects of the system. Davis (1976) makes the point that the individual job is not necessarily the right unit for diagnosis and intervention, since technology and organisational core structures may be the critical determining factors.

PARADIGM TWO : PREVENTION VERSUS CURE

Most efforts in the field of job redesign are curative rather than preventive. Typically, management takes no action until the problems in the relationships between the employees and the production system become overwhelmingly obvious, for example, in terms of absenteeism or labour turnover. To demonstrate the point, three job design projects are placed along a time axis in figure 5.1. If we assume that the re-design project is started a number of years after the new product is introduced and that it takes one or two years to implement the change, we can see the new systems of working have only just become operational before the product life cycle begins to run down and the production process is changed. New products and production methods are then introduced, typically using traditional systems and the cycle starts all over again.

The significant point to be made here is that Quality of Working Life activities have to be incorporated into ongoing management processes (for example, see Swedish Employers' Confederation, 1975). They should be introduced at the moment the system is being designed (van der Does de Willebois, 1968), even though this period is already a highly uncertain one. This is a point clearly recognised by the Central Workers' Council of the Dutch Philips organisation who state:

> If it is decided to apply work structuring, then allowance must be made for it from the beginning (e.g. in connection with product design, mechan-isation, factory layout, etc.) and not just at the last moment, adding it as a kind of sauce to make a dish a little tastier. We may call this aspect 'integration in time' or 'preventive work struct-uring' (Philips COR, 1973, p.22).

Examples of 'preventive job design' are scarce at this moment. The first attempts in this field, mostly originating from Scandinavia, seem promising (Swedish Employers' Confederation, 1975). Within the Philips television factory described earlier, a development in the same direction can be observed. The essence of this development is that the layout of each new production system is discussed and evaluated in advance, utilising job design criteria. The involved groups are system designers (for layout, machines, and information), system users or operators, and social scientists.

Because this approach is a very recent one, trade-offs

93

FIGURE 5.1

Job Redesign in the 'Life Cycle' of the Product:

Three Examples

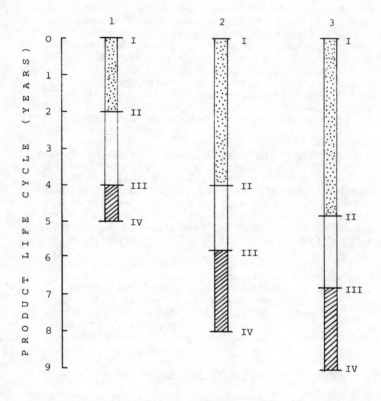

PROJECT

I   Start of Production

II   Preparation of WS

III   Implementation of WS

IV   End of Production

between cost, system effectiveness and work humanisation cannot yet be evaluated. A description of the preventive approach to job design and some interesting illustrations can be found elsewhere (see van Assen and Wester, 1980; and van Eijnatten and den Hertog, 1979). The alternative strategy for creating more meaningful work in a factory, by setting-up small experiments on a piecemeal basis, has now been rejected within Philips.

PARADIGM THREE : LEARNING

Job design is often described as a central strategy for Organisational Development (see for example, Vansina, 1976; and Zwart, 1972). To discuss extensively the relationships between various OD concepts and the practice of job design is beyond the scope of this chapter. Instead we will elaborate on one of the principles central to Organisational Development: learning. We agree with Allegro (1973) and Thorsrud (1972) that job design is more than the implementation of a carefully prescribed set of procedures. Job design requires continuous monitoring and the regular adaptation of the ideas which govern those actions.

Two case studies will be used to illustrate the argument. (For fuller descriptions of these studies, see den Hertog, 1978). The first concerns a department which assembles complicated electronic equipment in small batches. Work cycles are long (from a few hours to several days), and job learning times for new employees vary from half to a whole year. This work is 'semi-skilled' and there were acute difficulties in finding people suitable for this kind of job. According to the personnel manager and the local head of production, job design could provide a solution to this selection/placement problem, because a new category of worker would become interested in the redesigned jobs: especially trainees from the internal junior technical college.

The decision was made to start a small-scale experiment with a product which had just finished pilot production and which was not too complicated. The main elements of the new working arrangements were:
- the creation of a product-oriented group of ten operators;
- job rotation; and,
- job consultation or 'Werkoverleg'.
Unfortunately, the experiment was not as successful as people had hoped. Job redesign was utilised in this instance as a standard prescription for a clearly defined ailment. Without any previous study of the specific character of the production organisation, a number of elements were introduced into a single section of the department. The strategy was concerned only with short-term problems and possibilities. The under-lying philosophy was summed up by the phrase: 'if only the group gets going properly'. The project, which was tightly

95

controlled by a staff manager, did not fit into any broader policy plan.

When it became clear that the required production standards would not be achieved, the experiment was regarded by local management and the rest of the factory as a failure of work restructuring. The evaluation report was used by management in the same way as the school report of a weak pupil who failed the course. 'Proof' had been obtained that job redesign had not worked and therefore was not feasible in small-batch production because (in particular) job cycles were too long to enable rotation. The question of why the experiment failed was never specifically addressed and was allowed to remain unasked. However, a thorough follow-up would have shown that extensive job rotation is indeed unsuitable for a factory with cycle times of one day, but it may also have suggested a better solution in terms of integrating jobs across departmental boundaries. Subsequent modification of the experiment might have helped considerably in the search for solutions to the particular problems of co-ordination and integration between the inter-related departments.

The second project took place in a large highly-mechanised department experiencing difficulties with machine operations. To analyse how the department was functioning, some of the machines were closely monitored for six weeks. All supervisory and auxiliary groups (such as fitters, machine-setters, foremen and chargehands) were banned from the machines for that period, and operation and maintenance became the exclusive job of the machine operators (except in emergency situations). The other machines continued to operate normally (acting as a control group). The department head, who operated in close consultation with the machine operators and their supervisors, acted as analyst and observer.

The results revealed a 2% drop in productivity and a 25% increase in rejects which would generally be regarded as proof of complete failure. However, a carefully conducted follow-up showed that the machine operators could handle the increase in responsibility and required less supervision than had been assumed. The operators also needed less technical help, and their interest in their work increased as a direct result of their enhanced responsibility. In addition, a number of indirect tasks could be done by the machine operators themselves after some training. On the basis of this 'unsuccessful experiment' a number of radical steps were taken. Most significant were the elimination of two levels of management, the allocation of maintenance and inspection tasks to trained operators, and the transfer of skilled staff employees from the maintenance department to the shop floor to take appropriate action in the case of more serious machine faults. The project was gradually expanded to the entire production department (employing 400 people) and in time proved highly successful.

In this instance the approach to the project was characterised to a much larger degree by the need to solve practical problems using the broad strategy of job redesign, and to do it incrementally by progressive change and modification. Instead of drawing hasty conclusions and apportioning blame, a genuine attempt was made to develop the change participatively and those involved felt that the whole experience had been of a learning character.

In conclusion, both experiments were set up to solve problems and to gather experience with alternative work systems which constituted a first step in the process of organisational renewal. As often happens in practice, the aims of one of the projects (that involving small batch production) shifted: it was no longer viewed as one (albeit significant) part of a wider change process, but became an issue in itself. The job redesign exercise was seen as a means of resolving the problems and it had to justify and prove itself very quickly. As a means to a short-term end it provoked rejection from its immediate surroundings and was evaluated purely in terms of its local direct effects. A bad report meant that, so far as the particular department was concerned, job design was laid to rest in the grave for organisational techniques which have been 'tried out' and have failed. Real learning did not take place, largely because real learning was not attempted.

Argyris (1976) makes a useful distinction here between single and double-loop learning. The first learning style is rather egocentric in character: goal-oriented actions are based on the desire to control others without accepting feedback from them. The typical purpose is to win. The case of the small-batch production project is typical of this approach. The second learning style, 'double-loop' learning, Argyris describes as a style in which: "Articulateness and advocacy are coupled with an invitation to confront one another's views and to alter them, in order to produce the position that is based on the most complete, valid information possible and to which participants can become internally committed" (1976, p.369).

The experiment in machine operating constitutes a clear example of double-loop learning. The involved manager and the departmental members genuinely wanted to know what was happening and were keen to learn and develop from their problems. As a group they were not afraid to ask fundamental questions and to take risks in modifying a change which at first sight appeared a definite failure.

PARADIGM FOUR : PARTICIPATION

Participation of employees in the setting-up and subsequent monitoring of projects has become more and more recognised as another essential condition for successful job design. The word 'condition' is perhaps a little too weak. Experiences in Northern and Western Europe have shown that participation in decision-making can be regarded as a pre-requisite for successful job design (for example, see Emery and Thorsrud, 1969).

To quote 'Job Reform in Sweden': "The involvement of specialists in work design can be of great value, but the active participation of those affected by the changes is of even greater importance. The development of optimal solutions can be facilitated by the utilisation of knowledge possessed by those at different levels and in different skill categories. It is only common sense that a workplace can best be designed by using the contributions of those who know about the work - those who do it" (Swedish Employers' Confederation, 1975, p.24). From this standpoint, Herzberg's (1976) view is clearly rejected, at least in Europe. Herzberg argues that employee participation in projects leads only to temporary feelings of being involved, and diverts managerial attention from the core of the matter, that is professional informed analysis of the work itself.

In contrast, critical European studies show that a large number of failures to enhance the quality of working life can be attributed to a lack of employee participation. Thus Ramondt (1974) speaks of 'work democracy without workers'. This notion is also consistent with the fact that the demand for participation in job and organisation redesign has now become a political reality. A study by the Central Workers' Council of Philips in 1973 makes this point very clear. It was noted that until then, those directly concerned with significant changes, were given little opportunity to exert influence on the plans. The Council claimed the right for the strong involvement of employees at the earliest possible moment in the development of any projects which would impinge upon them and their work. In this way job redesign has to be seen as a step in a process of industrial democratisation. Ramondt (1974) points out that job design and other humanisation programmes demand an institutional form of worker influence but he is not prescriptive with regard to the concrete form in which worker participation has to be organised. In an earlier study, den Hertog (1978) has described a number of possibilities, the choices of which will be determined, to a large extent, by the prevailing industrial relations context. Examples are:

- Via collective bargaining: in Italy and Germany there are instances of collective agreements which contain specific job design elements and considerations.
- Via legislation: issues concerning the quality of working life and the involvement of employee representatives in the processes of organisational change, are included in recent legislation in different countries (such as Norway, the Netherlands and France).
- Via workers' councils: these can play important roles, both as stimulators as well as controllers of the job design process.

- Via internal consultation structures: Likert's link-ing-pin model has been used in a number of organisations to help design structures for the purpose of communicating proposals, comments and ideas up and down the hierarchy (see Likert, 1961). The case study below offers an illustration of this type.

This particular project involved the redesign of a tool factory (see Alink and Wester, 1978). A combination of internal and external pressures led top management of the machine tool division of Philips to reconsider the entire divisional operation. There had been increasing pressure upon the plants to be more flexible and to shorten delivery times. Over a number of years a lot of internal problems had also become apparent: for example, poor working relationships between supervisors and craftsmen; unnecessarily formalised interactions between departments; long throughput times; burdening bureaucratic procedures and so on. One plant was selected for a pilot project and the subsequent redesign aimed at:

- changing the working arrangements to meet the wishes and needs of the craftsmen, and,

- improving the delivery times and product prices by increasing the organisation's flexibility.

A new plant manager was given the explicit task of making the project a success. The management team, supplemented by a workers' council representative and by both an internal and external consultant, acted as a steering group. The project started with an intensive diagnosis, and seven diagnostic groups were instituted for this purpose. The members were elected from all departments and levels. They gathered an enormous amount of information about social, economic and technical aspects of the organisation. This material was integrated by a subgroup of the management team, including the plant manager aided by the internal and external consultants. At the same time an extensive linking-pin consultation structure was set up (see figure 5.2). On the basis of the diagnostic information, the management team developed a very broad outline plan for change. The plan was discussed and deliberated throughout the newly created consultation channels. Throughout the project the outline plan had the status of draft posposals, to be discussed and modified continuously. After discussion of the first and second version, the main proposals for the project were agreed and authorised. They involved the creation of four highly autonomous project groups in which different line and staff functions were integrated. The steering group decided to allow the composition of these groups to be determined by a democratic election procedure in which members of different functions and organisational levels participated. These groups were then given the task of making their own plans for the redesign of the internal organisation of their own project group. From time to time proposals were brought back to the steering group for discussion at every

FIGURE 5.2

The Communication and Project Structure in an
Organisation Redesign Programme

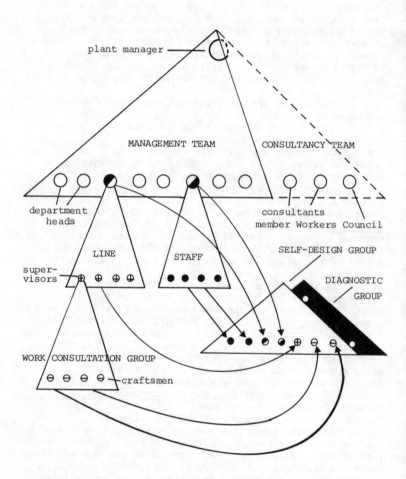

STEERING GROUP

plant manager

MANAGEMENT TEAM   CONSULTANCY TEAM

department
heads

consultants
member Workers Council

LINE   STAFF   SELF-DESIGN GROUP

super-
visors   DIAGNOSTIC
GROUP

WORK CONSULTATION GROUP

craftsmen

level. On the basis of these discussions the management team
came to a final decision and authorised the plans. This
project displays a combination of management initiative and
monitoring, and employee participation in the redesign process.
Managerial, clerical and shopfloor employees were involved in
and responsible for the programme. It is notable that in
projects such as this, good top management of the project is
accompanied most of the time with a high level of employee
participation (den Hertog and Wester, 1979).

The classic organisation development dichotomy between
the bottom up and top down approaches seems hardly adequate to
describe the plurality of the change strategy adopted here.
In this context, planned organisational change is best seen as
an iterative process in which proposals not only go up and
down the hierarchy, but are also exchanged horizontally.

From our experience, we conclude that the participation
of employees in the job design process is an important condition for success, both from an ethical as well as from a functional point of view. Employees have the right to a say in
the way their own work situation is altered. Furthermore, it
is logical to involve those who understand practical details
of the existing work system and who have to make the new
system work. In practice, participative job design, or self-
design, is not a one-way process. It implies an ongoing
interaction between management interventions and employee
responses within a well developed consultation structure.

PARADIGM FIVE : CONFLICT HANDLING

It has become quite usual in organisational change projects to
call for the 'participation of the employees involved' and
indeed, we have elaborated on this theme above. The word
participation is most commonly used in the sense of 'participation in decision-making', i.e. "procedures which will give
each person the opportunity to exert influence on matters that
concern him" (Swedish Employers' Confederation, 1975). This
same group point out that: "Almost everyone is eager to express
an opinion regarding his own work situation and it is only
logical for managers to try to satisfy this basic wish" (p.24).

It is, however, quite remarkable that in the discussion
on participative job redesign, or self-design, so little
attention has been paid to conflicts that can arise in the
course of such a programme. The Organisation Development
movement has had an enormous and unfortunate impact in this
respect. It made many of us (especially managers and consultants) believe that conflict represents some form of "misunder-
standing", or "miscommunication" or some lack of "authentic
and open relationships" (see Clark, 1972, pp.14-15). OD tends
to ignore the fact that conflicts can be based upon essentially different interests of groups and individuals. It also
tends to omit the fact that participation is a change in the
internal political system of an organisation which can involve

alterations in the distribution of power.

In organisation practice, 'power' and 'conflict' are dirty words. As Dale (1963) says, "the power process in management is like sex in the Victorian Age. Everyone knows about it, nobody ever talks about it". (For a discussion of this issue, see van Aken, 1978). Yet as Pettigrew (1973) points out, innovations in organisations are likely to trigger political activity: "Innovations are likely to threaten existing parts of the working community. New resources may be created and appear to fall within the jurisdiction of a department or individual who had previously not been a claimant in a particular area. This department or its principal representative may see this as an opportunity to increase his power, status and rewards in the organisation. Others may see their interests threatened by the change and needs for security or the maintenance of power may provide the impetus for resistance. In all these ways new political action is released and ultimately the existing distribution of power is endangered" (p. 192).

The case of the tool factory is illustrative in this respect. The project showed again and again differences in the interests of groups and individuals. These differences partly originated in the changes of roles, positions and tasks. Thus for many people in the project it was a matter of 'give and take'. Some however had to give more than they received in return. For example, in this case study, the decentralisation of staff to smaller, relatively autonomous product groups, necessitated the transfer of many staff specialists from their central position in the office block to positions on or adjacent to the shopfloor. It was perceived by them as a loss in status, influence and security.

More attention is given to the types of conflict that can arise in such projects by Chris Clegg (in chapter 6) and by Mike Fitter (in chapter 7). They demonstrate that these distinct plural interests may be experienced vertically (i.e. between managers and managed) and also laterally (i.e. between one function and another). On many occasions, however, such differences of interest are ignored, but sooner or later they become manifest and often result in the cancellation of the planned changes. Such failures are then usually explained in terms of 'resistance to change'.

Here we focus not on the different types of conflict that may arise, but on the ways in which the differences may be expressed and handled. Thus our interest here is in mechanisms and procedures for coping with conflicts of interest. Organisational change in this respect is not the fostering of harmony: rather it focusses on finding ways of dealing with inevitable conflicts (den Hertog and Wielinga, in press).

In the project we described above, new proposals from management and the design groups were continuously monitored and discussed by staff, supervisors and craftsmen. Inevitably, some situations required the co-operation of 'remote' central staff departments, which usually were not willing to create exceptions to company rules and procedures for a single factory. For example, a proposal by plant management to enlarge the array of promotion opportunities (in terms of job grades) for craftsmen, was turned down by the central personnel department because of the implications elsewhere.

The framework described by Walker (1974) for classifying alternative methods of participation is useful in this context. He distinguishes between mechanisms which are direct (i.e. face-to-face) or indirect (i.e. through representatives), formal or informal, and integrative (i.e. co-operative) or disjunctive (i.e. conflictual). For example, in a small-scale project it may be possible to handle most of the differences of interest (especially the vertical ones) using a direct, informal and integrative mechanism. In larger projects (such as in the tool factory above) the principal method was indirect, formal and integrative. Moreover, as Clegg (1980) points out, different issues at different stages in a project may require different sorts of mechanisms. (For example, issues of pay and skill differentiation will almost certainly be referred to collective bargaining procedures).

The essential point is that conflicts of interest of different types will arise during job redesign experiments, and there needs to be some mechanism (or inter-related set of mechanisms) which enable the differences to be aired, recognised and addressed. In Philips we recognise that such conflicts are inevitable and that they need to be managed.

CONCLUDING REMARKS

This chapter has deliberately not tried to present straight-forward, well-prescribed strategies for job and organisation redesign. Those who expected to find them will be very disappointed. Furthermore, when they go on looking for 'recipes for success', they will remain disappointed, because there are no <u>simple standard strategies.</u> The two main reasons for this statement conclude the chapter. In the first place strategic choices about complex issues concerning the process of change necessitate a search for the right strategic mix. Job redesign demands changes in technological and organisational processes as well as in cultural patterns and power relations. This means that one has to find the right balance of expertise, participation, planning, learning and conflict handling. The specific situation influences to a large degree the kind of balance that has to be created. In one case, for example, job design might only be possible if certain technological problems are solved. Such situations place a heavy demand on expertise concerning the man/machine interface. Other cases, however, may demand less technological change because basic changes are required in the dominant cultural patterns. It is clear that in those situations more emphasis has to be put on interpersonal relations, participation and learning processes. The second reason for not offering cut-and-dried solutions can be inferred from the paradigms themselves. These imply that the consultants or managers in the field of job design, have to share the structural control of the process with the other people who are directly involved. Participants in the projects have to learn to shape their own strategic choices.

What we have offered in this chapter are some practical paradigms derived from our experiences, which hopefully will enable people to make effective choices as they attempt to resolve their own specific problems. The refinement of these heuristics will best be furthered by their direct application in action research projects of the type we have described above. In time, the improvement of paradigms such as these should make it easier for the participants in a job redesign exercise to cope with and manage the process of change.

Chapter 6

MODELLING THE PRACTICE OF JOB DESIGN

Chris W. Clegg

INTRODUCTION

Much of the published literature on job design reveals an
artificial separation between 'theory' and 'practice'. To
some, theory is best advanced by empirical investigations
which adhere to the canons of experimental psychology with a
clear emphasis on control and rigour. In these instances
'experimentation' may involve study in field settings but
this is by no means always the case. Thus laboratory
simulations of 'real' situations are sometimes undertaken.
(For example, see Umstot, Bell and Mitchell, 1976; and
Seeborg, 1978). A central feature of such studies is that
typically they report on a limited range of variables with
psychologists in particular concentrating on the relationships between the characteristics of jobs, performance and
satisfaction.

    To others, the focus is on understanding the practice of
job design. The resulting lengthy case-study descriptions of
'what actually happens' may (or may not) accurately capture
the realities and complexities of the multi-variate
situation, but in any case these experiences may be such that
it can be extremely difficult to disentangle the causal
interrelationships, and thereby to apply the lessons learned
elsewhere.

    The dilemma for the researcher is obviously not unique
to this subject area and has been neatly captured by Benne,
Chin and Bennis (1976): "we may need to sacrifice some
'comprehension' in achieving a high degree of 'verification',
and (more typically), accept some lower degree of 'verification' in order to achieve maximum 'comprehension'" (p.137).
The central point is that the researcher is trading-off two
highly desirable qualities such that, for example, he will
face circumstances where his efforts to comprehend the
sequence of events and identify the interactions among the
critical variables, and subsequently report them, may by
their very complexity, reduce his ability to verify his

conclusions to the satisfaction of both himself and others. Of course, the choice of relative emphasis will be contingent upon the research problems: thus, if one is examining the performance of a specific model in a particular situation, clearly the emphasis is on verification (see for example, Wall, Clegg and Jackson, 1978). Nevertheless the writer believes that the 'current state of the art' in relation to job design, is such that the need is to place more emphasis on comprehension, i.e. to improve our understanding of the practice. (For reviews of the current state, see for example, Klein, 1976; and Lawler, 1976).

In this context the distinction between theory and practice, labelled above as 'artificial', can be bridged if the former is developed and used as an aid in the latter. As such, a "crucial test is the ability of a theory to explain the practice" (Singh, 1978, p. 63). In addition theories can be seen as tools to aid the pursuit of desired goals and to help predict future outcomes. It is in this sense that by definition, "there is nothing so practical as a good theory" (Lewin, 1952, p. 164), to which one might add 'there is nothing so useful for a theorist as the experience of practice'.

With this orientation of a reciprocal and dynamic relationship between theory and practice in mind, the principal aim of this chapter is to present an example of a model[1] which may further our understanding of the practice of job design. Specifically the objectives are:

1. to describe, using a case study, the major practical consequences of how jobs are designed, both before and after planned changes;

2. to develop a list of requirements for a model of job design;

3. to present an example of such a model derived from experience of the project;

4. to use the model to place the redesign exercise in its organisational context;

5. to match the model to both the list of requirements developed previously, and to the relevant literature; and,

6. to consider the methodological and research management implications of these points.

To these ends the next section outlines the case study.

A CASE STUDY

This project[2] took place within a single department in a medium-sized, family-owned, partially unionised confectionery firm in the North of England. The firm is renowned for the manufacture of high quality sweets and is highly successful, although acute problems were experienced within this particular department which produces and packs over 40 lines of hard-boiled sweets using a batch-production system. It was organised in two adjacent rooms separated by a partition, one for production staffed by men, and one for packing staffed by women. Each room had a supervisor who reported to the departmental manager and in addition there was a chargehand in the production area. Approximately 40 people were employed in the department on a regular basis.

The problems of the department were variously characterised in terms of 'attitudes', 'atmosphere' and 'climate'. Whilst there was widespread recognition that something was wrong with it, and that it was different to all the other departments in the firm, there was no coherent view of the causes, or of what could be done to make improvements. The factory manager however felt that the way in which the work was organised and managed might lie at the core of the difficulties. Thus when the researchers wrote to the organisation outlining their interests in job redesign, this led directly to the successful negotiation of an action research contract.

Research Contract and Method

The speculative contact by the researchers led to their meeting first the factory and departmental managers, and subsequently all the departmental staff in an informal meeting. At these meetings the researchers described their interests and their normal method of working. This method specified, for example, that any group could veto the project, that any written reports would be openly and freely available and that the researchers would accept no fees. This 'contract' proved acceptable to everybody and the researchers over a period of three years:

(i) undertook a detailed diagnosis of the problems in the department;

(ii) as members of a steering group representing a range of interests in the firm, helped redesign the work of the department and implement the new method of working; and

(iii) undertook a detailed evaluation of the new organisation that emerged from the redesign which centred upon two semi-autonomous working groups.

The research process was highly informal and participative and included the collection of large amounts of data. (For a fuller description of the process, see Clegg, 1980). Primarily this entailed a great deal of observation, large numbers of informal discussions and meetings, a planned programme of interviews (both with people within the department and from elsewhere), and three administrations of a questionnaire. This instrument was based on the Job Diagnostic Survey (Hackman and Oldham, 1975 and 1976), and was used in the form of a structured interview, 12 months before the changes, and 6 months then 18 months after the changes. In addition a variety of performance measures were gathered continuously over the period, and both absence and turnover were monitored. The researchers were actively

involved in the project from its inception until the second
survey. They then withdrew until returning to gather data
using the third survey. Since then (approximately one year)
they have maintained infrequent contact to 'keep in touch'
with developments both within the department and in the firm
as a whole.

Described below are the way the department used to work,
the changes that were made, and the way it now functions
(including a brief evaluation of the changes).

The Old Method of Working

To understand how the department worked it is necessary to
recognise the strong drive for production which emanated from
senior management and which was transmitted throughout the
organisation. Thus managers and supervisors were judged
primarily in terms of their ability to meet production targets
as efficiently as possible. In this department the manager
and supervisors responded to this pressure by keeping very
tight control over the production process. For example, the
production supervisor set the pace of work, allocated people
to the various tasks (usually the task at which they performed best and hence the same one each day), and decided the
timing and duration of any breaks. The packing supervisor
kept a similar degree of control and in practice together
they made almost all the daily operating decisions, acting as
working foremen.

This meant that the people on the shopfloor had no
control over events and usually did the same small part of the
overall task, although with over 40 different product lines
they experienced some variety. Their jobs were perceived as
lacking in autonomy (i.e. opportunities for personal
decision-making) and in task identity (i.e. opportunities to
complete a whole task). This overall lack of 'job complexity'
according to conventional theory would create low levels of
motivation. This proved to be the case in practice: for
example, people often claimed they could organise the work
better if left to themselves, and their own perceived lack of
control over the job led them to abrogate responsibility when
things went wrong ('we told them so'). This insular (but
understandable) outlook led to low levels of performance
which in turn made the supervisors and departmental manager
try even harder to tighten up their control over the work.

This self-perpetuating spiral of events was exacerbated
by two factors. First, the production information systems
were designed such that the shopfloor workers were usually
unaware of their targets and of their subsequent performance
against them. And secondly, the two groups of packers and
producers were physically separate from one another which
further reduced task identity as well as creating problems of
co-ordination. These difficulties were accompanied by low
levels of satisfaction and high levels of strain amongst

108

the people working there. For all these reasons the department was widely regarded as the 'worst' in the whole factory.

The Changes

A number of changes were implemented prior to the new method
of working and, in addition, the department has continued to
develop since. The first major change was to pull down the
partition between the two rooms and to organise the whole
department into 2 semi-autonomous work groups (or teams).
Each group worked on separate equipment, comprised both men
and women and was made responsible for the complete production
process (from processing the raw materials to despatching the
packed sweets to the warehouse). The work roles of these
teams were defined so that they had almost total control over
daily operating decision-making within certain constraints.
These specified that they should meet agreed daily targets
for each product line (based on work study standards) and
that they should operate within company standards with regard
to safety, hygiene and discipline. In practice this meant,
for example, that the teams allocated jobs and overtime
amongst themselves, set their own pace of work, and decided
on the timing of breaks and meals.

The issue of targets, i.e. "the negotiated agreement on
group objectives" (Emery, 1980, p.27), in particular was
crucial to the whole project. It was fortunate that the
perceptions of 'fair targets' on the shopfloor matched the
work study timings for almost all the product lines. In
addition the groups needed assurance that if they repeatedly
met their side of the bargain, the targets would not be raised
by management.[3] Another significant feature of this new
system was that the targets were flexible, such that if there
were interruptions to smooth working which were beyond the
teams' control, the targets were adjusted accordingly.
Similarly if higher targets were required these were met by
increases in overtime working. (See Fitter, chapter 7).

To match the new work roles of the teams, the job
descriptions of the manager and the supervisor[4] were altered
such that they were made responsible for maintaining overall
standards and performance, were used as expert advisors by
the teams, and spent most of their time managing the
'boundaries' of the department (for example, by ensuring the
materials were readily available, by checking the production
plans were optimal, and by improving the quality of service
provided by the maintenance engineers). In time it became
clear that only one person was needed for this job and the
supervisor became the new manager, the old one being
transferred to an equivalent position elsewhere in the
factory. The post of clerical assistant was also created.
This person took responsibility for the local management
information systems, which were improved so that the teams
had a clear idea of their daily targets as well as feedback

on their progress against them, both during and at the end
of each day. (For a fuller analysis of the target and feedback systems, see Clegg and Fitter, 1978). Minor changes
were also made to the grading structure with the aim of
increasing flexibility.

The New Method of Working

With some minor difficulties the changes were assimilated by
all the parties. For example the teams responded eagerly to
their freedom and much preferred their new found autonomy and
their responsibility for the complete production process. It
was readily apparent they were more efficient at organising
themselves than management had been, but also much more
highly motivated. Not surprisingly levels of scrap (which in
a sense reflects wasted effort) fell sharply and productivity
as a department rose significantly.

Although the departmental manager experienced difficulty
with this new devolved style of decision-making (and indeed
came under considerable pressure from his peers to 'take
control' again) the improvement in performance gave him the
confidence to continue, and, more significantly perhaps,
persuaded senior managers to continue their support of the
project. In time the whole atmosphere in the department
became much more relaxed but also much more purposeful. In a
rather low-key way the whole emphasis was on getting the job
done with the minimum of effort and as efficiently as
possible. It is important to recognise that this was not
because the shopfloor and management came to share the same
perspective but rather because there were sufficient advantages for both sides for them to want to continue the project.
Thus the shopfloor were quite happy to perform more product-
ively in return for their freedom to operate autonomously, a
method which they much preferred. Similarly senior management were prepared to risk the devolution to the shopfloor of
daily operational decision-making in return for overall
improvements in the department, both in terms of performance
and 'climate'. As the project progressed levels of job
satisfaction rose significantly, and levels of general strain
fell.

The principal changes that took place, along with notes
on their timing are tabulated below.

In summary, the redesign exercise has been highly
successful: the control over daily operational decisions
passed from management to the shopfloor; the management
structure became much 'flatter' with one manager and a
clerical assistant running the department previously
managed by one manager, two supervisors, and a chargehand;
the teams described their jobs as incorporating more autonomy,
task identity and feedback, with none of them wishing to
return to the old method of working; the grading system was
changed such that some individuals received a pay rise;

TABLE 6.1

The Principal, Practical Consequences in a Job
Redesign Project

Variables	Notes on Changes and Timing
Management Control and Structure	1. Control of day to day operational decision-making was passed to the groups. As such control over efficiency was delegated. 2. Management concentrated on providing a service to the groups to maximise their opportunities for uninterrupted working. Managerial control shifted to focus on 'utilisation'. 3. Between time 1 (t1)and time 3(t3), the departmental management structure became much 'flatter'. Thus one manager, two supervisors and a chargehand were replaced by one manager and a clerical assistant.
Job Characteristics (measured using a modified version of the Job Diagnostic Survey of Hackman and Oldham, 1975, with certain additional items)	1. Group autonomy, group task identity and group motivating potential scores each increased significantly between t1 and t2.* 2. Group feedback from superiors increased between t2 and t 3. (These changes were significant on the independent t-tests only).
Pay	1. Regrading (and therefore an increase in pay) occurred for some (but not all) people in each group between t1 and t2.

TABLE 6.1 (cont'd)

Variables	Notes on Changes and Timing
Motivation (measured using the J.D.S.)	1. Motivation increased significantly between t1 and t2.*
Productivity	1. Significant increases in productivity took place comparing the year before the change with the year after.* 2. Analysis of the first half of the next year showed these improvements were maintained.
Production Information Systems	1. The target and feedback systems changed gradually after the job redesign. The new systems became fully operational between t2 and t3. They ceased to be a purely management concern and became more comprehensive, accurate and useful.
Knowledge and Understanding	1. Changes here were slow to occur but gradually there were increases in understanding of the production information systems (e.g. the meaning of efficiency and how it is calculated); of how and why the department worked as it did; and of the external factors affecting the department (especially planning, maintenance and marketing).

TABLE 6.1 (cont'd)

Variables	Notes on Changes and Timing
Relations with Maintenance Engineering	1. Changes here were slow to occur. More accurate recording of information led to costing machine breakdowns and pressure on engineers to improve utilisation (between t2 and t3). 2. Since t3 an organisation-wide programme includes the notion of making engineers report direct to departmental managers.
Job Satisfaction (measured using the JDS)	1. Increases occurred gradually over the period, becoming significant between t1 and t3.*
General Strain (measured using the General Health Questionnaire developed by Goldberg, 1972)	1. Significant decreases occurred in reported strain symptoms between t2 and t3.*

*These statements are supported by statistical analyses using one way analysis of variance for repeated measures as well as independent and matched pairs t-tests. The data from which these conclusions are drawn are reported more fully in Wall and Clegg (1981).

motivation within the department increased significantly as
did overall productivity; the production information systems
were no longer a purely managerial prerogative - they became
useful to and used by the shopfloor, and at the same time,
more systematic and accurate; knowledge and understanding of
how and why the department worked as it did and was evaluated,
increased for most employees; relations with the maintenance
engineering function slowly improved such that the departmental manager had more say over maintenance workload
priorities; and reported levels of job satisfaction were
higher, and levels of general strain lower than before the
changes. Finally, the company is now seeking to extend the
principles of devolved decision-making throughout the rest of
the factory.

REQUIREMENTS OF A MODEL OF JOB DESIGN

The first point to note is that 'model' has supplanted
'theory'. This is quite simply because 'theory' would require,
among other things, that one could specify which relationships
are important and which are not, under what circumstances
certain variables behave the way they do, what sort of causal
links pertain (e.g. necessary or sufficient, lagged or
immediate), etc., etc.. In bald terms there is not sufficient
knowledge available for one to present a 'theory of job
design' and something less ambitious is appropriate at this
time. As such, the emphasis in this chapter is on developing
a heuristic model of job design. The second point to
recognise is that models may fulfill different functions. In
this context the role of a model is seen as helping further
the understanding of practice within organisations and thus
the question is: 'What is it we require of such a model?' A
number of properties seem desirable although it should be
noted the list below is not intended to be definitive. (For
examples of similar lists, see Chin, 1961; Gouldner, 1961;
and Bennis, 1966).
     1. The model should define its purpose and its level of
analysis. Clearly these two issues are inter-related. For
example, if one is developing a model to describe the growth
of interest in job design in Western Europe over the last
10-15 years, the level of analysis will be different to that
incorporated in a model aimed, as in this chapter, at understanding the practice of job design within particular
organisations.
     2. In this context the model should address both the
subject of job design and that of job redesign. Thus it
should enable the user to describe and understand the current
and historical impact of job design, whether the jobs be low
or high on complexity and tightly or loosely controlled. And
it should be capable of describing both 'stable' states (be
they good or bad) and 'unstable' states (be they improving or
worsening). Furthermore such a model should assist the under-

standing of the process of redesign, again whether the
changes are towards more or less complex jobs. For example,
it should point to the 'action levers' (Cummings and
Salipante, 1976) which interventionists can use to move from
one state to another. Thus it should give practitioners and
researchers specific guidance on what can be done to make
changes, and on what the likely effects will be.

3. Related to the above, the model should clearly
define its context, i.e. its sphere of operation. Thus, is
it universally appropriate or contingent upon circumstances?
(and if so, what circumstances?). For example a model
appropriate in a batch production firm may not be applicable
in process industries.

4. A model should specify a number of salient variables
which map onto the complex reality rather than to arbitrary
disciplinary boundaries. Thus the variables may be of
different types (e.g. economic or psychological) and on a
number of different levels (e.g. individual or group). As
such it should encourage/necessitate the crossing of disciplinary boundaries wherever necessary. (This is not without
its problems however laudable the aim: see for example,
Ehrenberg, Hamermesh and Johnson, 1977; and Derber, 1964).

5. In addition, the model should be flexible enough to
allow one to add in additional subsystems of variables where
particular circumstances dictate the need. Thus for example,
payment systems, management information systems, training
programmes, and technological changes may be differentially
relevant in different studies, and a useful model will be
able to handle the varying situations.

6. The model should reflect the complex reality in a
meaningful way. Thus, if there are, in practice, complex
causal relationships, the model should also be complex. As
well as defining the range of variables that are causally
implicated, the model should also give guidance on the
particular order of events in which things take place, incorporating feedback loops where they are hypothesised to exist.
At the same time, however, it should be an abstraction of
reality such that it is manageable and comprehensible. Thus,
it should be capable of being assimilated by the users and
clients in a project, most of whom will be non-specialists in
this area. In ideal circumstances the model in use should be
open and available to the participants (although this may
raise methodological problems).

7. And finally, a model should also be specific enough
to encourage the collection of data of a variety of types
(e.g. attitudinal, performance, observational etc.) and
thereby enable empirical testing of it, with a view to
confirmation and/or disconfirmation of parts or all of it.[5]

A MODEL OF JOB DESIGN

In this context the model presented will reflect the orientation, the case study and the requirements described above. Thus its purpose here is to further our understanding of the practice of job design and it should go some way to meeting the rather formidable list of requirements described in the previous section. It should however be recognised that the model described here was developed by the researchers as the project progressed. Thus although a modified version of the Job Characteristics Model (Hackman and Oldham, 1976; Hackman, 1977) was explicitly used and tested throughout the project, it was found to be severely limited in scope in that it addresses itself only to the intrinsic characteristics of jobs. Thus whilst the specificity of the J.C.M. is admirable from the criterion of 'testability', it is limited as a guide to practice.

The model described here is the one the researchers became aware was (sometimes) implicitly and (sometimes) explicitly guiding their actions and the project as a whole. It therefore remains a subjective interpretation of certain events and certain relationships between variables, as the result of lengthy involvement in and direction of the project. The nature of its development means that the study was not designed to test this particular model and hence it has less than ideal empirical support. Nevertheless it does have some external validation. First because it has been presented to members of the organisation who find it both plausible and useful. And secondly because the data analyses (briefly described in table 6.1) are consistent with the model. (For a more detailed analysis and presentation of the relevant data, see Wall and Clegg, 1981). This is not to say that alternative explanations do not exist. The most 'plausible rival hypotheses' (Campbell and Stanley, 1963) are discussed later.

The model is presented in figure 6.1, and can be most clearly described in three parts. (For a fuller description of the model see Wall, 1980). The first part focusses on the short-term cycle of changes and forms the core of the model. Here it can be seen that the nature of internal departmental control over daily operations and the operators' tasks (i.e. the closeness or remoteness of supervisory style), is hypothesised to influence job complexity, i.e. the more rigid the control, the less job complexity. By implication the key job characteristics here are autonomy and task identity since, in this case study, these were the ones affected by supervisory behaviour. The level of job complexity is hypothesised to affect motivation, i.e. the more complex the job, the greater the motivation to do it well. This hypothesis is central to the literature on job redesign. The next proposed link in the chain is that individual motivation affects levels of performance (where performance can vary). The

116

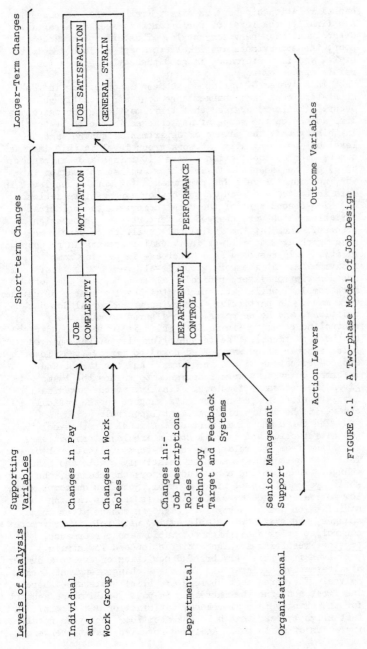

FIGURE 6.1 A Two-phase Model of Job Design

causal relationship here is direct (rather than inverse).
And finally, the level of performance is seen as a partial
determinant of supervisory style. Thus, if performance is
poor, the supervisors are likely to adopt a close directive
style, and if performance is good the style becomes more
remote and delegatory.

This system of variables is seen as operating in the
short-term such that changes here can be reasonably quick to
occur. (It is recognised that there may be technological
limitations on the scope of any changes in the short-term).
In this system, the nature of departmental control and the
level of job complexity (at work group level in this instance)
can be seen as the 'action levers' (Cummings and Salipante,
1976) or the independent variables; whilst motivation (at
the individual level) and performance (at work group level in
this instance) are seen as outcome or dependent variables.

The second part of the model comprises the principal
variables which were changed to support the job redesign
process. Thus, at the individual level, there were some
grading changes to reflect individual increases in responsibility. This resulted in an increase in pay for some
individuals. At the work group level, work roles (i.e. team
job descriptions) were radically altered to make the jobs
more complex, whilst at departmental level a number of changes
were made. In particular, supervisory/managerial job descriptions, and hence roles, were altered to make their
control more remote (in fact to shift it to the 'boundaries'
of the department). The technological layout was changed
(i.e. the partition was pulled down) to improve task identity
and co-ordination within the teams. And the target and
information systems were redesigned to ensure the teams were
given the necessary feedback. Finally, at the organisational
level, senior management lent its support to the radical
change in the nature of departmental control.

The third and final part of the model hypothesises that
job satisfaction and general strain are long-term outcomes
resulting from the relatively short-term cyclical system.
These two outcomes are seen as relatively stable and slow to
change. Thus, in the case study before the changes, the
whole system of close, rigid control, jobs low on complexity,
low motivation and low performance, is seen as causing low
satisfaction and high strain. Eighteen months after the
changes, the system was stable again, with relatively remote
control, complex jobs, high motivation and performance,
together resulting in high satisfaction and low strain.

Even from this very brief description of events a number
of alternative explanations for these changes suggest themselves. The three most obvious are briefly discussed here.
The first concerns the increases in pay. Could these account
for the changes in performance, satisfaction and strain? In
fact slightly less than half the shopfloor employees received
increases of up to 10%. Analyses revealed that there were

no significant differences between those receiving and those not receiving pay increases, on any of the individually measured variables. Furthermore it seems unlikely that changes of this order can account for the radical alteration to the working,and indeed the atmosphere,of the department. One interpretation is that with increased responsibility a pay increase may be a <u>necessary</u> part of the process of job redesign, but is by no means <u>sufficient</u>.

A similar argument applies to the improvement in the target and feedback systems. Improvements in performance and motivation (in particular) had already occurred (by time 2) before the new information systems became fully operational (between t2 and t3). Again the interpretation favoured by the researchers is that improvements to these systems may be necessary in the long run to support devolved decision-making, but again are by no means sufficient <u>in themselves</u> for changes of this order. (See Fitter, chapter 7).

The third alternative explanation is usually labelled the 'Hawthorne effect' (see Roethlisberger and Dickson, 1939; and Mayo, 1946), wherein improvements of this type are explained largely in terms of the presence of the researchers and the interest the project generates. This can be dis-counted in this instance because the very substantial effects continued at the same level for eighteen months after the changes, and the researchers rarely visited the department during the last 10 of those months. It is significant also that a year after the researchers completely withdrew from the situation, the high levels of performance and the changes in working practice had been maintained.

This then is the rather speculative model the researchers offer to promote better understanding of the practice of job design. Quite appropriately it emphasises changes <u>within</u> the particular department. It is however apparent that many of these changes have had an impact on other parts of the organisation, and hence the project needs setting in a broader context.

JOB REDESIGN IN THE ORGANISATIONAL CONTEXT

Mapping job redesign onto an organisational context is a difficult exercise, but nevertheless it is an activity which people managing the project must necessarily undertake (be it implicitly or explicitly). As such this section of the chapter takes a broader systemic view of the project, and attempts to trace the principal effects of the changes on three different functions within the firm. (Others were also affected, but less dramatically).

<u>Production Planning</u>. This function was told by the product-ion director to balance the production plans for the depart-ment over the whole year so as to even out the seasonal peaks and troughs in demand. This enabled the departmental manager

to maintain a balanced workload and thereby keep his work groups stable and intact. Under the normal system of planning, departments followed fluctuations in the market by borrowing staff from elsewhere or by loaning them out. This balancing exercise meant that other production departments, still operating under the normal system, could not borrow staff from this one (and hence saw this change as a loss in flexibility). Furthermore this policy caused complications over managing the shelf-life of certain product lines, and raised overall inventory costs. The planners also collaborated with the departmental manager in the implementation of the target and feedback systems described by Fitter in chapter 7.

Engineering. This function comprised two groups. The Development Engineers were least affected by the project but handled the problems of altering the layout of the department. The Maintenance Engineers were affected much more. As the information systems became a more accurate reflection of what was happening, the departmental manager exerted a great deal of pressure on this function to improve machine availability (and hence utilization). It was the improvements in availability, coupled with changes in team performance (i.e. efficiency) that led to the increase in productivity. (Productivity equals utilization x efficiency). These changes subsequently encouraged senior management to continue with the project. The significance of the impact of maintenance on productivity is now formally recognised in the organisation by the attempts to make the maintenance engineers directly responsible to line management. They are now seen as a service function to production. As such the maintenance engineers have lost a substantial part of their own autonomy - for example, the freedom to set their own workload priorities.

Marketing. This function was affected in two ways. In the first place the production director persuaded it to drop certain low turnover product lines which were not compatible with relatively stable-sized teams. More recently, very strong pressures have been exerted on Marketing by the departmental manager who can now produce more hard-boiled sweets than are being sold. He has been pressing for some time for better promotions, better packaging, more competitive pricing and for more adventurous new product development. In this he has the strong support of his department.

Descriptions at this level can be incorporated in the model, though the result must be regarded as very tentative. The three examples described above are added to the model in figure 6.2. They are characterised in the model as three highly significant subsystems which interact with the department in various specific ways. For example, Production Planning are requested to plan such that regular and even

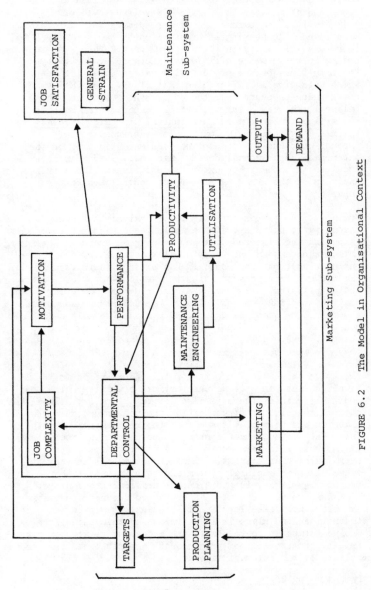

FIGURE 6.2　The Model in Organisational Context

121

targets can be adopted. Such a balanced workload enables the departmental manager to operate a devolved style of decision-making within the parameters of agreed targets. In addition Maintenance Engineering is pressurised by the department to improve availability/ utilization which together with improvements in performance/efficiency, increase productivity. At the same time, better productivity raises potential output which outstrips sales in the market place. Thus Marketing comes under pressure from the department to redress the balance. The key point is that the departmental manager is now trying to exert much more control over his immediate external environment, in particular the functions of production planning, maintenance and marketing. Thus the pattern of departmental control has shifted from an internal focus to an emphasis on external conditions. For a fuller analysis of the changing pattern of control see Fitter (chapter 7).

Summary. The purpose of this brief analysis has been to demonstrate, using specific examples, the range of functions affecting and affected by a job redesign exercise. For some this has been on a once-and-for-all basis, (e.g. development engineering), but for most, it has altered their work practices and/or relationships in the long-term (e.g. production planning, maintenance engineering and marketing). In many descriptions of job redesign the underlying assumption appears to be that the interested parties (usually defined as management and the shopfloor) share a common view on such changes. Where differences are recognised in the literature, they are almost always identified in hierarchical terms (e.g. between top management, middle management, the shopfloor and the trade unions). The point of this description is to highlight that as well as the vertical pluralism which undoubtedly exists, there is also lateral pluralism. Thus the natural sequel to the recognition that job redesign takes place in one part of a system, is the realisation that the different parts of that system, in both vertical and lateral dimensions, will have separate and distinct interests. The over-riding characteristic of redesigning jobs is that it takes place in a plural system and this is one of the major reasons why it is, in practice, so difficult to achieve.
    This section has also attempted to demonstrate using examples, how these functional interactions may be added in to the model to place it in a broader organisational context. The next task is to return to the model and relate it, very briefly, to the list of requirements described earlier, as well as to the relevant literature.

MATCHING THE MODEL

In some ways the model stands up fairly well alongside the listed requirements. In the first place it does define its purpose and level of analysis adequately. Thus it is concerned with understanding the practice of job design within firms, and hence considers variables at job, group, department and organisation level. It does not however give any clues as to the context within which it is appropriate. In particular it excludes such organisational features as technology (unit, batch or process - see Woodward, 1965) and design (organismic or mechanistic - see Burns and Stalker, 1961). This particular case study describes a small-batch production system designed and managed on mechanistic lines.

The model addresses both the subjects of job design and redesign. Thus it attempts a description of the situations before and after the changes, as well as pointing to those independent variables which can be manipulated as action levers. One weakness here is that, as it stands, the model gives no real clue as to why, or at what level, the system stabilises. Also whilst it specifies a number of variables on a number of different levels (individual, group, departmental and organisational), it remains a predominantly psychological model insofar as the short-term system of variables and the longer term outcomes are central to a long psychological tradition in this area. It does however attempt to reveal the particular causal links between variables, as well as approximately defining the sequence of events in the change process.

With regard to flexibility there is no reason why the model should not be extended to include other subsystems of variables. For example, a more complex analysis of performance in terms of efficiency (how effectively people are working) and utilization (how long they are working for) has been included above. This has enabled a description of how the changes allowed the teams to manage their own efficiency, with management concentrating on increasing utilization (by improving the service from maintenance engineering etc.).

Whether the model is 'sufficiently' complex to match reality is almost impossible to assess. From the other side of the coin however, it is certainly a manageable and comprehensible abstraction. As stated earlier, the model has been described to the organisation and has proved useful to them. Thus to the organisation, it appears sufficiently 'realistic' and at the same time sufficiently 'abstract'. And finally, the model is specific enough, both in terms of the causal relationships and the timing of the effects, to encourage detailed empirical testing. Thus, for example, it will be possible to examine elsewhere if performance changes precede longer-term changes in satisfaction and general strain. Ultimately of course, such a model cannot be scored against a list of requirements. It is presented speculatively, but hopefully it is worthy of further development and testing. In practice it will doubtless be judged as a more or less useful tool.

Furthermore the model presented fits extremely well with the psychological literature on this subject. Thus it relates directly to the work which has attempted to demonstrate the links between job characteristics (or job complexity) and outcome variables such as motivation, satisfaction and performance. Thus it shares the perspective adopted by writers such as Turner and Lawrence (1965), and Hackman and Oldham (1976), as well as those subsumed under the heading of 'sociotechnical theorists' such as Trist and Bamforth (1951), and Emery and Trist (1969). Moreover the model is relevant to the performance/satisfaction debate in occupational psychology. It implicitly rejects the view that satisfaction causes performance,aligning itself more closely to the performance causes satisfaction thesis. (For examples from this literature, see Brayfield and Crockett, 1955; Porter and Lawler, 1968; Locke, 1970; and Wanous, 1974). In the model, performance is seen as a partial determinant (i.e. as one part of a subsystem of variables) of satisfaction, as well as of general strain.

In addition this model is consistent with much of the literature relating performance and supervisory style. The hypothesis here is that performance has causal priority over leadership behaviour rather than vice versa. As such it complements the work of researchers such as Lowin and Craig (1968); Mohr (1977); and Barrow (1976). It also matches the literature relating target setting to outcome variables such as motivation and performance. (See for example, Locke, 1968; Ivancevich, 1976; and Umstot, Bell and Mitchell, 1976).

Furthermore it incorporates consideration of those other parts of the environment which may need changing either to allow a redesign exercise to take place, or to promote its effectiveness. As such it complements the work of writers such as Birchall (1975); and Cummings and Salipante (1976). And finally, the model draws from a longer tradition which has examined the impact of the type of work people do on their psychological well-being, in this case measured by the amount of strain they experience (see, for example, Fraser, 1947; Kornhauser, 1965; and Karasek, 1979).

As implied above however, the model does not align itself to certain other developments in the literature. For example it currently excludes any consideration of the moderating effects of individual differences, as exemplified in the work of Turner and Lawrence (1965), Blood and Hulin (1967), Stone (1975), and Hackman and Lawler (1971). And it ignores the literaure on task-organisation fit which relates job design to technology and to organisation design (see for example, Porter, Lawler and Hackman, 1975; Nemiroff and Ford, 1976; Pierce, Dunham and Blackburn, 1979; and Aldag and Brief, 1979).

IMPLICATIONS FOR METHODOLOGY AND RESEARCH MANAGEMENT

With the orientation described in this chapter, and the model presented above, a number of prescriptive points follow. In the first place it becomes clear one is working within a highly complex interdependent system of variables. For example, many of the changes, either alone or in combination, created the circumstances within which other changes could take place. This makes it difficult to give clear definitions of which are the dependent and which are the independent variables. The point is that it is almost impossible to conceive of a research methodology which would 'prove' the existence of certain causal links amongst these variables. The best one could hope for is to present data which are consistent with a particular interpretation. Thus verification becomes equivalent to consistency, plausibility and parsimony. And plausible rival explanations will almost certainly exist, which may only be excluded by a research strategy employing a number of studies (rather than within the context of any single one).

One direct implication of this 'systems view' is that researchers should consider a much broader range of variables than is typically the case at present. Thus comprehension will only be advanced by developing beyond, for example, the satisfaction-performance debate. At the same time researchers need to try to improve their objective and subjective measures of certain variables (e.g. job complexity) as well as examining new ways of measuring variables that currently go unmeasured (e.g. knowledge and understanding). The objective here is to improve the opportunities for verification.

A further implication from the model is that researchers should engage in change programmes to monitor effects over longer periods of time, as well as taking measures at regular intervals. The intention here is to examine the sequence of events as a project develops and hence assist both comprehension and verification. Also there is a need to promote better understanding through empirical research in a range of organisational settings, for example, by considering different sorts of jobs within different technologies and different organisation designs.

It would also improve understanding if research teams collaborated so that their inputs and outputs were broadly comparable. In the extreme this might involve empirical testing of common models, whilst at the minimum, the collaborators could examine a common core of key variables and major issues. And finally, it would aid verification if techniques for analysing complex causal networks were improved. For example developments in the area of time-series analysis (e.g. cross-lagged correlation analysis) may prove beneficial.

If these prescriptions were adopted, it might help action researchers in their efforts to achieve both comprehension and verification, and thus to overcome the doubts expressed by Foster (1972) whose view is that "action researchers are still learning how to cope with their self-imposed task of successfully combining contributions to immediate problem-solving and to scientific knowledge" (p. 74); and those, more pungently voiced by Lawler (1976), who characterised action research projects by saying, "the action part is very visible, but the research side is not" (p. 229).

SUMMARY

This chapter has argued that there is an outstanding need to develop models which further our understanding of the practice of job design.

One such model, developed from the experience of an action research project, has been presented and placed in an organisational context. An attempt has been made to match this model to a list of requirements and to the relevant literature. And finally, the implications of this perspective have been drawn for the methodology and approach which might be utilised by others trying to relate theory and practice in this area.

Clearly the model presented is not definitive. From both theoretical and practical perspectives, it most obviously lacks a coherent structural or contextual component. As Mitchell (1979) observed when reviewing the field of organisational behaviour, "we still have little understanding or closure about the interrelationships of behaviour and the organizational context" (p. 271).

Nevertheless the model is presented in the hope it may prove a useful tool for researchers and practitioners. At the least it presents a more systemic, complex and long-term view than that which usually pertains, as well as offering the possibility of integrating the findings from a range of relevant psychological theoretical traditions.

NOTES

1. 'Model' has supplanted theory for reasons which are given later in the chapter.

2. The project was undertaken jointly by Dr Toby Wall and the author.

3. The issue of targets is central to projects of this type. Clearly if there is no correspondence between managerial and shopfloor definitions of a reasonable workload, then the type of informal working contract that emerged here is not possible. The agreement was that providing the groups met their targets, they maintained their autonomy. Quite clearly any attempts to raise targets subsequent to satisfactory performance will cause conflicts which may destroy such

agreements.

4. Prior to the changes the packing supervisor, for personal reasons, transferred to another department and, with changes of this kind imminent, she was not replaced.

5. Ideally a model should also include the notion of individual differences by offering guidance on differing personal responses to alternative types of job design. This requirement is omitted in this context partly because the model offered in this chapter does not address this issue, but, more importantly, because this research area, to date, has proved notoriously difficult and unproductive. For a review of the research into personality and individual differences within the area of organisational behaviour see Mitchell (1979).

Chapter 7

INFORMATION SYSTEMS AND THE ORGANISATIONAL
IMPLICATIONS OF JOB REDESIGN

Mike Fitter

INTRODUCTION

Much psychological research in the area of job redesign has
focussed on the potential and actual psychological benefits to
individuals. The approach has been essentially individualistic,
by and large ignoring systemic, economic and political factors.
Thus, for example, the Job Characteristics Model (Hackman and
Oldham, 1976; Hackman, 1977) has been used to examine deficiencies in jobs (lack of autonomy, variety, feedback etc.) and to
indicate the requirements for redesign. This model was used by
Wall and Clegg (1981) as the starting point for a redesign
project in a confectionery firm which resulted in significant
improvements in psychological variables such as job satisfaction. Clegg (in chapter 6) discusses the limitations of the
Job Characteristics Model for the practice of job redesign as
well as placing the project in a more organisational context.
    In this chapter I shall examine the same redesign project
but with a somewhat different emphasis. I shall concentrate
on the ways in which the redesign changed the information and
control systems in operation in the department. The analysis
of the control systems will also be used as a medium for
understanding the implications of job redesign for wider
organisational change.
    Using an open socio-technical systems perspective, it is
demonstrated that for the department to function effectively,
changes are required to the information and control systems
over and above those resulting from the job redesign initiative.
These changes need consideration of the cognitive models and
skills of the operators who must process information, make
decisions, and exert control over the production process. It
is argued that the overall improvements in performance and
satisfaction that resulted from the job redesign occur partly
because the new control system is more capable of meeting the
task requirements and partly because the new work organisation
is more motivating to members of the department.
    Before introducing the case study I will outline the

socio-technical framework by which the project is analysed.
The task system has variously been called the primary task
(Miller and Rice, 1967), the technological system (Trist, 1959),
operations technology (Hickson, Pugh and Pheysey, 1969), and
the work system.

> The basis of socio-technical systems design is that
> organisational systems have, first and foremost, a
> technical function to perform in a turbulent and
> complex environment. This function is usually
> expressed in terms of the product (e.g. clean
> laundry, hot meals, treated patients), which results
> from the transformation of an input. In this light
> the organisational system responsible for that
> product is called the work system. (Taylor, 1978,
> p. 97).

Although this chapter considers primarily the inter-
relation between psychological (socio) and technical factors
as manifested in the task system, it should not be forgotten
that the objective underlying the task system is fundamentally
economic; and therefore when evaluating information systems
the essential criteria in practice for their design include
that:
    (i) performance measures should relate directly to
profitability; and,
    (ii) measures should be able to indicate the need for
change.
    The task system (outlined in table 7.1) has a 'physical'
manifestation in the transformation process that converts the
inputs into outputs thus achieving the primary task, and also
a control system that co-ordinates and maintains the components of the transformation process. The transformation
process has essentially three components: the materials being
processed, the physical environment and machinery in which the
processing is done, and the labour of the people who operate
and service the process. The control system also has three
distinguishable components. The targets, which derive from
the objectives of the primary task, are set as standards
against which performance can be assessed. The controllers
of the system and its parts must make regulatory actions in
order to control the process, correcting for perturbances
where necessary, to ensure that the targets are achieved. To
do this, system states must be monitored and communicated to
controllers by the measurement and transfer of information.
This includes, on the one hand, the informal observations
made by an operator as s/he regulates a process or reports a
fault to a supervisor, and also the more formal measures
recorded and analysed by a Management Information System.
    It will be argued that in the case study to be described,
the primary motivation for change occurred in component 1a
(labour), but that every other component also changed to a

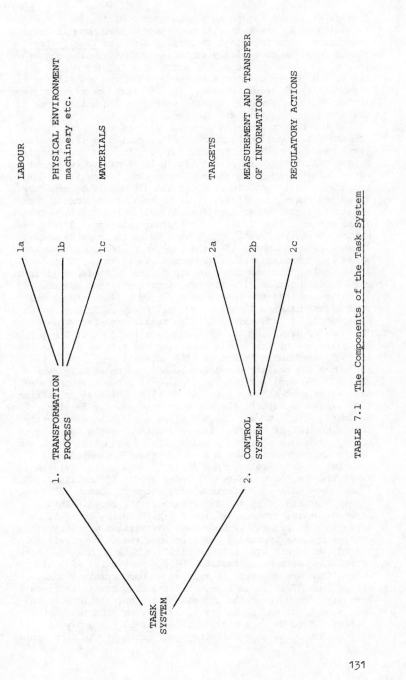

TABLE 7.1 The Components of the Task System

TASK SYSTEM

1. TRANSFORMATION PROCESS
- 1a — LABOUR
- 1b — PHYSICAL ENVIRONMENT machinery etc.
- 1c — MATERIALS

2. CONTROL SYSTEM
- 2a — TARGETS
- 2b — MEASUREMENT AND TRANSFER OF INFORMATION
- 2c — REGULATORY ACTIONS

131

greater or lesser extent as a consequence of the job redesign initiative. Although significant changes were made to several components it is important to realise that the task system itself remained essentially unchanged. That is, the objectives of the task system remained the same and the way in which subsystems interconnect via boundary transfers was not structurally changed. However, the internal operation of task system components was re-organised and the content of some of the boundary transfers was changed.

Job redesign seems to be primarily concerned to improve the content of jobs making them better suited to the psychological needs and skills of individuals. Thus if, for example, a particularly low and dissatisfying level of job complexity or autonomy is identifed amongst a working group, it is reasonable to attempt to redesign the jobs, thereby changing these job characteristics. It might seem, from some of the writings of the 'Human Relations School', that the objective is to maximise individual or work group autonomy. It has been argued, however (Trist, 1959), that there is an optimum level of work group autonomy (for example) which can only be determined by an analysis of the requirements of the task system. Although 'optimum' is not formally defined, its focus is on the requirements for an effective and functional task system. Trist argues that the task system places constraints on what work organisation will be effective. However, in any but the most simple of task systems, there remain some degrees of freedom for designing the work organisation to suit the psychological needs of the people operating the system, i.e. technological determinism is not totally pervasive.

Once the preferred changes to one component have been decided, the implications for changes to other components of the system must also be considered. The design of an information system to support the new work organisation is vital since as Emery (1980) has argued, "To allow any degree of autonomy in the absence of an effective information system would be simply to induce anarchy, a laissez-faire situation where each of the interdependent parts went their way". Despite the importance of control systems there is very little guidance available for the would-be job redesigner. Oldham and Hackman (1980) have stated, "Unfortunately, there is almost no research available in the literature on the relationship between control systems and the design of work, so it is impossible at present to know just how serious a problem control systems typically pose for work redesign activities. Indeed, we do not even have descriptive data on how the characteristics of control systems and the properties of jobs within them are empirically related across organizational units" (p. 257). It is hoped that the case study described here will demonstrate the importance of the relationship and shed some light on the interactions between jobs and control systems. Moreover, as will be illustrated, there may be dysfunctional and unsatisfactory components of the task system

which are revealed only when the redesign is implemented.
These must also be dealt with in a way that results in a
functional task system. The changes introduced are consistent
with the socio-technical design principles outlined by Cherns
(1976).

To summarise, the approach of job redesign theorists may
be thought of as 'person centred', focussing on the changing
of jobs, with possible consequential changes to the technology;
whilst the engineering approach is traditionally 'technology
centred', and has been criticised for its failure to take
sufficient account of people. The approach in this chapter is
essentially 'control centred' and focusses on the relationship
between individuals and the information and control systems
which shape their environment.

THE CASE STUDY

The project introduced changes into the hard boiled sweets
department (HB) of a medium-sized confectionery firm. It was
initiated and carried through by Toby Wall and Chris Clegg,
(details of the firm and changes introduced are given by Clegg
in chapter 6). My substantial involvement with the project
began soon after the new work organisation had come into
operation and it had become apparent that additional changes
to the information and control systems were necessary to
prevent regression to the old and, by general agreement,
unsatisfactory ways.

The objective of the project as outlined by Wall and
Clegg (1981) was:

> Within the organisation the principal shared
> objective was to ameliorate a problem in one
> particular department in the firm, which shop-
> floor and management alike characterised in
> terms of "low morale", "poor shopfloor/management
> relations", "poor work attitudes", "low work
> motivation" and "work apathy". This rather poorly
> defined but keenly felt deficiency had manifested
> itself in mutually recognised unco-operative
> attitudes between the two interest groups, the
> appointment of six different managers during the
> previous eight years, and a labour turnover rate
> much in excess of that elsewhere in the organis-
> ation. The department was generally regarded as
> the least desirable one in which to work in the
> whole factory and all internal attempts to improve
> the situation had failed to produce any recognis-
> able change. Those on the shopfloor wished to
> find new ways of working which they would find
> personally more rewarding, or less costly and
> stressful. (pp. 31-32).

The principal attack on these mainly 'psychological' problems was made through job redesign. That is, by informal discussions, interviews, and the administration of a question-naire (which included psychometric measures of job character-istics), it became apparent that job complexity and motivation were low and therefore the redesign programme concentrated on increasing job complexity by the creation of semi-autonomous work groups.

AN OPEN SYSTEMS VIEW OF HB AND ITS ENVIRONMENT

Figure 7.1 gives a systemic view of the routine activities in the environment immediately surrounding HB. The Sales Depart-ment forecast future requirements which form the basis for weekly production targets calculated by the Production Plann-ing Department using production standards provided by Work Study. Prior to the redesign the principle means of varying targets, whilst requiring a fairly consistent level of perfor-mance, was to use the Labour Pool to vary the number of labour hours available for production. That is, workers were drafted in and out of the department according to the demand forecast by the Sales Department. The HB manager arranged the transfer of operators and ensured the supply of necessary raw materials to meet the weekly targets by liaising with the material stores.

The HB manager was responsible for keeping clerical records which were sent to Management Services who routinely calculated performance measures which were fed back to the HB manager and to the factory manager. Typically the feedback would be received two to three weeks after the week in question. The actual measures used will be dealt with in some detail later. If the figures indicated that performance was particularly poor the factory manager would intervene (he adopted a management by exception philosophy) by putting pressure on the HB manager to make improvements. With this feedback delay however no-one had adequate memory of the events that had led to the apparently poor performance and thus myths were propagated. In general, the performance measures were not understood by the HB manager, supervisors or operators. When performance seemed poor (the department was assessed primarily by the efficiency with which goods were produced and were packed), the standard response was for the production supervisor to attempt to increase the work rate by increasing the cooker speed which controlled the rate of the batch process. However the main effect of this action was to create more 'scrap' and induce feelings of cynicism and help-lessness in the operators who felt they had little or no control over the production process. They were told to do things they knew to be ineffective and believed they could organise the work better themselves. As will be demonstrated later, the performance measures were systematically inaccurate, unfairly depressing apparent performance, and created a dysfunctional control system which was operated by the manage-

FIGURE 7.1

A Systemic View of HB and its Surrounding Environment

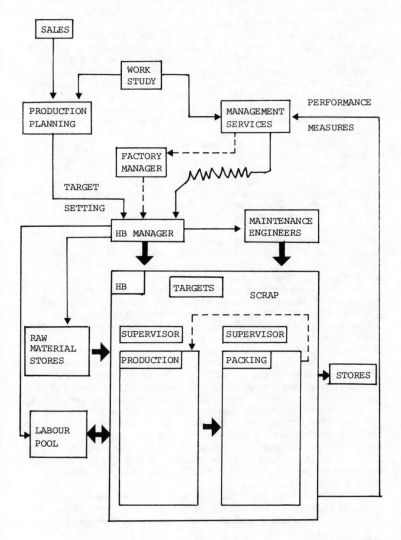

ment without any real understanding of its actual nature.

The other important part of the environment supporting HB was the Maintenance Engineering Department which supplied engineers and parts to fix machinery which broke down. The engineers were called in by the manager or supervisors and a record was kept of the time a machine was out of operation. However, because of the general lack of understanding and of confidence in the information system, the recording of break-downs was very lax, (they were often not recorded or were underestimated) which had the effect of making the performance measures systematically inaccurate.

The work organisation before redesign is shown schematically in figure 7.1. Within the department there were two subsystems, production and packing, each with their own supervisor and operating relatively independently of each other. Independence was reinforced by a number of factors:

(a) due to technical requirements (concerned with the humidity in the packing area), the producers and the packers were separated by a physical barrier thus making communication difficult;

(b) possibly for cultural reasons, all the producers were men, all the packers were women, and they saw themselves as distinct social groups;

(c) the Management Information System measured and evaluated the performance of production and packing separately.

The men produced sweets in batch units (of approximately 50 kg) which were then put into hoppers ready for packing. These hoppers provided a small buffer stock for packers and, within certain limits, allowed them to work independently. However, if the hoppers became full because the men were producing at a high rate, the women would not have time to pack directly from the hoppers and would temporarily put sweets in trays as an additional buffer. This 'traying up' necessarily increased the packers' workload and they resented having to do it. On such occasions the packing supervisor might attempt to influence the production supervisor to slow down production, although she was normally unsuccessful (which led to further resentment) and so coerced the packers to reduce the stockpile by working at what they considered to be an unreasonable rate. In addition to the primary flow of goods through the department, the packers also returned unsatisfactory sweets to production as scrap for reprocessing.

Thus, to summarise, neither packers nor producers had control over either their own work roles, or their work rate, and the production supervisor, often under the direct influence of the manager, attempted to regulate the rate of production by controlling the cooker speed. However, attempts to increase production often resulted in the production of more scrap.

In the redesigned work organisation, two teams were created (named red and white) each team being responsible for the total (production and packing) process. Through a number

136

of stages (see chapter 6) the supervisory roles were eliminted and the departmental manager liaised directly with an elected 'spokesman' from each team.

In addition the role of clerical assistant, which had been created at the initial implementation of the redesign, was expanded to include the collection, processing and feedback of information on performance. In response to the perceived lack of job complexity, each team was made responsible for allocating tasks between members. Each member had a number of skills that they were trained in (the pay was based on the number of skills acquired) and, in principle, people had the opportunity to move between tasks. To encourage further the integration of production and packing, technical problems were overcome which allowed the removal of the physical barrier between production and packing, and changes were made to the information and control systems to reinforce the concept of teamwork. In practice, the cultural distinction between men as producers and women as packers tended to predominate despite some pressure from the researchers to encourage its breakdown. This led to limited mobility between production and packing tasks.

The inadequacies of the original Management Information System (MIS) and the introduction of a new Departmental Information System (DIS) will now be described in some detail.

THE ORIGINAL MANAGEMENT INFORMATION SYSTEM

Prior to the redesign, basic information on labour hours, the number of batches produced and weight packed, were kept routinely. This data was processed by the Management Services Department and, two or three weeks later, derived performance measures were fed back to the department. Figure 7. 2 shows these measures which are defined in more detail in Appendix 1. With the exception of OUTPUT which was a direct measure of the quantities of each product line (in kilograms) reaching the stores, separate measures were used for Production and Packing. However, for clarity, figure 7.2 shows only the measures for Production, although directly equivalent figures were processed for Packing. The HOURS AVAILABLE was a direct measure of the number of labour hours in principle available during a week (normal time and overtime). The HOURS LOST represented deductions for "allowable" stoppages (e.g. machine breakdowns) and the HOURS WORKED was the resulting number of labour hours in practice available for work. These figures in conjunction with the WEIGHT PRODUCED (the number of batches produced x the notional weight of a batch for a given line), were used to calculate the performance measures of UTILIZATION and EFFICIENCY. (EFFICIENCY being derived using STANDARD TIMES for each line provided by the Work Study Department). Feedback was provided on the separate performance measures for Production and Packing and also averaged over the whole department. Although it was not routinely fed

FIGURE 7.2

<u>HB and the Original Management Information System</u>
(See appendix 1 for definitions of performance
indices. The surrounding environment remains as
described in Figure 1.)

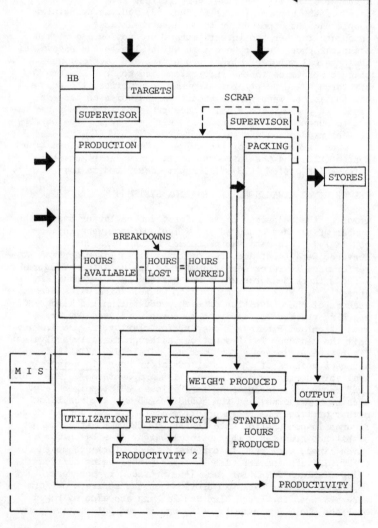

back to HB, senior management also evaluated the department by calculating productivity (the product of UTILIZATION and EFFICIENCY) which is labelled as PRODUCTIVITY 2 in figure 7.2. However it is also possible to calculate productivity directly from OUTPUT and HOURS AVAILABLE (for the whole department). This is labelled PRODUCTIVITY in figure 7.2 and, in principle, should be numerically very similar to PRODUCTIVITY 2. This turned out not to be the case, and the reasons for the discrepancy gave us insights into the inappropriateness and dysfunctional nature of the MIS.

Following the introduction of the new work organisation, substantially the same performance measures were calculated from the same basic data, although the measure WEIGHT PRODUCED was for a whole team (Production and Packing combined) and was therefore equivalent to WEIGHT PACKED. Also, separate performance measures were calculated and fed back for each team which was provided with daily production targets which, if they were achieved, should have led to at least 100% efficient performance.

During the first few months it became apparent that on some occasions at least, the teams were meeting their targets yet their measured efficiency was considerably lower than expected. Furthermore, when an early assessment was made of the change in productivity following the redesign, the measure PRODUCTIVITY (total weight packed/total hours available) showed a 20% improvement post-teamwork, whereas the other measure, PRODUCTIVITY 2 (standard hours produced/total hours available) showed no change. To us as researchers this discrepancy was of considerable concern for two reasons:

(i) although there was no explicitly stated aim to increase productivity, it clearly mattered, to senior management at least, whether there had been a 20% rise or no change;

(ii) the lack of understanding of "what was going on" at all levels in the firm seemed ominous for HB since an evaluation of performance that was fair, and was seen to be fair, was becoming more important because of the increasing involvement of the operators.

It was found that the discrepancy resulted from the way in which production and packing performance measures had been combined into a single index for each team. This had, in effect, led to a tightening of standards, one reason being that prior to the changes credit had been given for scrap produced. The details of the analysis, which give some insights into the complexity and level of misunderstandings, are given in Appendix 2.

As a result of these findings, we proposed that in future the assessment of performance should be directly linked to the achievement of targets (i.e. enough sweets packed) and that PRODUCTIVITY would provide an appropriate comparison of performance before and after teamwork. Any comparison of EFFICIENCY or PRODUCTIVITY 2 before and after would be systematically misleading.

As a consequence of the lack of understanding of the information system, the recording of data was lax at the best of times. When a machine broke down the effects were quickly felt by all people on the production line. Thus if a machine in the middle of the process broke down, people working after that machine were soon waiting for work and people before it had to stop working so as to prevent a pile up of sweets that would quickly cool down and become scrap. During such interruptions, supervisors and operators were busy trying to put things right and no attention was given to detailed and careful recording of information necessary to provide an accurate picture of events that would give a fair reflection of performance and allow problem diagnosis later.

The operators received a time allowance only for the actual period during which a machine was broken down, even though after repair there might be a considerable lead time before the process was operating smoothly again. Moreover, frequently no allowance was made for batches that had to be scrapped as a result of a breakdown. Thus there was a systematic bias in recording which underestimated EFFICIENCY and over-estimated UTILIZATION. It is not entirely clear to us whether the HB manager fully understood the nature of this trade-off. However, even if he did, any attempt to make transfers from one to the other would only have been robbing Peter to pay Paul since he was held responsible for maintaining both measures at a satisfactory level. There was a suspicion that because the senior manager in charge of maintenance in the firm was an extremely forceful figure, the HB manager was particularly concerned that UTILIZATION should appear to be as high as possible. The operators in HB were evaluated primarily by their EFFICIENCY. Not surprisingly the systematic depression of this performance measure led to a general lack of interest and cynicism amongst the staff.

It was surprising that analysis revealed a <u>negative</u> correlation between EFFICIENCY and PRODUCTIVITY over the 36 week period immediately prior to teamwork (Pearson r=-0.18). Thus although EFFICIENCY was being closely monitored and interventions made when it was low, this was in fact inappropriate since it was negatively related to the measure that the firm wished to maintain at a high level (i.e. productivity).

This is a clear example of a dysfunctional control system which proved to be highly demotivating. The explanation for the negative correlation is complex and tentative. Of greater consequence here however is that the need for redesigned <u>functional</u> information and control systems has been demonstrated.

THE NEW DEPARTMENTAL INFORMATION SYSTEM

The introduction of semi-autonomous work groups had itself changed the information and control systems operating in HB. Operators were now directly responsible for regulation of the

140

production process and therefore any uncertainty emanating from the process could be controlled much nearer to its source rather than having to deal with problems via a supervisor or manager. (Before teamwork supervisors had spent an average 85% of their time on detailed control of the department. Afterwards there were no supervisors and the manager rarely needed to intervene; on occasions the department would run satisfactorily for two or three days in his absence and without a replacement manager).

In addition the smoothing of production requirements to provide stable targets over the year had led to a much reduced weekly variance in manning levels. (The standard deviation in HOURS AVAILABLE for the 36 week period before teamwork was 244 hours per week, whereas for the corresponding period after teamwork was introduced, it fell to around 135 hours per week). This was a necessary change that permitted the creation of stable groups who could learn to work together in teams.

However, the teams were not provided with adequate feed-back and thus, although they were being given realistic targets and had agreed to take responsibility for achieving them, they could not regulate their performance to do so satisfactorily. Nor was there an adequate control mechanism by which targets could be modified in response to allowable stoppages. Thus we proposed the following principles as guidelines for the design of a new DIS.

PRINCIPLES UNDERLYING THE DESIGN OF THE NEW DIS

1. "It should provide information consistent with the concepts used by the operators, i.e. it should match their view of their work".

Using the original MIS, senior management assessed performance in terms of the kilograms packed, production efficiency and plant utilization. These concepts were, by and large, not understood by the operators in HB. The production men made subjective assessments of their own performance in terms of the number of batches produced. The female packers tended to assess their performance in terms of the number of cages they packed (4 cages were approximately equal to one batch). But some of the women said they didn't bother to monitor their progress because they had to pack whatever arrived. The DIS therefore needed to provide feedback in terms of batch and/or cage performance.

2. "It should be consistent with,and further development of,the desired work organisation, in this case teamworking".

It was important to assess performance of a team as a whole and not to make any distinction between Production and Packing. We wanted a single performance measure for each team and decided to use batches packed since the majority of operators used this concept and all were familiar with it: thus the second principle took priority over the first in that 'cages packed' was not used as a measure of performance.

3. "It should be accurate or at least not have any systematic biases ".

The original MIS had been shown to have systematic biases (resulting from poor recording) and it was crucial that the DIS should not be biased either for or against the teams.

4. "It should be perceived as fair by both management and teams".

Where there was disagreement over what had been produced, what the targets should be, or what allowances should be made, the information and control system should be flexible enough to allow negotiation between management and the teams to influence it, i.e. the DIS should be able to respond to the outcomes of negotiations.

5. "It should be responsive to events or mishaps as they occur and thus allow teams to regulate their behaviour based on the feedback they receive".

The previous principles should be implemented in a way such that with the minimum practical delay, the teams are aware of their achievements and any modifications to targets, e.g. targets that are decreased following an allowable stoppage or increased as a result of the allocation of overtime.

6. "It should be straightforward, i.e. it should be possible to collect and disseminate information routinely".

The regulation of targets etc. should be made by simple rules whenever possible. The occasions when it is necessary to negotiate over such changes should be kept to a minimum. To this end a 'ready reckoner' was devised so that for each line, a breakdown resulting in a loss of labour could be immediately translated into the equivalent number of batches (that would have been made assuming 100% efficiency) and the targets decreased by this amount. Similarly a loss of a given number of batches could be translated into the equivalent number of standard hours so that the loss could be recorded and used by the MIS.

This principle was also invoked by management over a problem that arose because it was sometimes necessary to pack sweets on the day following the one when they were produced. Usually credit for work is given only when finished goods are packed, so if daily performance is calculated and fed back, a misleading estimate will result, efficiency being too low one day or too high the next. This problem of goods left-over provides an example of the relationship between work organisation and the information and control systems. From the outset the teams chose to rotate daily between the long line (which was harder) and the short line (which was easier). Unfortunately this created problems with recording who had done what, when there were sweets left over, because one team produced them and the other packed them. The manager, wishing to give each team quick and accurate performance feedback on a daily basis, wanted the teams to rotate weekly so that these problems of left-over goods would be minimised. The teams accepted the manager had a problem in such circumstances but suggested the information system should be changed to meet the desired work organisation and not vice versa. For his part the manager argued such changes to the information system would be hard to administer, as unpacked sweets would need traying up, weighing,and special allowances either crediting or debiting to the teams almost everyday. In the end the manager insisted the teams rotate weekly thus altering the work organisation to match the information system.

7. "It should be consistent with the existing MIS as well as meeting the needs of the department".

The MIS was used factory-wide and any decision to significantly change it, even in HB alone, would have had implications extending beyond our brief. We wanted to provide a DIS that would satisfy the needs of HB whilst recognising that senior management would continue to use the measures in the original MIS. Therefore it was vital that the two systems should run in parallel and be closely coupled so that any events recorded in the DIS would be directly reflected in the MIS. To this end the ready reckoner was used to convert between batch units (used by the DIS) and standard hours (used by the MIS).

8. "It should not be prohibitively expensive to administer ".

This principle recognises the need for pragmatism. The costs of running a DIS must not exceed the benefits. A degree of caution must be exhibited over the implementation of principles 3 and 4, and where possible principle 6 should be used to minimise the cost of running the system.

THE IMPLEMENTATION OF THE DIS

The DIS,which was implemented over a period of several weeks, is shown schematically in figure 7.3 (for one of the teams). The feedback allows the teams to regulate their work and stop for the day when the BATCHES PRODUCED (i.e. sweets packed or trayed up) equalled the TEAM TARGET, which was the target set at the beginning of the day and modified by the occurrence of breakdowns, the allocation of overtime etc..

The implementation of the DIS created some revealing problems. Initially there was conflict between the clerical assistant and the supervisor (at this time there was a manager and a supervisor in HB although the supervisory role was soon found to be unnecessary) over the modification of targets. Previous to our proposals on feedback, the clerical assistant was recording allowable losses for the MIS. This was used by Management Services to calculate efficiency so, in effect, was causing a modification of targets. However, because changes in targets were not being fed back to HB, implications of recorded losses were not brought to the supervisor's attention, and he was happy for the clerical assistant to record them. Now that targets were modified directly, the supervisor argued that the decision was his responsibility and should not be

143

FIGURE 7.3

A Systemic View of HB, the MIS, the New Work
Organisation and the New Departmental
Information System.
(Shown for one team only. The surrounding
environment remains as detailed as Figure 7.1)

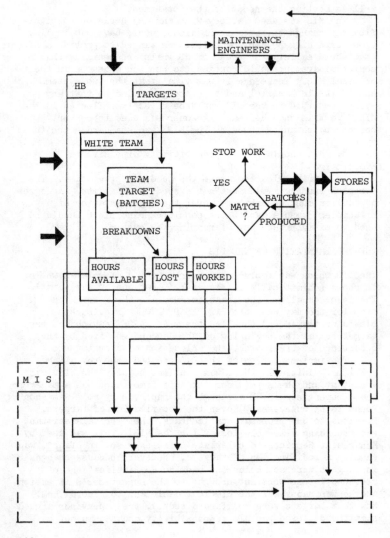

made by the clerical assistant. The issue was resolved by agreeing that the clerical assistant could make allowances for routine stoppages, but any unusual target modification be referred to the supervisor or manager (see principles 4 and 6). When things settled down, the DIS was easily maintained by a clerical assistant who on occasions had spare time to help out with packing. The manager was required very rarely to step in and negotiate over standards or fair allowance for any losses.

Another potential problem arose because the new information system improved the ability to diagnose problems and thus increased the possibility of effective control of the department. There was some concern (perceived by some of the operators and by the researchers) that if any problems arose, management might be tempted to tighten control over the teams, eroding their new discretionary areas, and conflicts would have resulted. How the manager investigated and handled legitimate interventions into the workings of a team, would have been crucial to the goodwill that all parties had displayed during the project. As an example, the teams sometimes met their targets with time to spare. They then cleaned their machinery and relaxed. The manager, not being used to such a situation, was unclear how to book this time, and chose to record it as cleaning time. This led to senior management observing that HB was now spending more than the budgeted time on the cleaning of equipment. They wanted the situation rectified and put pressure on the manager to cut down these 'lost' hours. The result was that unworked time at the end of the day is now booked to production. Provided the targets are met the teams should still remain 100% efficient. This resolved the problem although certain senior management and staff from other departments, still find it disturbing if they visit HB towards the end of the day and the teams are relaxing. These ingrained attitudes are being well coped with by the HB staff, although the new work organisation is having a catalytic impact on attitudes in other departments.

AN ANALYSIS OF THE CHANGES WITHIN AND OUTSIDE OF
THE HB SYSTEM

Although all these changes were initiated from within HB, they had a number of consequences that resulted in additional changes both within HB and elsewhere in the factory. The information systems are largely responsible for the effects being transferred across the departmental boundaries. A number of interconnected changes took place as a result of the job redesign. The internal organisation has been modified and the content of some boundary transfers has been changed, but it is essentially the same system in terms of its objectives and structure.

Although the initiative for change took place in component 1a of table 7.1 (labour), it resulted in complementary changes occurring in all the other components. The changes to the physical environment have already been mentioned. Other changes, mainly concerned with the control system are outlined in table 7.2, which also shows whether the particular component of the task is primarily concerned with <u>within</u> boundary control, or with <u>across</u> boundary control.

Although the final design of the control systems was arrived at by an interactive and iterative process (see Clegg and Fitter, 1978) without formal reliance on any theoretical model, it is instructive to compare the actual control mechanisms that were implemented with the control mechanism <u>prescribed</u> by sociotechnical systems theory. Applying this framework would lead to all decisions <u>within</u> the HB system being made by the semi-autonomous teams, whereas control decisions that <u>crossed</u> the HB system boundary would be made by the departmental manager, possibly in conjunction with relevant people from outside the department (Trist, 1959). The boundaries that have been imposed by the analysis (as for example shown in figures 7.1-3), although in no sense absolute, have been determined by essentially functional (task) considerations. This functional division is consistent with the boundaries of the existing management authority structure. By and large the changes moved control nearer to this situation, although in some areas the teams got more involved in across boundary decisions than might be expected purely from the theoretical framework. For example the teams became involved in the following areas:

a) Resource utilization - the teams became concerned to ensure that fair allowances were made for stoppages. Being at the 'work face', they were in the best position to respond to mishaps and were motivated to see that adequate allowances were made. The manager recently estimated that on nine out of ten occasions, the maintenance engineers were called in by team members without involving him. However, it can be argued that so long as these are routine problems, the operators are only executing an agreed procedure and are not making across boundary control decisions.

b) Work study standards - during the project the operators took a more active interest in the standard time allowed for each line. There was open discussion and a degree of bargaining with the work study engineers, whereby the standard on some lines was reduced in return for an increase on other lines. Although these are across boundary decisions (involving an outside department) they are often considered to be a legitimate issue for union negotiations. Interestingly, during the process of the project, there was an increase in union membership within the firm. This may also have contributed to the increased interest in work study standards although the negotiations were entirely informal. (Although in this particular case study, the union did not play a significant role, it is not clear how sociotechnical systems theory would incorporate such a relationship were it relevant!).

146

TABLE 7.2

The Principal Changes to the Control of the Task System
and Their Consequences

	Area of Change	Component of Task System Affected (see table 7.1)	Control "Before"
1.	Work organisation and job allocation	1a & 2c	management control
2.	Work rate (efficiency)	1a & 2b	management attempted to control
3.	Resource utilization (normal functioning)	1b	management control
	Resource utilization (maintenance)	1b	management control
4.	Materials	1c	management control
5.	Work Study standards	2b	external (Work Study) control
6.	Targets	2a	management control
7.	Labour pool	1a	management control
8.	Marketing	–	external management

TABLE 7.2 (cont'd)

	Control "After"	Control Classification	Other Changes
1.	teams control within agreed constraints	within boundary	some team members up-graded; more skills acquired; greater flexibility in work roles
2.	teams responsible	within boundary	improved measurement and feedback of per-formance; higher productivity
3.	teams responsible	within boundary	resulted in reduced scrap
	management respon-sible, teams and clerical assistant operate routinely	across boundary	more accurate measure-ment; seen more as a service function (i.e. less autonomy)
4.	management control though teams decide when to fetch materials	across boundary	production smoothing places greater demands on stock control
5.	as before but to some extent negotiable	across/ outside boundary	accidental tightening of standards; rectifi-ed by intervention of researchers
6.	management control but more related to resources available	across boundary	targets smoothed
7.	management control	across boundary	stabilised by product-ion smoothing and policy of keeping teams together; other managers less able to 'borrow' team members
8.	as before but HB manager and teams applying pressure	outside boundary	Sales Department discouraged from making unplanned demands

c) Marketing - the teams were concerned that the Sales Department should continue to obtain sufficient orders to maintain the teams at full strength (avoiding the transfer of members to other departments). They made visits to retail shops to see how their lines were being sold and put forward ideas for their promotion. The control of marketing decisions is outside the boundary rather than across it, but the link across the boundary is via targets which can be regarded as an input parameter to the HB system, regulated from the outside. Thus the teams attempt to influence decisions made outside their boundaries with the intention of maintaining targets in order to keep manning levels steady.

The need to reduce the flow of labour across the departmental boundary and the need for an improved service from the maintenance engineers, can both be seen as consequences of the redesign which crossed the departmental boundary and resulted in pressure for changes outside. These two areas are elaborated below:

d) The reduction of work flow - the desire to create two teams with a stable labour force was achieved because the Production Planning Department created a production schedule which balanced seasonal variations in demand and smoothed production requirements over the year. Although this more complex scheduling method stabilised HB's production, it had other effects. Firstly, to some extent it pressurised the Sales Department to stick to its demand forecasts; and it required the stores to carry more stock. Secondly, the reduction of labour flow in and out of HB, was seen by some managers in other departments as a disadvantage because it cut down their ability to 'borrow' staff when they themselves were under pressure. Moreover, the operators in these other departments became aware of their own lack of autonomy (for example, they couldn't stop work when they chose to). This itself created problems for their managers who did not see active support of the HB project as in their interests.

e) Maintenance engineering - the realisation that HB was not getting an adequate allowance for machine down-time, led to an increase in recorded lost time. Thus the maintenance engineers' performance appeared to have deteriorated since now the total effective loss of production was being recorded. They were under pressure to improve their performance, and one result is that maintenance engineering is now seen as more of a service function directly responsible to line management. As such the maintenance engineers have lost a substantial part of their autonomy - for example, the freedom to set their own work priorities.

Thus it would be excessively idealistic to argue that everyone will individually gain from a job redesign project. There are no redesign panaceas (see also the section on conflict handling in chapter 5 by den Hertog and van Eijnatten).

The changes to the HB system resulted in a considerable

149

increase in PRODUCTIVITY. Over an eighteen month period immediately following the introduction of teamwork, productivity was on average 22% higher than in the 12 month period before. The measures of EFFICIENCY and PRODUCTIVITY which had previously been negatively correlated became significantly and positively correlated (r = 0.42 over 36 weeks). In addition there were marked and significant improvements in psychological variables related to job characteristics. These were assessed by questionnaires administered to all members of HB at intervals 12 months before, 6 months after, and 18 months after the changes. (For a full description of these results see Wall and Clegg, 1981).

There is clearly no simple or single reason for these improvements. The complex set of interacting factors is comprehensively described by Clegg (in chapter 6) where he derives a model of the interactions. The conclusions I shall draw here however concentrate on the relevance of changes made to the control system. These changes in their various ways add up to a dysfunctional control system being converted into a rather more functional one.

The critical factor is the way in which the system handles unplanned and unanticipated events (or variances as they are called in systems terminology). For example, if a machine unexpectedly breaks down, a series of responses must be made to deal with it. During the project it became apparent that throughout the organisation, there was very little understanding of the ways in which such variances occurred and they were not controlled effectively. The redesign, although intended primarily to improve psychological variables directly, also had an important effect on the control system. Giving the teams responsibility to regulate the production process directly without reference to the manager, enables variance to be controlled nearer to its source. This led to a reduction in variance within the department because unplanned events could be dealt with more quickly and more effectively.

The other major effect was to stabilise operations within HB by reducing variance across the departmental boundary. The target smoothing led to a stabilised labour force by reducing the variance in HOURS AVAILABLE. This itself led to a more skilled workforce since the influx of temporary staff from other departments would decrease the overall level of appropriate skills. This strategy of creating semi-autonomous units is one of Galbraith's (1973) four strategies which an organisation can use to cope with a complex and uncertain environment. Thus the teams had greater autonomy within the department and the departmental boundaries were made clearer by more controlled and stabilised regulation of the boundary traffic.

These factors provided the mechanisms necessary for effective control of the production process, but severe problems still remained with the performance measures and the

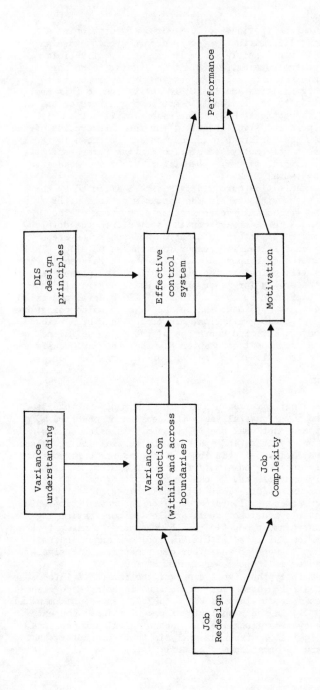

FIGURE 7.4   The Hypothesised Causal Links leading from the
Job Redesign Initiative to Improved Departmental
Performance

151

way feedback was provided to the teams. By developing a Departmental Information System in accord with the design outlined, it was possible to implement an effective information and control system. This, it is argued, is no more complex than the original MIS, but is more appropriate to the new work organisation and is itself motivating to team members in comparison to the extremely demotivating nature of the original dysfunctional MIS. (The team's satisfaction with feedback increased significantly after the introduction of the DIS). Thus the performance improvement can be seen to result from a more highly motivated staff operating a more effective and stable control system. (See figure 7.4 for a schematic view of the causal links).

The organisation more widely has been affected by the redesign which originated in the dissatisfactions of HB members and spread into several other subsystems of the organisation. This outward growth stemmed from the development of more satisfactory information and control systems within HB and resulted in pressure for change outside. This pressure, although responded to at times with reluctance, has had a catalytic effect on the organisation, and plans are currently under way for major changes which may result in several departments being run along the lines developed in HB. It is hoped that, by focussing on the ways in which change has crept through the organisation, the project has been placed in a broad context and thus meets one of the major deficiencies of previous projects (see chapter 5), that they are considered too much in isolation from the rest of the organisation.

CONCLUSION

The changes that have taken place in HB may be characterised as follows. Over several years the department operated a stable but dysfunctional control system. This led to dissatisfaction, cynicism and apathy. The initial job redesign, based on psychological principles, improved the work roles of individuals and created a more functional system, but was essentially unstable and in danger of drifting back to the old work organisation. The additional changes to the information and control systems created an organisation which was both stable and functional, and led to more satisfying jobs and increased productivity. Furthermore, changes to the control system initiated within HB, led to changes in the relationship between HB and other departments, and to significant changes in those departments.

Increasingly the significance of the impact of information and control systems for job designs is being recognised (see for example, Lawler and Rhode, 1976). Indeed Hackman and Oldham (1980), in their analysis of organisational context, place such systems alongside the technological and personnel systems. It follows from the analysis in this chapter, that not only are information and control systems central to the design of jobs, but they also provide a medium for understanding the interrelationships between job designs and wider organisational systems.

APPENDIX 1

Definitions of the information system measures used to calculate performance are given below. Lower case measures are
directly recorded by staff within HB, with the exception of
"standard hours per kilogram" which is the standard of each
individual line assessed by Work Study. The upper case
measures are the derived performance indices.

STANDARD HOURS $=$ no. of
PRODUCED $\quad$ batches $\quad$ x $\quad$ batch $\quad$ x $\quad$ standard hours
$\qquad$ produced $\qquad$ weight $\qquad$ per kilogram

HOURS WORKED $\quad=\quad$ hours $\quad\quad$ hours
$\qquad\qquad$ available $^{-}$ lost

OUTPUT $\qquad=\quad$ weight (in kilograms) received by
$\qquad\qquad$ stores

UTILIZATION $\quad(\%) = \dfrac{\text{HOURS WORKED}}{\text{hours available}} \quad$ x $\quad$ 100

EFFICIENCY $\quad(\%) = \dfrac{\text{STANDARD HOURS PRODUCED}}{\text{HOURS WORKED}} \quad$ x $\quad$ 100

PRODUCTIVITY $\quad(\%) = \dfrac{\text{OUTPUT}}{\text{hours available}} \quad$ x $\quad$ 100

PRODUCTIVITY 2 $(\%) = \dfrac{\text{EFFICIENCY x UTILIZATION}}{100}$

APPENDIX 2

The measure PRODUCTIVITY was directly related to OUTPUT whereas PRODUCTIVITY 2 was directly related to EFFICIENCY. Since the success at meeting targets was assessed by OUTPUT, the achievement of targets resulting in inefficient performance could possibly be explained if the discrepancy between the two productivity measures could be explained.

Although PRODUCTIVITY is an important measure of performance (being directly related to OUTPUT which will result in income), PRODUCTIVITY 2 is potentially the more accurate measure of performance because it corrects for the relative difficulty of lines. This suggests two alternative hypotheses to account for the discrepancy between measures:

(i) the increase in PRODUCTIVITY could have resulted from a coincidental move post-teamwork towards making simpler lines which have easier Work Study standards. Thus the change in PRODUCTIVITY would not reflect a true increase in performance;

(ii) there is a real increase in productivity but it is masked in PRODUCTIVITY 2 because of change in the Work Study standards used to calculate STANDARD HOURS PRODUCED.

There was no suggestion that there might have been a deliberate increase in standards but one may have been inadvertently introduced during the teamwork changes.

We tested these hypotheses as follows:

(i) Analysis of the proportions of each line produced before and after teamwork showed no change in the average difficulty of lines produced (there was a change of 0.75%, not nearly enough to account for the 20% discrepancy). Therefore the measure PRODUCTIVITY does not seem to be at fault.

(ii) A calculation was made of weekly average standard times (i.e. standard hours/kilo = performance x hours available) for a 36 week period before teamwork and a 24 week period after teamwork. Comparison revealed that the average standard hours per kilo had reduced from 0.0473 to 0.0404; this represents an effective tightening of standards by 16.5% which seems sufficient to mask a 20% improvement in productivity.

An alternative illustration of the discrepancy was made by selecting at random, three weeks of pre-teamwork production and for each week comparing performance as originally calculated with performance using the new work study standards. For these three weeks the differences in performance averaged out at 19.5%, again indicating that an effective change in standards had masked a genuine improvement in performance of the order of 20%.

The new work study standards had arisen because of the need for a combined (Production+Packing) standard for each line, whereas prior to teamwork there had been separate standards for Production and for Packing so that their performance could be measured separately.

In the face of the above evidence we suspected initially that the combined average was a higher standard than the individual production and packing standards. However, this turned out not to be the case; the difference arose because prior to teamwork, production was credited according to WEIGHT PRODUCED (number of batches x batch weight) whereas after teamwork only production that was packed was credited to the team. This is, we believe, the more appropriate measure since the firm is primarily interested in saleable goods. Previously production was credited to the men even if it was later rejected as scrap, and also any systematic bias in estimating the weight of a batch would give an unrealistic estimate of the weight actually produced.

Chapter 8

JOB REDESIGN AND SOCIAL POLICIES

Frank Blackler

INTRODUCTION

The subject of this concluding chapter is the future of job
redesign, especially the directions in which job redesign
theory and practice might usefully develop. Before it is
possible to tackle the issue directly however, it is necessary
to consider certain basic themes that, either explicitly or
implicitly have recurred repeatedly throughout this book.
    As illustrated by the previous contributions job design
can be studied from a number of different perspectives. Much
work in the area begins from the idea that conventional
approaches to the design of work are based on mistaken
assumptions of human psychology. Accordingly the effectiveness of new approaches to the design of work has been studied,
with both psychological and organisational outcomes the focus
of enquiry. One result of such work has been to highlight the
complexity of issues which may arise when jobs are redesigned
with guidelines emerging concerning ways in which dependent,
independent and "supportive" organisational variables can be
managed. (The papers by Clegg, Fitter and den Hertog and van
Eijnatten discuss these themes). An alternative approach (see,
in this volume, the papers by Kelly, Gregory and Roberts and
Wood) has been to study the practice of job design in its
historical, economic and sociological contexts. At first
sight this second approach would appear to complement the
first. However, it has tended to highlight the importance of
power and control in the organisation of work and has pointed
towards the possibility that job design changes inspired by
new psychological insights have, in practice, been rather more
conventional than the supportive rhetoric would have led one
to expect.
    Throughout the variety of topics that has been consider-
ed in the previous papers therefore, for example, job design
and its organisational implications, environmental effects on
motivation and satisfaction, contextual factors and problems
for change, management and sectional interests and the

157

relationships between different forms of social scientific
analyses, two related issues emerge as crucial. Firstly,
there is the question of how significant previous work in the
area of job redesign has been for social and organisational
policies. It is this theme that is at the heart of issues
discussed in the book. Has previous effort to improve the
quality of working life by redesigning jobs been of some
general importance? If well intentioned efforts to redesign
jobs to include increased areas of worker discretion have had
only marginal impact on the quality of work experiences, one
might well conclude that job redesign is not worth the effort.
The second question is related to the first. Early hopes that
social science in this area had "come of age" have generally
proved disappointing. Will the position remain this way or is
it possible that more useful prescriptions may be found?
Radical social theories, of course, are normally to be found
at the macro-level of analysis. Do the arguments presented in
this volume imply that approaches which focus on the primacy
of individual experience inevitably come to little? In the
following two sections these issues are explored before turning directly to the question of the future of job redesign in
the concluding section.

SOCIAL SCIENCE AND THE QUALITY OF WORKING LIFE

It is fair to say that psychology applied to organisations has
received a fair amount of criticism in recent decades.
William Gomberg's 1957 address to the Industrial Division of
the American Psychological Association posed the question
"psychology for what purpose?" and argued that a moral
philosophy had to be found for the subject to work within. In
a far-sighted paper that anticipated many of the problems
still faced by psychologists, he pointed out:

> The manager is now faced with a dilemma. To what
> extent does he sacrifice productivity to being
> loved and vice versa. It will be interesting to
> find out what will be the decision of the future
> managers. The psychologists can no longer sell
> a bromide without any question, that happy workers
> are necessarily productive workers. The question
> that now has to be answered is in what sort of
> society do we want to live. To what extent do we
> sacrifice our human values for economic objectives?

Three years later Loren Baritz published a book in which he
argued that industrial psychologists had contented themselves
with a very limited role to service management "problems".
He claimed employers' costs and workers' loyalties were the
issues psychologists working in industry predominantly
concerned themselves with. They were in all significant
aspects said Baritz "the servants of power".

At around this time some psychologists certainly were concerned with the ethics of their profession. The famous debate between Rogers and Skinner (1956) was to prompt Kelman's (1965) more specific concern with the value dilemmas facing applied psychologists. But these were the exception rather than the rule. Industrial psychologists did not respond to the points Baritz and Gomberg made. And just as they ignored their points so did the bad press for industrial psychology continue. Consider the following newspaper report of October 1978.

Questions asked during a job interview seemed to Mrs. Nicola Wilson to have 'nothing to do with cleaning out railway carriages'.
Mrs. Wilson, unemployed, of Hove, had replied to an advertisement for cleaners on British Rail Southern Region. She had expected to be tested on her ability to wield a broom and erase graffiti. Instead, she found herself filling a question which said: 'Would you be embarrassed if you had to strip off in a nudist colony? Answer (a) Yes, (b) Doubtful, (c) No'.
British Rail also wanted to know whether she liked watching team games, whether she preferred people who were (a) reserved, (b) in between, (c) made friends quickly, and whether she preferred having lunch (a) with a lot of other people (b) in-between, or (c) by myself.
Mrs. Wilson persevered through the form, which contained 78 questions, until she came to: 'Would you like to be (a) a bishop, (b) doubtful, (c) a colonel?'
Later she said forlornly 'I did not want to be a bishop or a colonel and I certainly wasn't doubtful about either fact. I only wanted to clean trains'.
So she left the question blank and she didn't get the job. Mrs. Wilson is still unemployed. Southern Region is still short of carriage cleaners. What Mrs. Wilson had encountered was the spreading of the psychological questionnaire - long familiar among business executives, servicemen and mental patients - to more ordinary walks of life, railway cleaning and porterage.
British Rail was spurred into introducing it experimentally 18 months ago by the high staff turnover rate.
Asked about the questions on team games and solitary lunches, a British Rail official said that BR recruits would 'quite possibly' have to lunch in large groups.

The "Guardian" article ends, somewhat abruptly at this
point. So quite why aspiring cleaners were being asked about
their ambitions to take the cloth as clerics or to shed it as
nudists is not really explained. It seemed sufficient to
indicate, apparently, that such silly questions were just
another of those "psychological" tests "long familiar" amongst
such assorted (and, presumably, long suffering) groups as
business executives, servicemen and mental patients.

It does appear that while psychologists working in other
fields, like education or clinical work, have been viewed
respectfully and with a certain awe, psychologists working in
industry have, as a general rule, tended to attract suspicion
and hositility, or to be discussed as an irrelevancy. A well
known example of this is, of course, Elton Mayo's "human
relations" approach to industrial problems, often held up as a
prime example of unquestioning managerialism. The more recent
phenomenon of "organisational development" (OD) is a similar
case. OD developed from a series of ideas pioneered by Kurt
Lewin (1948) who argued that social changes could be encouraged when people who are likely to be involved in change are
given the opportunity to study relevant issues for themselves,
and are not expected blindly to follow the advice of outside
experts. His "action research" approach was later developed
by Argyris (1970) who stated that organisational consultants
should not understand their task to be the promotion of
change as such. Change might be an outcome of their work,
but basically they should act as catalysts for their clients,
helping to provide "valid and useful information", assisting
the client to exercise "free and informed choices" and
providing conditions under which an "internal commitment" to
decisions might be possible. It seems strange that such fine
ideals should have become associated with yet another management fad. But inspired with the belief that the most crucial
area where "useful and valid" information is not normally
available, was interpersonal relations, OD consultants became
primarily associated with human relations training (see
Stevenson, 1975; Strauss, 1976; or Mangham, 1978). A brashly
optimistic movement developed which (despite Gomberg's warning
of fifteen years previously) assured managers that through OD,
organisations can be run "in such a way that the goals and
purposes of the organisation are attained at the same time
that human values within organisations are furthered" (French
and Bell, 1973, p.xiii).

We have seen in this collection of papers, Kelly's
suggestion that job design has developed to fit a partial and
distorted ideology reflecting the interests of a particular
class interest. Economically based conflict is excluded from
its scheme of things. Co-operative endeavour is promised as
a feasible outcome. From the foregoing comments however it
would seem that such a state of affairs is not peculiar to
job design alone. In the broad context of the uses of social
science in industry this may be a rather usual outcome. One

conclusion from this would be the one drawn by Braverman (1974), whose thesis on deskilling tendencies has often been referred to in this book. He says:

> From their confident beginnings as sciences devoted to discovering the springs of human behaviour the better to manipulate them in the interests of management, they have broken up into a welter of confused and confusing approaches pursuing psychological, sociological, economic, mathematical or "systems" interpretations of the realities of the workplace, with little real impact upon the management of worker or work (p.145).

It is by no means clear however that such a view does justice to the pioneering spirit that drove Mayo (see Ackroyd, 1976), Lewin (see Marrow, 1969) or for that matter that inspired the work of important job redesign theorists. As Cherns (1979) has pointed out, developments in organisational psychology have been influenced not only by theoretical and methodological advances in the discipline itself but by prevalent social problems and by prevailing ideologies also. Social scientists who are interested in applied subjects will not be displeased by Cherns' emphasis on problems and ideologies. His analysis does suggest however that past practices are bound to look dated as different problems emerge, new ideologies predominate and the discipline progresses in sophistication. Indeed if the state of development within a particular applied social science is not sufficiently sophisticated to draw attention to factors relevant to its usage, then, no matter how progressive it might originally have seemed, as time passes it will come to look rather naive. Applied social science theories are inevitably, in important parts, products of their time.

At root it is developments in ideology, an awareness of new problems and a growing sophistication in applied social science that have led to the shift in attitudes towards job redesign that dominates the first half of this book. The psychological benefits of enriched jobs impressed the pioneers of job redesign theory. In the papers by Kelly, Gregory and Roberts and Wood however, the issues of power and control provide an alternative framework against which to judge the effectiveness of job design endeavours. In his review of historical developments in the job design area, Wall reports the influence of American work in redirecting social scientific thought. The work of Walker and Guest (1952), Herzberg (1966), Davis, Canter and Hoffman (1955), and Hackman and Lawler (1971), was undoubtedly of considerable influence. But the explosion of governmental interest in job design that Wall records (in chapter 1) and that occurred simultaneously in many different countries in the mid 1970's, did not occur "out of the blue". There was a very considerable effort made

161

around this time by prominent academics and others who had become convinced that job redesign was a crucial social issue.

A brief history of the activities of the group that was to become most influential in the area is as follows. Working at the Tavistock Institute of Human Relations in London, Fred Emery and Eric Trist in the early 1960's had developed a package of ideas that warned of developing social problems, offered a series of prescriptions for dealing with them, and suggested ways by which these might be introduced. The bulk of this analysis is to be found in Emery and Trist (1965), Emery (1967), Emery and Oeser (1958), and Emery and Trist (1972). They suggested that social changes were proceeding at such a pace in modern industrial states that conventional approaches to management were likely to fail. Largely because of their own activities in centralising resources, investing in new technologies, creating wealth, stimulating expectations of social services and life opportunities, a situation was developing where the environments in which organisations worked were becoming unstable and uncontrollable. This sounds somewhat similar to present day fears of social collapse as new technologies rip the fabric of our society and threaten to stimulate changes, the final nature of which remains unknown. Two ways forward suggested themselves to Emery and Trist in the early sixties. In the first place they believed companies should adopt new roles in society, behave less competitively, recognise the legitimacy of other organisations, and collaborate with them to find arrangements that all could find mutually acceptable. In this suggestion a near anarcho-syndicalist system of values was being proposed to replace that of free market capitalism. Secondly, they thought that new values should guide the internal management of companies, in particular those of McGregor's (1960) "theory Y" that emphasises people's capacity for self-motivation and direction. Sociotechnical forms of job redesign would be the concrete way in which such values could be expressed. Emery and Trist believed it was very important that people should begin to become more self directing in their lives and that once they had experienced the pleasure of increased self-determination through new forms of job design (usually semi-autonomous work groups as it happened), they would begin to demand increased self-management opportunities in other walks of life also. In this it is quite clear that, in aims and ideology, Emery and Trist were far removed from the charges of managerialism that subsequently have been levelled against them.

Regarding the problem of introducing such ideas, Emery and Trist believed that as social changes were proceeding at a faster pace than man's apparent capacity to adapt his values, change was itself a major issue. From his studies of technical innovation in Australia (influenced by Lewin's approach) Emery did have one idea however. If opinion leaders could be influenced this would, he felt, be far more effective than any educational campaign directed more indiscriminately. People

162

would, on this view, be far more likely to imitate people they respected than they would to go along with "experts".

At about the time Emery and Trist were putting this package of ideas together, two magnificent opportunities arose for them to put it into practice. One was in Norway where, with Einar Thorsrud, Phil Herbst and others, Emery began work on a programme designed to do nothing less than introduce a national policy of manpower utilisation and industrial democracy along the lines his analysis suggested was desirable. The other was in Shell U.K. Refining, a company in a large multinational group that approached the Tavistock Institute with the unprecedented request for them to help the Company to write a new philosophy of management (see below).

In the Norway project, Emery and Thorsrud conducted a survey of industrial democracy practices in Europe, and concluded that board representation made no difference to the working experiences of employees being represented. They concluded that direct involvement in shop floor matters would be a better idea, and set about trying to introduce semi-autonomous work groups in Norway. Following Emery's ideas on how to introduce changes, a number of demonstration sites were selected. Sociotechnical theory provided the theoretical basis for the job redesign ideas. A number of pioneering projects were launched. Later, under the auspices of a steering committee composed of government, management and union representatives, a number of reports on the projects were published.

However as things were to turn out, dissemination of the new practices of job design did not follow in Norway on any scale. As this became clear, the social scientists involved in the programme experienced considerable disappointment. The writings of Elden (1972) and Herbst (1976) show how it had been firmly expected that semi-autonomous work groups would change people's expectations, confidence and skills, and lead to more generalised social changes. Why this had not happened was the subject of some disagreement. One commentator, a Dutchman studying events in Norway for his Ph.D., published his account (Bolweg 1976) in which he suggested that the fault partly lay with sociotechnical theory itself, failing as it does to draw attention to the conflicting interests and power bases of different interest groups associated with organisations. Management had wanted the job redesign for productivity reasons, and unions because they thought it might help in their general aims for industrial democracy (though otherwise it is correct to say they were somewhat reserved). Those affected by the new job designs usually were very pleased after sometimes doubtful initial involvement.

Interestingly, despite the apparent rigour of Bolweg's analysis, it failed to find favour with most of those who had been involved in the original programme. Herbst's (1976) analysis of the failure of the projects to diffuse, for example, does not propose any basic revision of sociotechnical

163

theory as a guiding framework. He concentrates instead on the
failure of Emery's model of diffusion through opinion leaders
that had guided the strategy of demonstration projects.
Amongst his suggestions was the observation that the experimental sites became thought of as "different", that social
scientists involved in them came to dominate developments
rather than acting as catalysts, that people who might have
copied the new forms of job design, found that the excitement
of a pioneering venture was in their cases replaced by the
fear of doing less well than had been achieved in the original
demonstration projects.

Very soon Herbst and his colleagues were able to put into
practice their views on why the change strategy had failed.
An international conference was convened in 1972 for academics
and others interested in improving the quality of working life.
The theme of the resulting two volumes of conference proceed-
ings that were later published (Davis and Cherns, 1975) was
consistent with Herbst's (1976) analysis of developments in
Norway:

> A number of U.S. and Western European organisations,
> some in association with university researchers have
> undertaken experiments that have changed conditions
> and relationships and led to enhanced satisfaction,
> more qualified people, and greater commitment at
> work. <u>The problem now is to determine how these
> pioneering changes can be generalised, built upon,
> and extended</u>. (p. 7, emphasis in original)

How to do it was inspired by the model of "network organisation" that Phil Herbst had been working on. "The basic
character of a network is the maintenance of long term
directive correlations, mutually facilitating the achievement
of a jointly recognised aim" (p. 33). People who are part of
a network come together only occasionally. However, members
may communicate quite frequently with each other and journals
or newsletters are able to keep people abreast of significant
developments. After a period people may drift in and out of
the network or old networks may be abandoned with new ones
emerging around new issues and new aims.

Given this analysis after the 1972 conference, a task
force was set up to form the "International Council for the
Quality of Working Life". As was stated in Davis and Cherns
Vol II:

> We may require national and international 'maps'
> which relate us with key groups and individuals,
> with unions, employer associations, schools and
> the media both nationally and at the internation-
> al level. The 'maps' will need to include the
> links between unions, government and employers
> associations, with special reference to multi

and trans-national corporations and international
organisations. Consideration should be given to
special problems of diffusion between countries
of different sizes and states of development and
to possible reasons for forming regional networks
(1975, p.360).

Although it would be wrong to over-estimate the influence
of this network in galvanising its members to action, there is
no doubt but that membership of the group gave people confidence and purpose in their activities to promote job redesign
activities. In accordance with a growing awareness of the
unacceptability of routinised and fragmented work, members of
the network campaigned (sometimes vigorously) for funds and
research centres to work to improve the Quality of Working
Life. "QWL" was to become a new watchword, taking over from
OD as the latest trend, or sometimes being used synonymously
with it. Yet while overenthusiastic presentation and lack of
precise analysis did undoubtedly allow the QWL movement to
become part of a managerialist ideology, as we have seen the
aims of many of those involved and the objectives that they
strove to meet were very different.
      Quite why these aims have not been achieved importantly
relates, in the present author's view, to the points raised by
Bolweg. This was illustrated by developments in the Shell
project, a project which had become somewhat overshadowed by
the excitement of the Norwegian exercise. As Blackler and
Brown (1980a) record in detail, the new philosophy Emery and
Trist wrote for Shell was not to succeed in transforming the
company's role in the modern world, nor was it to be successful in promoting the widespread introduction of participative
management and autonomous work groups throughout the organisation. Emery and Trist prepared a philosophy statement for
Shell that argued the company should act more as the custodian
of society's assets than as their exploiter, and that socio-
technical principles should be used in the design of jobs in
the company. The document was widely discussed in the
company, but after raising a lot of people's expectations it
came to little. Indeed this case provides a detailed example
of how the reforming intentions of job redesign theorists were
to lead to little widespread change of significance. Within a
short period the philosophy ceased to act as a force for
change in Shell. Explaining this Blackler and Brown point in
the first place to the "pseudo-innocence" of the philosophy
statement, emphasising as it did the technological constraints
on interesting jobs and the prospects for changing these, but
saying nothing at all about the nature of different interest
groups in organisations, the differential power bases available to them, and the control strategies which have evolved to
maintain the system along present lines. Secondly they point
to the enthusiasm of those directing the project, their
certainty that their views would convince others, and their

lack of appreciation of how significant the differences
between their objectives and those of Shell's management would
prove to be. Nowadays these errors look rather obvious ones
to make. But in the optimistic years of the 1960's, with
values in apparent turmoil,with flower power, counter cultures,
student riots and the May '68 Paris "revolution" dominating
public awareness, the "dynamic conservatism" of organisational
life (see Schon 1971) was not so self-evident. It did seem
that new value approaches could work. What else was there to
do but to initiate developments to show sceptics that new
approaches born of trust and mutual respect would be successful?

One approach to answering this question is to examine
what other psychologists interested in developing an
"emancipatory" theme to their work were doing at this time.
One of the negative effects of networks incidentally (that
Herbst does not discuss) is the tendency for people to rely
on them too much. In such cases rather than amounting to a
temporary system where shared learning is encouraged, the
network becomes an "old boy" network. In scientific circles
this amounts to people reading and quoting the works of only a
limited number of like-minded individuals. Although it would
be wrong to push the point too far, Blackler and Brown (1978)
have suggested that such a trend can be discerned in the work
of some people associated with QWL, as major criticisms of
theory and practice voiced by outsiders, have passed them by.
And certainly a number of distinct and contemporary approaches
to emancipatory psychology may be identified (van Strien 1980)
that are quite independent of the activities of job redesign
theorists and do not seem to have influenced them.

One such contemporary approach is phenomenology, including ethnomethodology. Since Berger and Luckman's (1967) "The
Social Construction of Reality" and Harré and Secord's (1972)
"The Explanation of Social Behaviour", a great number of books
and articles have appeared urging social psychologists to
value the points of view of the people whose behaviour they
are studying (e.g. Shotter,1975; Harré,1979). Such descriptions, it is suggested, are the data of social research. This
position is, of course, not that dissimilar from that of Kurt
Lewin (1948). However a major difference does arise in that
Lewin believed theory was a necessity for psychologists.
These"hermeneutic" approaches have proved rather disappointing
as a basis for social change programmes, perhaps because on
their own they can do little more than record peoples existing
self understandings. While this is undoubtedly a major
contribution it is perhaps the starting point for psychological enquiries and not its end (a point developed in the next
section).

The second approach to an emancipatory psychology is that
represented by the "Frankfurt School", including Adorno,
Horkheimer, Fromm, Marcuse and Habermas (see Jay 1973). These
writers have each developed their own social critiques but a

theme they share is the suggestion that a variety of constraints embedded in existing social structures conspire to prevent people from developing their full humanities. A concern with both psycho-analysis and Marxist critique typically informs this line of thought. Thus, for example, Adorno felt Freud had discovered much concerning individual socio-psychological development in the modern world, while Marx had revealed important truths concerning the context of that development. Habermas (1974) went as far as to suggest that emancipatory social science would serve the same function as psycho-analysis, revealing the true nature of a stultifying social reality and thereby enabling people to transcend the constraints they otherwise would have accepted. But as a programme for action the Frankfurt School has not been especially influential. During a brief period in the late 1960's, and most notably during the May 1968 uprising in Paris, Marcuse and others became popular with "new left" intellectuals. Later, however, the obscurity of his writings and the fact that the Frankfurt writers in general wrote only for an intellectual audience, have both contributed to the demise of the school as a significant force for social change.

The third approach is a Marxist psychology. Examples of this are provided in Armistead's (1974) collection of papers. The most articulate of such papers is one by Sedgwick (1974) who argues that "psychologists have to go outside the logic of their own training and take up explicit political positions in order to master an outlook on the social order of which they form an indubitable part" (p. 36). This indeed is the problem with the idea of a Marxist psychology. While it does not make the mistake of the Frankfurt School in failing to service a particular "clientele", Marxist psychology has a clear programme which already identifies what to study and indeed what to find. Much Marxism is concerned with analysis at the macro level; on this vision of things psychology can only operate in a servicing role, interpreting events at the psychological level on the basis of people's pre-defined needs as understood to have arisen from economic imperatives. Marxist psychology has not, to the present writer's knowledge, made much impact on social change practices although van Strien (1980) does mention some activity by Marxist psychologists in West Germany and Holland.

Clearly there is much that job redesign theorists interested in increased self determination, can learn from these other approaches. Marxist approaches emphasise the centrality of power variables and how change here is necessary to support other developments. Their emphasis on struggle also is provocative. The Frankfurt School can show that a great variety of factors inhibit personal development. Restricting organisational experience is but one of many; "fear of freedom" runs deep and is the result of fiercely strong socialisation processes. Ethnomethodological approaches emphasise the importance of personal interpretation and may help in the development of more appropriate action research techniques.

Yet what does stand out from this discussion, is that in comparison with other 'emancipatory' psychologies, job design theorists have made a major contribution to the development of a social psychology relevant to social policies. They offered a reasoned critique of social problems, a scenario of apparently attainable goals to be aimed for, and a programme of social action by which this might be achieved. The present writer is convinced that it is important vigorously to criticise the shortcomings associated with the approach so that future progress may be made. But as we have argued previously, social science is inevitably a product of its day and the element of fad or fashion associated with past approaches may tend to belie the more general significance of the work.

SOCIAL SCIENCE KNOWLEDGE AND ITS RELEVANCE TO
ORGANISATIONAL POLICIES

Discussion of job design theory in the context of other approaches in psychology inspired by values of individual emancipation, points towards the conclusion that it is limiting to think of job redesign as an end in itself. If one is not simply interested in redesign theory as a management technique but is concerned to increase people's opportunities and tendencies to become more active and influential, then it is appropriate to think of job redesign as merely one means to this end. Clearly there may be many other ways also in which people might become more self-directing. While undoubtedly an important topic, job redesign need not be regarded as the only or indeed as the most effective way in which this might be encouraged. Yet there has been a tendency for theorists working in this area to promote redesign itself as the aim to be sought. Gustavsen (1980) has acknowledged this tendency in the Norwegian programme. The quotation above from Davis and Cherns confirms how others also saw the diffusion of new forms of work organisation as the job in hand.

The point that it need not be job redesign as such that should be the primary concern, reflects a more fundamental point about social science and social policies. This involves consideration of the nature of social scientific knowledge and can be introduced by comparing important epistemological approaches within the subject. "Positivism" has been the dominant orthodoxy in much social science. The roots of positivism reach back to Locke and Hume through Newton, Comte, the Vienna circle and logical positivism and modern day behaviourism. According to this approach a scientist works with observable phenomena (in psychology "stimuli" and "responses") and abstracts from his many detailed observations general "laws" of behaviour. Hollis (1977) has pointed out how science is, according to positivism, concerned with the discovery of regularities of causes and effects, of the nature of reality in the social world. On this view basically the same methods of observation and abstraction are used in the social sciences as are understood to operate in the natural sciences. The raw materials of all sciences are thought to be facts and their regularities.

Although the positivistic approach has been very influential, an alternative approach does exist in the social sciences which also has a long and distinguished history. Stemming from Kant, through phenomenology, then for example through the work of Cassirer, Gestalt psychologists, Lewin, Piaget and Chomsky, this approach emphasises less the process of "abstraction" and more the process of "conceptualisation". According to this neo-Kantian approach, an understanding of purposes and intentions is central to the explanation of human behaviour. The processes by which people construct and order the world, discover relationships and create explanatory concepts, are considered crucial. On this view it is not sufficient simply to record the patterns of people's responses in certain situations. How they themselves conceive of their reactions is vital in explaining them. So too the social scientist is not simply recording observable events but is (or should be) developing concepts and appreciative frameworks to account for them. Science is a creative endeavour with understanding emerging from the development of new appreciation of the way things are and could become.

A number of approaches in the social sciences today subscribe to such views. "Action researchers", for example, reject positivism as an acceptable or workable framework. Action research (for example, see Susman and Evered 1978) involves the researcher in a collaborative relationship with his clients in a joint endeavour to solve problems of importance to them. (Positivistic approaches would encourage the researcher to remain detached, and to define for himself the objective of the study). In action research the relationship between the clients and their circumstances may change, as they study issues and engage with them. This is, of course, a major objective of such work. And given this process the action researcher is inevitably aware that much of the knowledge he is acquiring is of a specifically local nature.

Other non-positivistic approaches may not share the emphasis in action research on practical problem solving, but do also emphasise the localised character of much social scientific knowledge. The work of Harré and Shotter was mentioned earlier, for other examples see Ginsburg (1979) and Brenner et al(1978).According to such writers the well ordered rule bound system of knowledge sought by positivists is not possible in social affairs. Given that people have active capacities and interpret their circumstances through value frameworks which may themselves be changed, it is inappropriate to seek to abstract general "laws" of behaviour from an analysis of general trends. Reality is "socially constructed" to the extent that we learn and create meanings for situations, and such "situational definitions" help us to decide upon appropriate action.

Points such as these are central to a discussion of the relationship between social science and social policy. It is tempting to look to social science for definitive answers to social problems. But given the foregoing, it is evident that "off the peg" prescriptions will be the exception rather than the rule. When behaviours influenced by people's definitions of the situation are involved, social science concepts and models may help identify likely problems and approaches, but detailed study will be necessary before reliable interpretations of particular circumstances can sensibly be proposed. In the field of job design, for example, social science theory draws attention to the fact that in the Western industrialised world, factors like variety, ability to exercise skill and involvement in a significant part of a production or service process, are variables which are commonly associated with worker motivation and satisfaction. But such theory cannot say with certainty that such factors will always predominate, nor how much variety, discretionary elements or centrality in the total process should be regarded as essential in any given situation. To begin to decide how relevant factors are, in any particular instance, to people's reactions to their jobs, detailed study with the people involved must be undertaken. Such study will obviously centre around their existing and developing values and preferences.

It would be wrong to conclude from points such as these, however, that social reality is an arbitrary matter with behaviour entirely the function of idiosyncratic reaction or local custom. There may be very good reasons to predict reactions of a certain kind. This point has been well made by Tannenbaum (1980) who, in his review of organisational psychology from a cross cultural-perspective, wrote:

> . . . . common denominators do exist among all societies in the character of organisations and in the reactions of members. Furthermore the data of cross-cultural organisational psychology hint at principles that may transcend culture. The way in which these principles manifest themselves, however, may be different in different places, and attempts to apply these principles may require culture-specific techniques. For example, data suggest that people who have or feel that they have influence in their work situation will feel a corresponding sense of responsibility and will be motivated to perform well in the organisation. But it does not follow that the organisational arrangements that enhance the influence of members or that contribute to their feeling of influence in one culture will do so in another culture. Thus people in the inner city or in Peru may differ from middle class Americans, not

in their reaction to being influential, but in what
it takes to make them influential. General versus
close supervision and other techniques of human
relations may be culture-specific in this sense -
effective in some places but not in others. It is
conceivable that in some societies practicable
techniques cannot easily be developed. But if the
underlying principle is valid in these societies,
then a search for techniques might ultimately prove
fruitful even though many attempts will fail (p.323).

Tannenbaum's point therefore is not only that particular
techniques of job design need not be universally applicable.
His suggestion also is that "common denominators do exist
among all societies in the character of organisations".
Clearly, given the existence of common psychological "principles", general social problems are likely to appear in similar
circumstances. On this argument, as before, psychologists and
others should avoid proposing prescriptions, allegedly
universally applicable, of suitable ways forward. Rather,
their contribution to social policy-making is, on the one hand
to discuss and research the nature of general psycho-social
problems while, on the other, to encourage development of
localised solutions to them.

In this volume little has been said about the nature of
the general psychological principles relevant to organisations
and the design of work. Indeed it is difficult to do this well.
Herzberg's (1966) approach, for example, while sounding
humanitarian, succeeds only, as Carey (1977) points out, in
legitimising the convenient view that hard work is as essential
for "personal development" as ever it was for virtue and
salvation. In this volume Kelly, Gregory and Roberts and Wood,
point to problems of a similar nature. The difficulty
associated with such science is that, just as action research
requires a shift away from deduction and induction, explanation,
prediction, detachment and contemplation, towards conjecture,
understanding and engagement, it is not easy to make this shift
effectively. Expressed quite simply, it is impossible to
routinise social science as positivistic methodology attempts
to do, and a certain flair is required to be able to avoid
stating the mistaken or the obvious about human nature.

One successful example of this kind of analysis has been
provided by Herbst (1975). Observing that "the significance
of what we do is not always evident while we are doing it" he
points out that preoccupation in work with achievement and
success, with enjoyment and consumerism can be tragic. He
speculates:

The product of our adult life is like a shell, which
protects the growth of the fruit inside. As soon as
we realise that the shell is not essential value, we
may make use of what we find in ourselves. However,
it is possible that one uses work and inner strength

to produce no more than an outer shell of success,
possessions and pretensions, and then towards the
end of one's career, suddenly, one may quite
literally experience oneself as an empty, burnt-out
and rigid shell, and find that one has gained little
of value (p. 440).

Given the predominance of Western values of progress, achievement and satiation of appetites, Herbst's observations may
well lead towards the identification of one of Tannenbaum's
"principles". An analysis of similar quality has been offered
by Jahoda (1979). Reviewing reactions to the experience of
unemployment, she finds herself able to make some conjectures
about the general significance of "work" in people's lives.
Noting the predominance of literature criticising the experience of work (she mentions Braverman's thesis on deskilling,
Kumar's (1978) allegation that bureaucratisation has destroyed
the significance of work not only for blue collar but for
white collar workers also, and Anthony's (1978) conclusion
that "work, in a sense, is a joke, and like some other basic
functions, very difficult to take seriously unless its
performance breaks down"), she nonetheless cites the experiences of workers from several different cultures who, despite
the apparently trivial content of their jobs, take a deeply
felt pride in their work. Concluding that a profound ambivalence exists here and that people want to work even though
they may hate the present organisation of it, Jahoda concludes
by proposing that work serves certain "latent functions". A
time structure is imposed on the working day, regularly
shared experiences and contacts result, a person is linked to
goals and purposes other than his own, stature and identity
are acquired and activity (rather than idleness) is enforced.
While the details of her list may need revision, it nonetheless
has a certain plausibility linking insights into the human
condition with the opportunities for its expression that are
available in many modern societies.
    In conclusion to this section, two points about the
nature of social science knowledge need to be emphasised. It
is important to remember that social science can only point to
the likely relevance of certain factors in the formulation of
organisational and social problems. What it cannot do is
specify how much of these is essential. How much interest a
job should provide, how much responsibility, how much
influence people should have at work, is impossible generally
to say. Given the points made earlier about the nature of
social science knowledge, administrators should not expect
quantification of such factors. The second problem is
related to the first. Processes of socialisation being what
they are, sometimes people do not perceive what outsiders
might claim to be rather obvious. Prevailing situations may
not, by some criterion or other, be judged to be in participants' best interests even though those involved are quite

happy. Social scientists interested in an emancipatory psychology have (as the Norwegian and Shell cases discussed earlier show) a difficult role to play in exploring, as experts, alternatives to present arrangements while, as change agents, avoiding the temptation to impose their analysis on people who may not necessarily agree.

THE FUTURE OF JOB REDESIGN

Given the continuing existence of many fragmented jobs, job redesign is, and seems likely to remain, an issue of some importance. But given also that it is restricting to regard job redesign as an end in itself, it may be that other ways to involve people in the events that affect them should perhaps be sought. Assessment of this will, of course, depend not only on an understanding of psychology but also on an understanding of the significance of social developments.

Two issues seem, to the present author, to mitigate against the desirability of a major effort being directed to reforming the content of jobs. The first is unemployment, at the time of writing in excess of two million in the U.K. and forecast by the Cambridge Economic Policy Group (1980) as likely to rise to three million by mid-1982. Just to have a job may be a greater priority than the nature of what work is available. However, one should not push this point too far, for it can reasonably be argued that people have rights not only for jobs but for meaningful jobs. What it probably does signify though, is that if new (more interesting) forms of work organisation are less labour intensive, given the tendency for people to become more involved in them, to work harder and thus to restrict the total number of jobs available, then their usage without safeguards is somewhat dangerous.

The second issue is the changing nature of the world economy, particularly the increasing depletion of the world's resources and the fact that Western industrial nations by their actions are, as the Brandt report (1980) points out, holding the underdeveloped world in poverty. If comments such as Herbst's are to be taken seriously and if the truly social nature of work is to be emphasised by psychological theories inspiring job redesign, then the question "what's it all about?" must be asked. This suggests to the present author that in addition to reviewing the content of work, its purpose should be reviewed. The feasibility of alternatives to mindless consumerism is an urgent social issue (perhaps the social issue) and social science should be able to contribute to its study.

Yet two other issues underline the importance of job redesign theory. The first is related to both the issues just mentioned. The new technology of micro-processors promises to revolutionise work. Presently the possible effects of micro-electronics are not fully understood, and research is underway in various centres to plot likely and possible uses. But the history of new technologies does not inspire confidence. Taylor's "scientific management" at the turn of the century was specifically designed to take control of work from the working man, placing control in the hands of management. The tacit knowledge of many skilled craftsmen was such, however, that deskilling was not feasible beyond a certain level. Nowadays however, this is no longer the case. Experiments are in progress that will not only allow complex manual skills to be learned by robots, but will allow complex professional decisions, like medical diagnosis, to be undertaken by computer. Office work too, offers great opportunities for computerisation. The new technology promises indeed to revolutionise many aspects of organisations, from computer-aided design through computer-aided manufacturing, and quality control, to warehousing, purchasing and supply. Conceivably also, integrated computer systems can link one factory to another, confusing conventional union procedures, providing management with the greatly increased power that an efficient centralised information system may provide. The headline of an article in "The Engineer" of 17 January, 1980 sums up this point: "Keeping tabs on shop floor activity is a job for the micro-processor".

This is not to say that the new technology is necessarily to be deplored. Important choices have to be made, for improved computerised information systems could conceivably assist local decision-making on a scale not possible at the present time, with prospects for widespread and extensive involvement in it. A highly optimistic account of the implications of the new technology for job design has been provided by Davis and Taylor (1976), who conclude "modern technologies are associated with flexible, adaptive, more formless organisation . . . . or with bureaucracy based on a consensus and sense of industrial community" (p. 408). It may well be, however, that in common with other people involved in the QWL movement, Davis and Taylor grossly underestimate the strength of existing control structures and ideologies. One thing that, above all, stands out from all papers comprising this present volume is that a certain pessimism is in order concerning the ease with which new approaches to job design are likely to be incorporated within modern organisations.

A second social trend which underlines the importance of continuing concern with job design, is the trend towards the spread of bureaucracies in the modern state. This is particularly felt in the U.K. Despite the involvement of a few large firms (including Shell, Esso, ICI, Philips), who have consistently encouraged and used developments in the social sciences, Britain has never been amongst the foremost innovators in this field. OD never took a hold in the U.K. as it did in the U.S.A. Job design has never become a public issue as it has in Scandinavian countries. Such points led one commentator (Steele 1977) to suggest that a deep sense of the legitimacy of hierarchical authority is characteristic of British managers, who also believe that change cannot be planned for.

This picture of the deferential conservative Britisher does not fit the experiences of the present writer too well. A more penetrating analysis has been offered by Harries-Jenkins (1980). Observing that British bureaucracies have been criticised repeatedly and on various grounds, yet still continue to grow, he explains the trend as resulting from a combination of various factors. Given an "age of uncertainty" and a plurality of values more evident in the U.K. than ever before, Harries-Jenkins observes that in such circumstances governments have sought ways of controlling the means by which the society's resources are distributed. Highly centralised administrations have resulted, in central government, local government and in the public services like health and education (membership of the E.E.C. has of course, confirmed this trend). But his analysis does not stop at this point. He observes the strongly defended tradition in British bureaucracies to select leaders according to criteria favouring persons of a particular class background. This is justified by a guise of objective rationality (psychological test included). Similarly decisions made by the incumbent elite are justified by the dogma that, given the theory of rational bureaucracy, the decision-makers have the right to decide. An expert basis of authority is not used to justify decisions as, of course, one expert's view can be called against another's. The authority of traditional management prerogative is far less open to question.

Harries-Jenkins' analysis therefore suggests that more general processes are at work encouraging the spread of bureaucracy than simply local U.K. conditions. The bureaucratic form concentrates power in the hands of relatively few who can employ the ideology of rationality to justify selection of others to their ranks, and can project an "idealised apolitical image of bureaucratic structures and conceal the true political nature of organisational activities" (p. 327). At a time of increasing resource scarcity, changing values and urgent debate concerning resource allocations, the spread and consolidation of bureaucratic organisations may be expected. In these circumstances once again there is very good cause to be pessimistic about the chances of job redesign becoming common practice, though the need for a closely argued body of theory in this area is evidently strong.

Clearly therefore, there is a lot that should be done. However, as argued before, it would be a mistake for social scientists working in this area to seek to produce sets of prescriptions on how jobs should generally be redesigned. This point is underlined by Arbose (1979), who records the fact that, even in Scandinavian countries where job redesign has received much publicity, the general conclusion is that little now remains of the experiments of the 1960's. It would be foolish for social scientists to try to resurrect job redesign as a specific objective to be worked for. As argued in the last section, social scientists should, through critical studies and consideration of new possibilities, explore the general problems of worker detachment from work, and through consideration of ways in which changes might be made, encourage the development of local initiatives for their solution.

Regarding the former task a number of key research areas present themselves. The trend to increased bureaucratisation, and the uses of new technology are obvious issues. Additionally basic research could usefully be undertaken into the circumstances under which individuals and groups do become active and influential at work. The explicit model guiding job redesign work aimed at leading to increased worker autonomy (see Emery and Thorsrud, 1969), was that localised job design changes were just the start and from them people would become more interested in taking an active role in other spheres. What is extraordinary is that their basic model of self-awakening has been very little studied. Brousseau's (1977) study is one of the very few in this area. The few others are reviewed by Parker (1972) and more recently by Staines (1980). Despite optimistic assertions like Herbst's (1976) statement that the approach has proved itself, the case is by no means made. It is clear that experiences other than those in the work place determine the extent to which people choose to be self-directing. It is clear too that a stepwise model of personal learning is not the only possible way in which people learn to become autonomous. Rather than gentle guidance towards emancipation, struggle against oppression can awaken people's latent capacities and inclinations. More research should be undertaken into this matter, and studies at the individual level should be related to the study of pressure groups such as the Lucas aerospace stewards who have (perhaps to their cost) pioneered a vigorous and well-publicised campaign independent of support from management, unions and government. (Coates, 1978; Foster, 1979).

Apart from basic studies, important work also remains to be done at the practical level, to encourage local initiatives to overcome generally experienced problems. In this regard the papers by Clegg, Fitter and Den Hertog and van Eijnatten are of importance. They provide insights into the systemic nature of organisations, how changes in one sphere require changes elsewhere, and how there can be no one best way for introducing change.

Yet despite the importance of discussions such as these and the study generally of how job redesign ideas can become accepted in organisations (Walton, 1975, 1977), it is evident from other contributions to this volume that management initiatives in this area are limited in scope. On their own terms they may be very worthwhile. Yet economy, profitability and the need for management to retain strategic control, tend to provide the limits to management initiated reforms. Ways in which other criteria may be used to guide action need to be explored. Given that no generally applicable prescriptions for specific action are likely to be forthcoming from social science, locally inspired activities must be encouraged and supported. The strategy should be to make resources available to support self-managed change efforts.

In practice this approach leads to particular examples of what others would term industrial democracy. Three variants of the strategy can be cited. The first involves Governmental support for local initiatives. In Germany for example (see Klein 1977), some progress has been made through the provision of grant aid support for local experiments in new forms of work organisation. This has stimulated much interest amongst industrial engineers, and some experimentation. As an educational programme the approach has obvious merit though on its own is unlikely to lead to developments that may significantly challenge conventional management prerogatives. Another form of government support for locally controlled initiatives has been tried in Norway. The failure of the early efforts to introduce autonomous work groups throughout Norwegian industry, led to some distress on the part of the social scientists involved. However, they did not abandon their intention to introduce more autonomy and by the mid 1970's an opportunity developed for a new general change strategy to be developed. Health and safety at work became an important political issue in the country, and social scientists' advice was sought in the drafting of a new act of parliament. Gustavsen, whose work was referred to earlier, provided the guiding force here. Aware that conventional "rule following" models of law are not applicable in areas of health and well-being,he advised that a number of open-ended clauses be written into the new act (see Gustavsen 1977, 1980). Factories over a certain size have to constitute health and safety committees made up of workers'and management representatives. These committees are charged to consider relevant matters, and safety stewards have certain powers to demand action. Most importantly the committees are required continually to seek improvement of health standards; the burden of proof has shifted in some respects away from employees or factory inspectors having to demonstrate their acceptability, and in the area of job redesign the act states that "conditions shall be arranged so that employees are afforded reasonable opportunity for professional and personal development through their work. The individual employee 's opportunity for self determination and professional responsibility shall be taken into consideration when planning and arranging the work . . . ." (The Act, 1977, para. 12).

Seeking as it does to identify a general problem but to legitimise local solutions on issues of health and safety (topics of obvious importance to each employee), the Act is very much in the spirit of recommendations for the role of social science discussed here. However, as Gustavsen himself notes (1979), there are problems in this instance. Parts of the Act are very specific in their requirements, and those which are more open-ended look odd by comparison. The area of job design is specialised, and many managers and employees (as well as factory inspectors) do not understand what is intended by the section quoted above. Moreover, the requirement that continued improvements be sought is unrealistic as even in oil rich Norway there are limits to what may reasonably be afforded. This latter point has concerned the present author and a colleague who have concluded (Blackler and Brown 1981) that, contrary to the spirit of this Act, controls over developments are still held by central bureaucracy. It appears that the Government Health and Safety Inspectorate determines, through the level of vigilance of their factory inspectors, how rapidly many items are brought before the organisational safety committees. Given the inexperience of people sitting on the committees, the qualified factory inspectors play a crucial role in advising on relevant matters. Being a government agency of course, the inspectorate is exposed to political concerns and, generally speaking, the inspectors' willingness to press matters forward reflects the economic realities and political will of the moment. Long-term however, the Act may lead to significant changes in health and safety provisions in Norwegian industry. Indeed, if the stepwise learning model of worker autonomy does have validity, the Act may indirectly stimulate developments in other areas.

The second way in which social scientists may attempt to encourage local activities is in the area of union interest and involvements. In recent years much has been said about the lack of involvement by social scientists with trade unions. This is less true nowadays but important misunderstandings still remain. To constantly be on the receiving end of management inspired reforms allegedly undertaken for workers' own good, the academic presentation of some redesign projects, the extent to which shared interests are emphasised and the realities of competitive motivation ignored - factors such as these help account for union suspicion. But Gregory's chapter in this volume also hints at a certain ambivalence. Instances of job redesign that involve workers in decisions may make them less militantly inclined; if they are more efficient jobs may be lost; if workers become more confident they may rely less on their full time officials. Unions as large organisations are, after all, just as likely to be vulnerable to the processes Harries-Jenkins describes as are other bureaucracies. And, at a more general level, the philosophy of individual autonomy is not easily assimilated into a philosophy of collective action, and more flexible work designs are not easily compatible with collective bargaining.

Examples of union initiatives can be found of course. The Italian unions (Rollier, 1979) have pressed for alternatives to Taylorism and, while pleased with their success, are fully aware of the opportunities for increased management control that decentralised organisations can sometimes offer. Indeed there can be no prepackaged solutions to the relationship between social science and trade unions. Increased dialogue between the two groups, trade union funded basic research (as undertaken, for example, by the Arbetslivcentrum in Stockholm, see Viklund, 1980), trade union initiated action research, and opportunities for rank and file members to exchange information about social science projects they have been associated with, are amongst the useful things that might be attempted. It is evidently important that they are.

The third way forward that the author would suggest is in the area of organisational management, i.e. to change the rules of organisational governance. At the time of writing this is rather a dead issue in the U.K. (see Forester's 1980 comments on the demise of industrial democracy as an issue in Britain),but elsewhere this is not the case, especially in Scandinavian countries, where debate on possible ways forward is continuing at a lively pitch. The situation in Sweden is of particular interest where (see Albrecht,1980; or Asard, 1980), a recent programme of legislation has progressively eroded conventional management prerogatives. A shift has taken place in trade union policy. The traditional reliance on negotiations and bargaining has been supplemented with a strategy for legislative reform to alter the existing distribution of power in Swedish industry.

A number of provisions now ensure increased job security for employees, require joint consultation on ways to maintain employment levels, and shop stewards have increased powers. The previously held priority under Swedish law of employers' interpretations of collective agreements is reversed. Also employers are required to disclose more information on more organisational activities than ever before. Within the labour movement however, the issue of company ownership has become seen as the crucial obstacle to increased employee influence. Ways of overcoming this hurdle were discussed in the early 1970's and the suggestion by Meidner (1978), became union policy. Meidner's idea is that a proportion of company profits should each year be put aside into investment funds. These funds would be specific to each company and would be used to buy stocks in the organisation. In this way employees would gradually, through the funds, become the major shareholders in the company. The ideas are very controversial. Quite what the plan would mean for the conduct of the Swedish economy is not clear, nor is it clear how the new arrangements would affect company structures. Yet should anything like Meidner's plan be adopted, employees would become the economic participants in their organisation and private enterprise in Sweden (as conventionally understood) would disappear.

In this climate new forms of job redesign might be rather more easily introduced than is presently the case, given that job redesigns may flounder when traditional management prerogatives are challenged. Blackler and Brown (1980b) have provided a case example of this in Sweden, where a new approach to assembling trucks by autonomous groups was not adopted in Volvo despite evidence that it could be more cost effective than conventional line assembly. The basic reason for this was that the autonomous group assembly method made it difficult for management to control and direct the speed of production. Given an uninvolved work group, production targets might not be met. A motivated group's performance would be quite different of course - assembly time could be cut rather dramatically (by up to 30%). But in deciding how to make a major investment in a new truck plant, Volvo decided on "safety first" and produced plans for the factory that involved job designs which were, in Blackler and Brown's view, only marginally innovatory. Although, even in the climate that Meidner's form of economic democracy would provide, the vested interests of senior organisational groups would still no doubt create pressures to stifle shop floor autonomy, it should be easier to combat them. Presently the system of governance in Volvo (a most enlightened company in the job design field), does not encourage shop floor demands for autonomy from management. A new structure which allowed employees more control in strategic policy might provide the opportunity for worker demands for new forms of work organisation to be more clearly heard. The law in itself would do little more than provide a general climate for change. Local activity would be essential. But, as in Norway, such a "multi-level" strategy for work reform would help legitimate shop floor initiatives as management decision-making prerogatives are eroded.

SUMMARY

In this chapter past achievements and future prospects for job redesign have been discussed. It has been suggested that the task facing social scientists and others interested in job redesign, is for them to integrate their work into the more general context of employee emancipation at work. Given the nature of social science knowledge, it was suggested that a primary concern to provide general prescriptions about what should be done, is inappropriate. In the context of present day social conditions, general psycho-social problems should be studied. Such study should be combined with a search for localised solution to the issues, with a variety of approaches and a multi-level strategy for reform offering most potential for progress.

REFERENCES

Ackroyd, S. (1974). Economic rationality and the relevance
of Weberian sociology. British Journal of Industrial
Relations, 11, 236-248.

Ackroyd, S. (1976). Sociological theory and the human
relations school. Sociology of Work and Occupation, 3,
379-410.

Act Relating to Worker Protection and Working Environment
(1977). Norway.

Aken,van, J.E. (1978). On the Control of Complex Industrial
Organisations. Leiden:Nijhoff.

Albrecht, S.L. (1980). Politics, bureaucracy and worker
participation:The Swedish case. Journal of Applied
Behavioural Science, 16, 299-309.

Aldag, R.J. and Brief, A.P. (1979). Task Design and Employee
Motivation. Illinois:Scott, Foresman and Company.

Alexander, K. (1978). Introduction. In D. Gregory (ed.),
Work Organisation. London:Social Science Research
Council.

Alink, J.B. and Wester, P. (1978). Organisatieverandering in
een Gereedschapmakerij. Eindhoven:Philips.

Allegro, J.T. (1973). Sociotechnische Organisatie
Ontwikkeling. Leiden:Stenfert Kroese.

Amalgamated Union of Engineering Workers (TASS). (1979).
Computer Technology and Employment. Manchester:National
Computer Centre Publications.

Anon. (1975). Experiments to improve the quality of working
life in the Netherlands. European Industrial Relations
Review, 17, 8-9.

Anthony, P.D. (1978). The Ideology of Work. London:Tavistock.

Arbose, J. (1979). Is worker democracy working? International Management, November, 14-18.

Argyris, C. (1957). Personality and Organisation. New York:
Harper and Row.

Argyris, C. (1964). Integrating the Individual and the
Organisation. New York:Wiley.

Argyris, C. (1968). Unintended consequences of rigorous research. *Psychological Bulletin,* 70, 185-197.

Argyris, C. (1970). *Intervention Theory and Method*. Reading, Mass.:Addison-Wesley.

Argyris, C. (1973). Personality and organisation theory revisited. *Administrative Science Quarterly*, 18, 141-167.

Argyris, C. (1976). Single-loop and double-loop models in research on decision-making. *Administrative Science Quarterly*, 21, 363-375.

Armistead, N. (1974). *Reconstructing Social Psychology*. Harmondsworth:Penguin.

Asard, E. (1980). Economic participation in Sweden 1971-79. The issue of economic democracy. *Economic and Industrial Democracy*, 1, 371-393.

Assen, van, A. and Wester, P. (1980). Designing Meaningful Jobs: A Comparative Analysis of Organisational Design Practice. In K. Duncan, M. Gruneberg and D. Wallis (eds.), *Changes in Working Life:Proceedings of the NATO International Conference*. London:Wiley.

Association of Professional, Executive, Clerical and Computer Staff (APEX). (1979). *Office Technology:The Trade Union Response*. London:APEX.

Babbage, C. (1835). *On the Economy of Machinery and Manufacturers*. London:Charles Knight.

Baldamus, W. (1961). *Efficiency and Effort*. London:Tavistock.

Banks, T. (1974). Autonomous work groups. *Industrial Society*, 56, 10-12.

Baritz, L. (1960). *The Servants of Power*. New York:Wiley.

Barnes, R.M. (1968). *Motion and Time Study*, 6th ed.. New York: Wiley.

Barrow, J.C. (1976). Worker performance and task complexity as causal determinants of leader behaviour style and flexibility. *Journal of Applied Psychology*, 61, 433-440.

Benne, K.D., Chin, R. and Bennis, W.G. (1976). Science and practice. In W.G. Bennis, K.D. Benne, R. Chin and K.E. Carey (eds.), *The Planning of Change*. New York: Holt, Rinehart and Winston.

Bennis, W.G. (1966). Theory and method in applying behavioural science to planned organizational change. In J.R. Lawrence (ed.), <u>Operational Research and the Social Sciences</u>. London:Tavistock.

Berg, I. (1970). <u>Education and Jobs</u>. Harmondsworth:Penguin.

Berger, L. and Luckman, T. (1967). <u>The Social Reconstruction of Reality</u>. London:Allen Lane.

Berglind, H. (1975). Working conditions, employment and labour market policy. In L.E. Davis and A.B. Cherns (eds.), <u>The Quality of Working Life, Vol.I</u>. New York: Free Press.

Birchall, D. (1975). <u>Job Design</u>. Epping:Gower.

Birchall, D. and Wild, R. (1973). Job restructuring among blue-collar workers. <u>Personnel Review</u>, 2, 40-55.

Blackler, F.H.M. and Brown, C.A. (1978). <u>Job Design and Management Control</u>. Farnborough:Saxon House.

Blackler, F.H.M. and Brown, C.A. (1980a). <u>Whatever Happened to Shell's New Philosophy of Management?.</u> Farnborough: Gower.

Blackler, F.H.M. and Brown, C.A. (1980b). Job design and social change, the case of Volvo. In K.D. Duncan, M. Gruneberg and D. Wallis (eds.), <u>Changes in Working Life:Proceedings of the NATO International Conference</u>. London:Wiley.

Blackler, F.H.M. and Brown, C.A. (1981). Reflections on some Scandinavian legislation to improve the quality of working life. Paper presented at British Psychological Society Occupational Psychology Section Conference, January 1981.

Blackler, F.H.M. and Brown, C.A. (n.d.). <u>Job Redesign and Social Change:Case Studies at Volvo</u>. University of Lancaster.

Blackler, F.H.M. and Williams, R. (1971). People's motives at work. In P.B. Warr (ed.), <u>Psychology at Work</u>, 1st ed.. Harmondsworth:Penguin.

Blauner, R. (1960). Work satisfaction and industrial trends in modern society. In W. Galenson and S. Lipsett (eds.), <u>Labor and Trade Unionism</u>. New York:Wiley.

Blauner, R. (1964). _Alienation and Freedom_. Chicago: University of Chicago Press.

Blood, M.R. and Hulin, C.L. (1967). Alienation, environmental characteristics and worker responses. _Journal of Applied Psychology_, 51, 284-290.

Bolweg, J.P. (1976). _Job Design and Industrial Democracy_. The Hague:Nijhoff.

Bosquet, M. (1972). The Prison Factory. _New Left Review_, 73, 23-34.

Brandt, W. (1980). _North-South:A Programme for Survival_. London:Pan Books.

Braverman, H. (1974). _Labor and Monoply Capital_. New York: Monthly Review Press.

Brayfield, A.H. and Crockett, W.H. (1955). Employee attitudes and employee performance. _Psychological Bulletin_, 52, 396-424.

Brenner, M., Marsh, P. and Brenner, M. (eds.). (1978). _The Social Context of Methods_. London:Croom Helm.

Brousseau, K.R. (1977). Effects of job experience on personality. Technical Report No. 14, Yale University School of Organisation and Management, New Haven, Connecticut.

Brown, W. (1962). _Piecework Abandoned_. London:Heineman.

Burbidge, J.L. (1975). _The Introduction of Group Technology_. London:Heineman.

Burns, T. and Stalker, G.M. (1961). _The Management of Innovation_. London:Tavistock.

Butteriss, M. (1975). The quality of working life:The expanded international scene. Work Research Unit, Paper No. 5. London:Department of Employment.

Cambridge Economic Policy Group. (1980). _Cambridge Economic Policy Review_, 6, 1.

Campbell, D.T. and Stanley, J.C. (1963). _Experimental and Quasi-Experimental Designs for Research_. Chicago:Rand McNally.

Carey, A. (1977). The Lysenko syndrome in western social science. _Australian Psychologist_, 12, 27-38.

Centers, R. and Bugenthal, D.E. (1966). Intrinsic and extrinsic job motivations among different segments of the working population. _Journal of Applied Psychology_, 50, 193-197.

Centre for Alternative Industrial and Technological Systems. (1979). _Lucas Aerospace:Turning Industrial Decline Into Expansion_. London:North East London Polytechnic.

Cherns, A.B. (1976). The principles of socio-technical design. _Human Relations_, 29, 783-792.

Cherns, A.B. (1979). _Using the Social Sciences._ London: Routledge and Kegan Paul.

Cherns, A.B. and Davis, L.E. (1975). Assessment of the state of the art. In L.E. Davis and A.B. Cherns (eds.), _The Quality of Working Life, Vol.I._ New York:Free Press.

Chin, R. (1961). The utility of systems models and developmental models for practitioners. In W.G. Bennis, K.D. Benne and R. Chin (eds.), _The Planning of Change_. New York:Holt, Rinehart and Winston.

Chinoy, E. (1955). _Automobile Workers and the American Dream._ New York:Doubleday.

Clark, P.A. (1972). _Organisational Design, Theory and Practice._ London:Tavistock.

Clark, P.A. (1975). Intervention theory:Matching role, focus and context. In L.E. Davis and A.B. Cherns (eds.), _The Quality of Working Life, Vol. I._ New York:Free Press.

Clegg, C.W. (1980). The process of job redesign:Signposts from a theoretical orphanage? _Human Relations_, 32, 999-1022.

Clegg, C.W. and Fitter, M.J. (1978). Information systems: The Achilles heel of job redesign? _Personnel Review,_ 7, 5-11.

Coates, K. (1978). _The Right to Useful Work._ Nottingham: Spokesman.

Conant, E.H. and Kilbridge, M.D. (1965). An interdisciplinary analysis of job enlargement:Technology costs and behavioural implications. _Industrial and Labor Relations Review_, 18, 377-395.

Cummings, T.G. and Molloy, E.S. (1977). Improving Productivity and the Quality of Working Life. New York:Praeger.

Cummings, T.G., Molloy, E.S. and Glen, R. (1977). A methodological critique of fifty eight selected work experiments. Human Relations, 30, 675-708.

Cummings, T.G. and Salipante, P.F. (1976). Research-based strategies for improving work life. In P.B. Warr (ed.), Personal Goals and Work Design. London:Wiley.

Cunnison, S. (1966). Wages and Work Allocation. London: Tavistock.

Dale, E. (1963). Functions of the manager of tomorrow. Training Directors Journal, 9, 25-36.

Daniel, W.W. (1970). Beyond the Wage-Work Bargain. London: PEP.

Daniel, W.W. and McIntosh, N. (1972). The Right to Manage? London:MacDonald.

Davis, L.E. (1957). Towards a theory of job design. Industrial Engineering, 8, 305-309.

Davis, L.E. (1966). Job satisfaction research:The post-industrial view. Industrial Relations, 10, 176-193.

Davis, L.E. (1972). The coming crisis for production management. In L.E. Davis and J.C. Taylor (eds.), Design of Jobs, 1st ed.. Harmondsworth:Penguin.

Davis, L.E. (1976). Developments in job design. In P.B. Warr (ed.), Personal Goals and Work Design. London:Wiley.

Davis, L.E., Canter, R.R. and Hoffman, J. (1955). Current job design criteria. Journal of Industrial Engineering, 6, 5-11.

Davis, L.E. and Cherns, A.B. (eds.). (1975). The Quality of Working Life, Vols. I and II. New York:Free Press.

Davis, L.E. and Taylor, J.C. (1972). Introduction. In L.E. Davis and J.C. Taylor (eds.), Design of Jobs, 1st ed., Harmondsworth:Penguin.

Davis, L.E. and Taylor, J.C. (1975). Technology effects on job, work and organisation structure:A contingency view. In L.E. Davis and A.B. Cherns (eds.), The Quality of Working Life, Vol. I. New York:Free Press.

Delamotte, Y.P. (1975). Union attitudes toward quality of working life. In L.E. Davis and A.B. Cherns (eds.), The Quality of Working Life, Vol. I. New York:Free Press.

Delamotte, Y.P. and Walker, K. (1973). Humanisation of work and the quality of working life - trends and issues. International Institute of Labour Studies Bulletin, 11, 3-14.

Derber, M. (1964). Divergent tendencies in industrial relations research. Industrial and Labor Relations Review, 17, 601.

Does de Willebois, van der, J.L.J.M. (1968). Werkstrukturering als Organisatie-ontwikkeling. Eindhoven:Philips.

Drucker, P. (1970). The Practice of Management. London:Pan.

Dunn, W.W. and Swierczek, F.W. (1977). Planned organisational change:Toward grounded theory. Journal of Applied Behavioural Science, 13, 135-157.

E.E.C. Council of Europe, Consultative Assembly, May 9th, 1974 (5th sitting). Resolution 565.

Edwards, C.A.B. (1972). Readings in Group Technology. London:Machinery Publishing Company.

Ehrenberg, R.G., Hamermesh, D.S. and Johnson, G.E. (1977). Policy decisions and research in economics and industrial relations:An exchange of views:Comment. Industrial and Labor Relations Review, 31, 13.

Eijnatten, van,F.M. and den Hertog, J.F. (1979). Job consequences of technological choices in industry:A design perspective. Paper presented at the International Quality of Working Life Conference, Thessaloniki, 20-24 August, 1979.

Elden, M. (1972). Organisational self management:Governmental and political change implications of non hierarchical forms of work organisation. Paper presented to the First International Conference on Participation and Self Management, Dubrovnik, December, 1972.

Eldridge, J.E.T. (1975). Industrial relations and industrial capitalism. In G. Esland, G. Salaman and M.A. Speakman (eds.), People and Work. Edinburgh:Holmes McDougall.

Elger, T. (1979). Valorisation and deskilling. Capital and Class, 7, 58-99.

Emery, F.E. (1959). Characteristics of socio-technical systems. Document No. 527, London, Tavistock Institute of Human Relations.

Emery, F.E. (1967). The next thirty years. Human Relations, 20, 199-237.

Emery, F.E. (1980). Designing socio-technical systems for 'greenfield' sites. Journal of Occupational Behaviour, 1, 19-27.

Emery, F.E. and Oeser, O.A. (1958). Information, Decision and Action. Melbourne:Melbourne University Press.

Emery, F.E. and Thorsrud, E. (1969). Form and Content in Industrial Democracy. London:Tavistock.

Emery, F.E. and Thorsrud, E. (1975). Democracy at Work. Canberra:Australian National University.

Emery, F.E. and Trist, E.L. (1965). The causal texture of organisational environments. Human Relations, 18, 22-32.

Emery, F.E. and Trist, E.L. (1969). Socio-technical systems. In F.E. Emery (ed.), Systems Thinking. Harmondsworth: Penguin.

Emery, F.E. and Trist, E.L. (1972). Towards a Social Ecology. London:Plenum.

Esland, G., Salaman, G. and Speakman, M.A. (eds.). (1974). People and Work. Edinburgh:Holmes McDougall.

Flanders, A. (1964). The Fawley Productivity Agreements. London:Faber.

Ford, R.N. (1969). Motivation Through the Work Itself. New York:American Management Association.

Forester, T. (1980). Whatever happened to industrial democracy? New Society, 53, 120-122.

Foster, G. (1979). Lucas Aerospace:The truth. Management Today, January, 34-41.

Foster, M. (1972). An introduction to the theory and practice of action research in work organisations. Human Relations, 25, 529-556.

Fraser, R. (1947). The incidence of neurosis among factory workers. Report no. 90, Industrial Health Research Board. London:HMSO.

French, W.L. and Bell, C.H. (1973). Organization Development. Englewood Cliffs, N.J.:Prentice-Hall.

Friedman, A. (1977). Responsible autonomy versus direct control over the labour process. Capital and Class, 1, 43-57.

Friedmann, G. (1961). The Anatomy of Work. London:Heineman.

Galbraith, J. (1973). Designing Complex Organisations. Reading, Mass.:Addison-Wesley.

Galbraith, J.K. (1958). The Affluent Society. London:Hamilton.

Gallie, D. (1978). In Search of the New Working Class. Cambridge:Cambridge University Press.

Gardner, J.W. (1979). The United Kingdom's economic performance:Comparisons with other countries of the EEC. Economic Trends, 310, 90-98.

George, M. (1979). The pros and cons of workers' alternative corporate plans. Bulletin of the Institute for Workers' Control, No. 4.

Gilbreth, F.B. (1911). Brick Laying System. New York:Clark Publishing Company.

Ginsberg, G.P. (ed.). (1979). Emerging Strategies in Social Psychological Research. Chichester:Wiley.

Ginzberg, E. (1975). Work structuring and manpower realities. In L.E. Davis and A.B. Cherns (eds.), The Quality of Working Life, Vol. I. New York:Free Press.

Goldberg, D.P. (1972). The Detection of Psychiatric Illness by Questionnaire. Oxford: Oxford University Press.

Goldthorpe, J.H. (1966). Attitudes and behaviour of car workers: A deviant case and theoretical critique. British Journal of Sociology, 17, 227-244.

Goldthorpe, J.H., Lockwood, D., Bechhoffer, F. and Platt, J. (1969). The Affluent Worker in the Class Structure. Cambridge:Cambridge University Press.

Gomberg, W. (1957). The use of psychology in industry:A trade union point of view. Invitational address before the Industrial Division of the American Psychological Association.

189

Gomberg, W. (1973). Job satisfaction:Sorting out the nonsense. American Federationist, 80 (6), 14-20.

Gorz, A. (1976). Technology, technicians and class struggle. In A. Gorz (ed.), The Division of Labour. Sussex: Harvester Press.

Gouldner, A.W. (1955). Wildcat Strike. New York:Free Press.

Gouldner, A.W. (1961). Theoretical requirements of the applied social sciences. In W.D. Bennis, K.D. Benne and R. Chin (eds.), The Planning of Change. New York:Holt, Rinehart and Winston.

Gregory, D. (ed.). (1978). Work Organisation:Swedish Experience and British Context. London:Social Science Research Council.

Gregory, D. (1979). Safety representatives and safety committees:An extension of democratic control? Unit for Industrial Democracy, Western Australia.

Guest, R.H. (1957). Job enlargement-revolution in job design. Personnel Administration, 20, 9-16.

Gustavsen, B. (1977). A legislative approach to job reform in Norway. International Labor Review, 115, 263-276.

Gustavsen, B. (1979). A strategy for reform of working life. Unpublished manuscript, Work Research Institutes, Oslo.

Gustavsen, B. (1980). Legal administrative reforms and the role of social research. Acta Sociologica, 23, 3-20.

Habermas, J. (1974). Theory and Practice. London:Heineman.

Hackman, J.R. (1977). Work design. In J.R. Hackman and J.L. Suttle (eds.), Improving Life at Work. Santa Monica: Goodyear.

Hackman, J.R. and Lawler, E.E. (1971). Employee reactions to job characteristics. Journal of Applied Psychology, 55, 259-286.

Hackman, J.R. and Oldham, G.R. (1975). Development of the job diagnostic survey. Journal of Applied Psychology, 60, 159-170.

Hackman, J.R. and Oldham, G.R. (1976). Motivation through the design of work:Test of a theory. Organizational Behavior and Human Performance, 16, 250-279.

Hackman, J.R. and Oldham, G.R. (1980). Work Redesign. Reading, Mass.:Addison-Wesley.

Hales, M. (1974). Management science and the 'second industrial revolution'. Radical Science Journal, 1, 5-28.

Harré, R. (1979). Social Being:A Theory for Social Psychology. Oxford:Blackwell.

Harré, R. and Secord, P.F. (1972). The Explanation of Social Behaviour. Oxford:Blackwell.

Harries-Jenkins, G. (1980). Bureaucracy in Great Britain in the 1980s. Journal of Applied Behavioural Science, 3, 317-335.

Health and Safety at Work Act (1974). London:HMSO.

Hedberg, B. and Mumford, E. (1975). The design of computer systems. In E. Mumford and H. Sackman (eds.), Human Choice and Computers. New York:North Holland Publishing Company.

Heneman, H.G. and Schwab, D.P. (1972). Evaluation of research on expectancy theory of predictions of employee perform-ance. Psychological Bulletin, 78, 1-9.

Herbst, P. (1975). The product of work is people. In L.E. Davis and A.B. Cherns (eds.), The Quality of Working Life, Vol. I. New York:Free Press.

Herbst, P. (1976). Alternatives to Hierarchies. Leiden: Nijhoff.

Herrick, N.Q. and Maccoby, M. (1975). Humanizing work: A priority goal for the 1970s. In L.E. Davis and A.B. Cherns (eds.), The Quality of Working Life, Vol.I. New York:Free Press.

Hertog, den,F.J. (1966). Work structuring. In P.B. Warr (ed.), Personal Goals and Work Design. London:Wiley.

Hertog, den,F.J. (1978). Arbeitsstrukturierung, Experimente aus Holland. Bern:Huber.

Hertog, den,F.J. and de Vries, H.J.J. (1977). Breaking the Deadlock. Eindhoven:Philips.

Hertog, den,F.J. and Wester, P. (1979). Organizational renewal in engineering research:A comparative process analysis. In C.L. Cooper and E. Mumford (eds.), The Quality of Working Life in Western and Eastern Europe. London:Associated Business Press.

Hertog, den,F.J. and Wielinga, C. (1981). The computer as an ink-blot test. Accountancy, Organisations and Society, in press.

Herzberg, F. (1966). Work and the Nature of Man. Cleveland: World Publishing Company.

Herzberg, F. (1968). One more time:How do you motivate employees? Harvard Business Review, 46, 53-62.

Herzberg, F. (1976). The Managerial Choice:To be Efficient and to be Human. Homewood, Illinois:Dow Jones-Irwin.

Herzberg, F., Mausner, B. and Snyderman, B. (1959). The Motivation to Work. New York:Wiley.

Hickson, D.J., Pugh, D.S. and Pheysey, D.C. (1969). Operations technology and organisation structure:An empirical reappraisal. Administrative Science Quarterly, 14, 378-397.

Hill, C.P. (1972). Toward a New Management Philosophy. London:Gower.

Hollis, M. (1977). Models of Man. Cambridge:Cambridge University Press.

Hughes, J. and Gregory, D. (1978). Work organisation:Some issues of practice and concept. In D. Gregory (ed.), Work Organisation:Swedish Experience and British Context. London:Social Science Research Council.

Hull, D. (1978). The Shop Steward's Guide to Work Organisation. Nottingham:Spokesman.

Hyman, R. and Brough, I. (1975). Social Values and Industrial Relations. Oxford:Blackwell.

International Labour Organisation (1979). New Forms of Work Organisation 2. Geneva:I.L.O.

Ivancevich, J.M. (1976). Effects of goal setting on performance and job satisfaction. Journal of Applied Psychology, 61, 605-612.

Jahoda, M. (1979). The impact of unemployment in the 1930's and the 1970's. Bulletin of the British Psychological Society, 32, 309-314.

Jay, M. (1973). The Dialectical Imagination. London: Heineman.

Jenkins, C. and Sherman, B. (1979). The Collapse of Work. London:Methuen.

Jenkins, D. (1978). The West German humanization of work program:A preliminary assessment. Work Research Unit Occasional Paper No. 8. London:Department of Employment.

Karasek, R.A. (1979). Job demands, job decision latitude and mental strain:Implications for job redesign. Administrative Science Quarterly, 24, 285-308.

Katz, D. and Kahn, R.L. (1978). The Social Psychology of Organisations, (2nd edition). New York:Wiley.

Kelly, J.E. (1978). A reappraisal of socio-technical systems theory. Human Relations, 31, 1069-1099.

Kelly, J.E. (1979). Job Redesign:A Critical Analysis. University of London, Ph.D thesis.

Kelly, J.E. (1980). The costs of job redesign:A preliminary analysis. Industrial Relations Journal, 11, 22-34.

Kelly, J.E. (1981). Scientific Management, Job Redesign and Work Performance. New York:Academic Press. In preparation.

Kelly, J.E. and Nicholson, N. (1980). The causation of strikes:A review of some approaches and the potential contribution of social psychology. Human Relations, 33, 853-883.

Kelman, H.C. (1965). Manipulation of human behaviour:An ethical dilemma for the social scientist. Journal of Social Issues, 21, 31-46.

Kjellen, B. (1980a). Employee consultants and information disclosure:Some notes on the Swedish experience. Trade Union Research Unit Discussion Paper No. 21. Ruskin College, Oxford.

Kjellen, B. (1980b). Research on employees' conditions:A Swedish trade union view. Trade Union Research Unit Discussion Paper No. 22. Ruskin College, Oxford.

Klein, L. (1964). Multiproducts Ltd. London:HMSO.

Klein, L. (1976). New Forms of Work Organisation. Cambridge: Cambridge University Press.

Klein, L. (1977). Designing the jobs fit for the people who do them. The Times, June 20.

Koopman, P.L. and Drenth, P.J.D. (1979). Werkoverleg en Komplexe Besluitvorming. Amsterdam:The Free University.

Kornhauser, A. (1965). Mental Health of the Industrial Worker. New York:Wiley.

Kraft, P. (1977). Programmers and Managers. New York: Springer-Verlag.

Kumar, K. (1978). Prophecy and Progress. London:Allen Lane.

Kuriloff, A.H. (1963). An experiment in management:Putting Theory Y to the test. Personnel, 40,8-17.

Lafitte, F. (1962). Social policy in a free society. In W.D. Birrell, P.A.R. Hillyard, A.S. Murie and D.J.D. Roche (eds.), Social Administration. Harmondsworth: Penguin.

Larrain, J. (1979). The Concept of Ideology. London: Hutchinson.

Lawler, E.E. (1971). Pay and Organisational Effectiveness. New York:McGraw-Hill.

Lawler, E.E. (1976). Issues of understanding. In P.B. Warr (ed.), Personal Goals and Work Design. London:Wiley.

Lawler, E.E. and Rhode, J.G. (1976). Information and Control in Organizations. Santa Monica:Goodyear.

Lawrence, P.R. and Lorsch, J.W. (1969). Developing Organizations:Diagnosis and Action. Reading, Mass.: Addison-Wesley.

Levitan, S. and Johnston, W.B. (1973). Job redesign, reform, enrichment:Explaining the limitations. Monthly Labor Review, 96, 35-41.

Lewin, G. (ed.). (1948). Resolving Social Conflicts. New York:Harper.

Lewin, K. (1952). Field Theory in Social Science. London: Tavistock.

Likert, R. (1961). New Patterns of Management. New York: McGraw-Hill.

Lindholm, R. (1972). The Condemned Piecework. Stockholm:SAF.

Littler, C. (1978). Understanding Taylorism. British Journal of Sociology, 29, 185-202.

Locke, E.A. (1968). Toward a theory of task motivation and incentives. Organizational Behavior and Human Performance, 3, 157-189.

Locke, E.A. (1970). Job satisfaction and job performance: A theoretical analysis. Organizational Behavior and Human Performance, 5, 484-500.

Locke, E., Sirota, D. and Wolfson, A. (1976). An experimental case study of the successes and failures of job enrichment in a government agency. Journal of Applied Psychology, 61, 701-711.

Lowin, A. and Craig, J.R. (1968). The influence of levels of performance on managerial style. Organizational Behavior and Human Performance, 3, 440-458.

Lupton, T. (1963). On the Shopfloor. London:Pergamon.

Lupton, T. (1971). Management and the Social Sciences. Harmondsworth:Penguin.

Lyons, J.F. (1972). Turnover and absenteeism:A review of the relationships and shared correlates. Personnel Psychology, 25, 271-281.

McGregor, D. (1960). The Human Side of Enterprise. London: McGraw-Hill.

McLean, A.J. and Sims, D.B.P. (1978). Job enrichment from theoretical poverty:The state of the art and directions for further work. Personnel Review, 7, 5-10.

Mangham, I. (1978). The limits of planned change. Paper presented at the First European Forum on Organisational Development, Aachen, 1978.

Marriott, R. (1968). Incentive Payment Systems. London: Staples Press.

Marrow, J. (1969). The Practical Theorist:The Life and Works of Kurt Lewin. New York:Basic Books.

Marx, K. (1867). Capital. Moscow:Progress. (Reprinted 1970).

Marx, K. (1965). Capital, Vol. I. Moscow:Progress.

Marx, K. and Engels, F. (1975). Collected Works, Vol.3. Moscow:Progress.

Maslow, A.H. (1943). A theory of human motivation. Psychological Review, 50, 370-396.

Maslow, A.H. (1970). Motivation and Personality, 2nd ed..
New York:Harper-Row.

Mayo, E. (1946). The Human Problems of an Industrial
Civilisation. Harvard:Harvard University Press.

Meidner, R. (1975). The obligations of industry and society
in the Swedish labour market of the future. In L.E. Davis
and A.B. Cherns (eds.), The Quality of Working Life,
Vol. I. New York:Free Press.

Meidner, R. (1978). Employee Investment Funds. London:Allen
and Unwin.

Miller, E.J. and Rice, A.K. (1967). Systems of Organisation.
London:Tavistock.

Mitchell, T.R. (1979). Organisational behaviour. Annual
Review of Psychology, 30, 243-281.

Mohr, L.B. (1977). Authority and democracy in organisations.
Human Relations, 30, 919-947.

Montmollin, de,M. (1974). Taylorisme et anti Taylorisme.
Sociologie du Travail, 16, 374-382.

Myers, M.S. (1970). Every Employee a Manager. London:McGraw-
Hill.

Myers, M.S. (1976). Managing Without Unions. Reading, Mass.:
Addison-Wesley.

Nemiroff, P.M. and Ford, D.L. (1976). Task effectiveness and
human fulfilment in organisations: A review and
development of a conceptual contingency model. Academy
of Management Review, 1, 69-82.

Nichols, T. (1975). The 'socialism' of management:Some
comments on the new human relations. Sociological Review,
23, 245-265.

Nichols, T. (1976). Management, ideology and practice. In
People and Work, Block 4, Unit 15, Open University
Course. Milton Keynes:Open University Press.

Nichols, T. (1980). Capital and Labour. London:Fontana.

Nichols, T. and Beynon, H. (1977). Living with Capitalism.
London:Routledge and Kegan Paul.

Nicholson, N. (1977). Absence behaviour and attendance
motivation. Journal of Management Studies, 14, 231-252.

Nicholson, N., Brown, C.A. and Chadwick-Jones, J.K. (1976). Absence from work and job satisfaction. Journal of Applied Psychology, 61, 728-737.

Nord, W.R. (1969). Beyond the teaching machine:The neglected area of operant conditioning in the theory and practice of management. Organizational Behavior and Human Performance, 4, 375-401.

Oldham, G.R. and Hackman, J.R. (1980). Work design in the organisational context. In B.M. Staw and L.L. Cummings (eds.), Research in Organisational Behaviour, Vol. 2. Greenwich:JAI Press Incorporated.

Parker, S. (1972). The Sociology of Leisure. London:Allen and Unwin.

Paul, L. (1977). Sixteen-year-olds' image of work. Memo. No. 147, MRC/SSRC SAPU, University of Sheffield.

Paul, W.J. and Robertson, K.B. (1970). Job Enrichment and Employee Motivation. London:Gower.

Penzer, W. (1973). After everyone's had his job enriched, then what? Administrative Management, October, 20-22.

Pettigrew, A.M. (1973). The Politics of Organisational Decision-making. London:Tavistock.

Philips COR (1973). Wat doet Philips in Nederland aan Werkstrukturering. Eindhoven:Philips.

Pierce, J.L., Dunham, R.B. and Blackburn, R.S. (1979). Social systems structure, job design and growth need strength: Test of a congruency model. Academy of Management Journal, 22, 223-240.

Porter, L.W. and Lawler, E.E. (1968). Managerial Attitudes and Performance. Illinois:Dorsey.

Porter, L.W., Lawler, E.E. and Hackman, J.R. (1975). Behavior in Organizations. New York:McGraw-Hill.

Powell, R.M. and Schlacter, J. (1971). Participative management:A panacea. Academy of Management Journal, 6, 165-173.

Quin, R.P., Staines, G.L. and McCullough, M.R. (1974). Job Satisfaction:Is there a Trend? Washington:US Department of Labor.

Ramondt, J. (1974). _Bedrijfsdemokratisering zonder Arbeiders_. Alphen aan der Rijn:Sansom.

Ramsay, H. (1976). Participation:The shopfloor view. _British Journal of Industrial Relations_, 14, 128-141.

Rasmus, J. (1974). Why management is pushing 'job enrichment'. _International Socialist Review_, December, 23-25/43-44.

Reif, W., Ferrazzi, D. and Evans, R.J. (1974). Job enrichment: Who uses it and why. _Business Horizons_, 17, 73-78.

Rice, A.K. (1958). _Productivity and Social Organisation_. London:Tavistock.

Roethlisberger, F.J. and Dickson, W.J. (1939). _Management and the Worker-An Account of a Research Program Conducted by the Western Electric Company, Hawthorne Works, Chicago_. Harvard:Harvard University Press.

Rogers, C.R. and Skinner, B.F. (1956). Some issues concerning the control of human behaviour. _Science_, 124, 31-46.

Rollier, M. (1979). Taylorism and the Italian unions. In C.L. Cooper and E. Mumford (eds.), _The Quality of Working Life in Eastern and Western Europe_. London:Associated Business Press.

Rosen, H. (1963). Job enlargement and its implications. _Industrial Medicine and Surgery_, 32, 217-228.

Rosenhead, J. (n.d.). Job enrichment:It's a con. Unpublished manuscript, prepared for the British Society for Responsibility in Science.

Ross, A. and Hartman, P.T. (1960). _Changing Patterns of Industrial Conflict_. New York:Wiley.

Roy, D. (1952). Quota restriction and 'goldbricking' in a machine shop. _American Journal of Sociology_, 57, 427-442.

Roy, S.K. (1969). A re-examination of the methodology of A.K. Rice's Indian textile mill work reorganisation. _Indian Journal of Industrial Relations_, 5, 170-191.

Runciman, W. (1966). _Relative Deprivation and Social Justice_. Harmondsworth:Penguin.

Rush, H. (1971). _Job Design for Motivation_. New York:Conference Board (Report 515).

Schon, D.A. (1971). Beyond the Stable State. Harmondsworth: Penguin.

Sedgwick, P. (1974). Ideology of modern psychology. In N. Armistead (ed.), Reconstructing Social Psychology. Harmondsworth:Penguin.

Seeborg, I.S. (1978). The influence of employee participation in job redesign. Journal of Applied Behavioural Science, 14, 87-99.

Shephard, J.M. (1969). Functional specialisation and work attitudes. Industrial Relations, 8, 185-194.

Shotter, J. (1975). Images of Man in Psychological Research. London:Methuen.

Singh, R. (1978). Theory and practice in industrial relations. Industrial Relations Journal, 9, 57-64.

Sirota, D. (1973). Production and service personnel and job enrichment. Work Study, January, 9-15.

Skinner, W. (1971). The anachronistic factory. Harvard Business Review, 49, 61-70.

Sleigh, J., Boatwright, B., Irwin, P. and Stanyon, R. (1979). The manpower implications of micro-electronic technology. Department of Employment, London.

Smith, A. (1776). On the Wealth of Nations. (Reprinted 1974). Harmondsworth:Penguin.

Smith, C.T.B., Clifton, R., Makeham, P., Creigh, S.W. and Burn, R.V. (1978). Strikes in Britain. London:HMSO.

Social Science Research Council (1978). Research Needs in Work Organisation. London:SSRC.

Social Science Research Council (1979). Newsletter No. 40. London:SSRC.

Srivastva, S., Salipante, P.F., Cummings, T.G., Notz, W.W., Bigelow, J.D. and Waters, J.A. (1975). Job Satisfaction and Productivity. Cleveland:Case Western University Press.

Staines, G.L. (1980). Spillover versus compensation:A review of the literature on the relationship between work and non-work. Human Relations, 33, 111-180.

199

Steele, F. (1977). Is the culture hostile to OD? The UK
    example. In P. Mirvis and D. Berg (eds.), <u>Failures in
    Organisational Development and Change</u>. Chichester:Wiley.

Stevenson, T.E. (1975). Organisational development, a critique.
    <u>Journal of Management Studies</u>, 12, 249-265.

Stone, E.F. (1975). Job scope, job satisfaction and the
    protestant ethic:A study of enlisted men in the U.S. navy.
    <u>Journal of Vocational Behavior</u>, 7, 215-224.

Stone, E.F. (1976). The moderating effect of work-related
    values on the job scope-job satisfaction relationship.
    <u>Organizational Behavior and Human Performance</u>, 15,
    147-167.

Strauss, G. (1976). Organisational development. In R. Dubin
    (ed.), <u>Handbook of Work, Organisation and Society</u>.
    Chicago:Rand McNally.

Strien, van,P.J. (1978). Paradigms in organisational research
    and practice. <u>Journal of Occupational Psychology</u>, 51,
    291-301.

Strien, van,P.J. (1980). In search for an emancipatory
    psychology. Unpublished manuscript, University of
    Groningen.

Susman, G.I. (1973). Job enlargement:Effects of culture on
    worker response. <u>Industrial Relations</u>, 12, 1-15.

Susman, G.I. and Evered, R.D. (1978). An assessment of the
    scientific merits of action research. <u>Administrative
    Science Quarterly</u>, 23, 582-603.

Swedish Employers Confederation (1975). <u>Job Reform in Sweden</u>.
    Stockholm:Swedish Employers Confederation.

Tannenbaum, A.S. (1980). Organisational psychology. In
    H.C. Triandis and R.W. Brislin (eds.), <u>Handbook of Cross-
    Cultural Psychology:Social Psychology</u>. Boston:Allyn and
    Bacon.

Tanner, I. and Lupton, T. (1979). <u>Job Design</u>. Manchester:
    Manchester Business School.

Taylor, F.W. (1903). <u>Shop Management</u>. New York:ASME.

Taylor, F.W. (1911). <u>The Principles of Scientific Management</u>.
    New York:Harper.

Taylor, F.W. (1919). A piece rate system. In F.W. Taylor, Two Papers on Scientific Management. London:Routledge and Sons.

Taylor, F.W. (1947). Testimony before the house committee. In F.W. Taylor, Scientific Management. New York:Harper.

Taylor, J.C. (1977a). Experiments in work system design: Economic and human results. Part I. Personnel Review, 6(3), 21-34.

Taylor, J.C. (1977b). Experiments in work system design: Economic and human results. Part II. Personnel Review, 6(4), 21-41.

Taylor, J.C. (1978). The socio-technical approach to work design. In K. Legge and E. Mumford (eds.), Designing Organisations for Satisfaction and Efficiency. London: Gower.

Taylor, J.C. (1979). Job design criteria twenty years later. In L.E. Davis and J.C. Taylor (eds.), Design of Jobs, 2nd ed.. Santa Monica:Goodyear.

Tchobanian, R. (1975). Trade unions and the humanisation of work. International Labor Review, 111, 199-217.

Thorsrud, E. (1972). Job design in the wider context. In L.E. Davis and J.C. Taylor (eds.), Design of Jobs. Harmondsworth:Penguin.

Tiefenthal, R. (ed.). (1976). H.B. Maynard and Company, Production: an International Appraisal of Contemporary Manufacturing Systems and the Changing Role of the Worker. New York:Halsted Press.

Tiffin, E.J. and McCormack, J. (1975). Industrial Psychology, 6th ed.. London:Allen and Unwin.

Tourraine, A. (1962). An historical theory in the evolution of industrial skills. In C.R. Walker (ed.), Modern Technology and Civilization. New York:McGraw-Hill.

Trade Union Congress (TUC). (1979). Employment and Technology: A TUC Interim Report. London:TUC.

Trade Union Research Unit (TURU). (1980). The Duration and Pattern of Working Time in Selected Industries in Great Britain. The Possible Employment Effects Associated with Changing Present Patterns. To be published by the Anglo-German Foundation.

Transport and General Workers Union (1979). Micro-electronics, new technology:Old problems, new opportunities. London: TGWU.

Trist, E.L. (1959). On socio-technical systems. Reprinted in W.A. Pasmore and J.J. Sherwood (eds.), (1978), Socio-technical Systems:A Source Book. La Jolla:University Associates.

Trist, E.L. (1976). Critique of scientific management in terms of socio-technical theory. In M. Weir (ed.), Job Satisfaction. London:Fontana.

Trist, E.L. and Bamforth, K. (1951). Some social psychological consequences of the longwall method of coal getting. Human Relations, 4, 3-39.

Trist, E.L., Higgins, G., Murray, H. and Pollock, A.B. (1963). Organisational Choice. London:Tavistock.

Turner, A.N. and Lawrence, P.R. (1965). Industrial Jobs and the Worker. Cambridge, Mass.:Harvard University Press.

Turner, A.N. and Miclette, A.L. (1962). Sources of satisfaction in repetitive work. Occupational Psychology, 36, 215-231.

Umstot, D.D., Bell, C.H. and Mitchell, T.R. (1976). Effects of job enrichment and task goals on satisfaction and productivity:Implications for job design. Journal of Applied Psychology, 61, 379-394.

US Department of Health, Education and Welfare (1973). Work in America. Boston, Mass.: MIT Press.

Vansina, L.S. (1976). Beyond organisational development? In P.B. Warr (ed.), Personal Goals and Work Design. London: Wiley.

Viklund, B. (1980). Swedish centre for working life, reporting the first projects. Economic and Industrial Democracy, 1, 433-438.

Vroom, V.H. and Deci, E.L. (1970). Management and Motivation. Harmondsworth:Penguin.

Walker, C.R. and Guest, R.H. (1952). The Man on the Assembly Line. Cambridge, Mass.:Harvard University Press.

Walker, K.F. (1974). Worker participation in management-problems, practice and prospects. International Institute for Labour Studies Bulletin, 12, 2-35.

Wall, T.D. (1980). Group work redesign in context. In K. Duncan, M. Gruneberg and D. Wallis (eds.), Changes in Working Life:Proceedings of the NATO International Conference. London:Wiley.

Wall, T.D. and Clegg, C.W. (1981). A longitudinal field study of group work redesign. Journal of Occupational Behaviour, 2, 31-49.

Wall, T.D., Clegg, C.W. and Jackson, P.R. (1978). An evaluation of the job characteristics model. Journal of Occupational Psychology, 51, 183-196.

Walton, R.E. (1975). The diffusion of new work structures: Explaining why success didn't take. Organisational Dynamics, 3, 3-22

Walton, R.E. (1977). Successful strategies for diffusing work innovations. Journal of Contemporary Business, 6, 1-22.

Wanous, J.P. (1974). A causal-correlational analysis of the job satisfaction and performance relationships. Journal of Applied Psychology, 59, 139-144.

Weir, M. (ed.). (1976). Job Satisfaction. London:Fontana.

Weiss, R.S. and Rein, M. (1970). The evaluation of broad-aim programs:Experimental design, its difficulties and an alternative. Administrative Science Quarterly, 15, 97-109.

Wild, R. and Birchall, D. (1973). Means and ends in job restructuring. Personnel Review, 2, 18-24.

Wilson, N.A.B. (1973). On the quality of working life. Department of Employment Manpower Paper No. 7. London: HMSO.

Wood, S. (1979). A reappraisal of the contingency approach to organisation. Journal of Management Studies, 16, 334-354.

Wood, S. (ed.). (1981). The Degradation of Work?:Skill, Deskilling and the Braverman Debate. London:Hutchinson.

Woodward, J. (1965). Industrial Organisation:Theory and Practice. Oxford:Oxford University Press.

Wragg, R. and Robertson, J. (1978). Post war trends in employment. Department of Employment Research Paper No. 3. London:HMSO.

Wyatt, S., Fraser, J.A. and Stock, F.G.L. (1928). The comparative effects of variety and uniformity in work. Report No. 52, Industrial Fatigure Research Board. London: HMSO.

Zimbalist, A. (1975). The limits of work humanisation. Review of Radical Political Economics, 7, 50-59.

Zwart, C.J. (1972). Gericht Veranderen. Rotterdam:Lemniscaat.

AUTHOR INDEX

Ackroyd, S. 28, 161
Aken, van, E. 102
Albrecht, S.L. 179
Aldag, R.J. 124
Alexander, K. 18
Alink, J.B. 99
Allegro, J.T. 95
Anon. 36
Anthony, P.D. 172
Arbose, J. 175
Argyris, C. 2, 14, 22, 35,
    87, 97, 160
Armistead, N. 167
Asard, E. 179
Assen, van, A. 95

Babbage, C. 6, 7
Baldamus, W. 21, 24, 27,
    43, 44
Bamforth, K. 11, 124
Banks, T. 28
Baritz, L. 158, 159
Barnes, R.M. 34
Barrow, J.C. 124
Bechhoffer, F. 34
Bell, C.H. 105, 124, 160
Benne, K.D. 105
Bennis, W.G. 105, 114
Berg, I. 31
Berger, L. 166
Berglind, H. 31
Beynon, H. 29, 32, 66
Bigelow, J.D. 14, 15
Birchall, D. 14, 15, 21,
    33, 88, 124
Blackburn, R.S. 124
Blackler, F.H.M. 12, 29,
    33, 63, 65, 66, 165,
    166, 178, 179, 180
Blauner, R. 10, 24, 32
Blood, M.R. 124
Boatwright, B. 61
Bolweg, J.P. 5, 163, 165
Bosquet, M. 30, 67, 68,
    73, 81, 82
Brandt, W. 173
Braverman, H. 2, 8, 16, 24,
    25, 29, 32, 49, 50, 65,
    66, 67, 68, 81, 161, 172

Brayfield, A.H. 123, 124
Brenner, M. 169
Brenner, M. 169
Brief, A.P. 124
Brough, I. 27
Brousseau, K.R. 176
Brown, C.A. 12, 29, 35, 63,
    65, 66, 165, 166, 178,
    179, 180
Brown, W. 33
Bugenthal, D.E. 24
Burbidge, J.L. 12
Burn, R.V. 34
Burns, T. 123
Butteriss, M. 3

Campbell, D.T. 116
Canter, R.R. 8, 24, 161
Carey, A. 171
Centers, R. 24
Chadwick-Jones, J.K. 35
Cherns, A.B. 8, 16, 18, 21,
    133, 161, 164, 168
Chin, R. 105, 114
Chinoy, E. 24
Clark, P.A. 19, 88, 101
Clegg, C.W. 19, 87, 102,
    103, 106, 107, 110, 113,
    116, 129, 133, 146, 150,
    157, 176
Clifton, R. 34
Coates, K. 176
Conant, E.H. 23
Craig, J.R. 124
Creigh, S.W. 34
Crockett, W.H. 123, 124
Cummings, T.G. 14, 15, 23,
    28, 115, 118, 124
Cunnison, S. 34

Dale, E. 102
Daniel, W.W. 33, 50
Davis, L.E. 5, 7, 8, 16,
    18, 21, 24, 31, 32, 93,
    161, 164, 174
Deci, E.L. 33
Delamotte, Y.P. 16, 29
Derber, M. 115
Dickson, W.J. 119

205

213